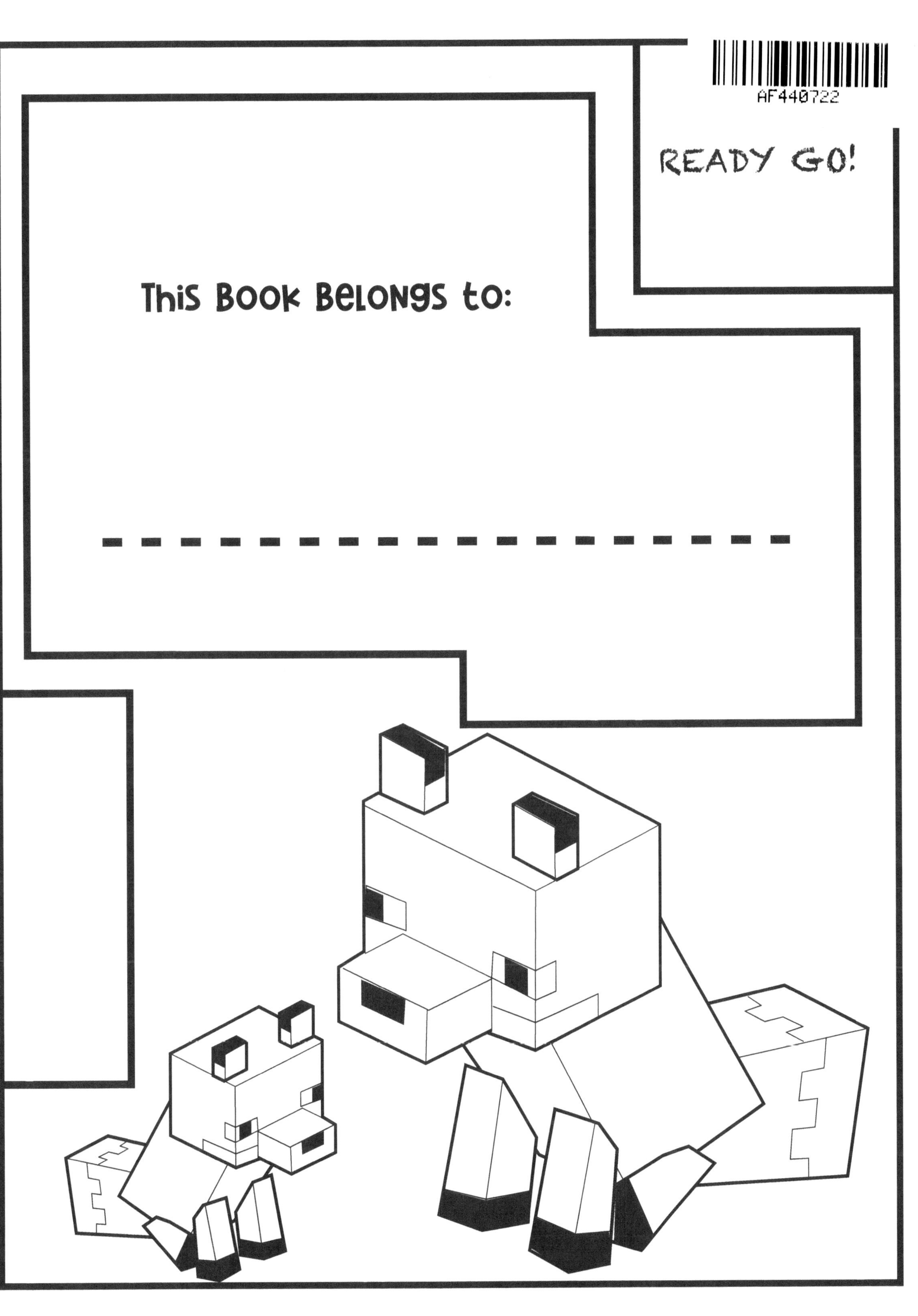
AF440722
READY GO!
This Book Belongs to:
. . . .

GETTING READY- WHAT YO

Welcome to the start of the journey where you will learn to draw the world of Minecraft! We will start from the simple most easy forms moving towards more complex characters! Here are presented the few tools you will need to accomplish great results... no worries it is nothing special only things that lay around the house! Yay! Can't wait to start!

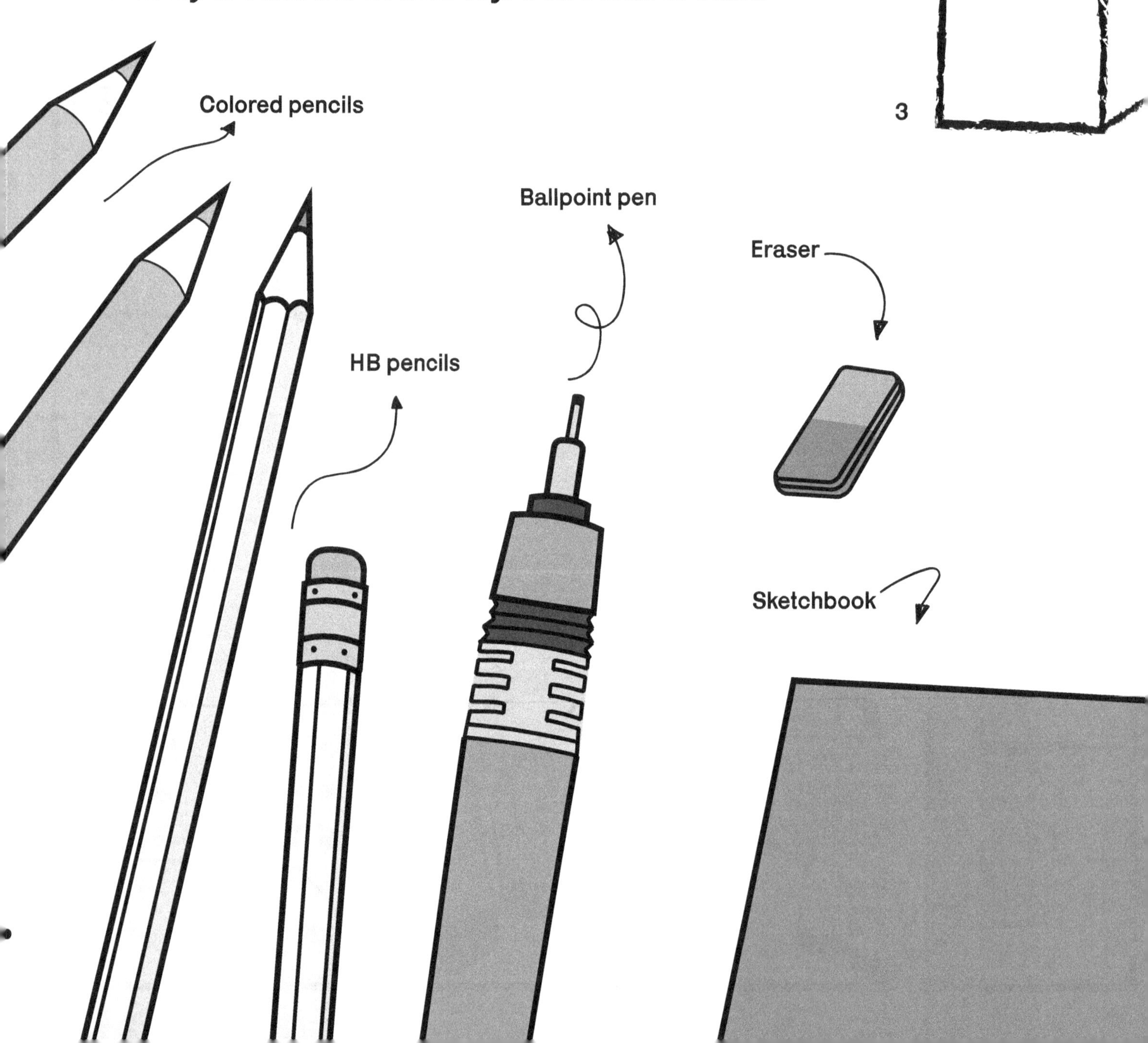

The Ultimate Guide for Minecrafters

DRAWING MOBS

Step-by-Step

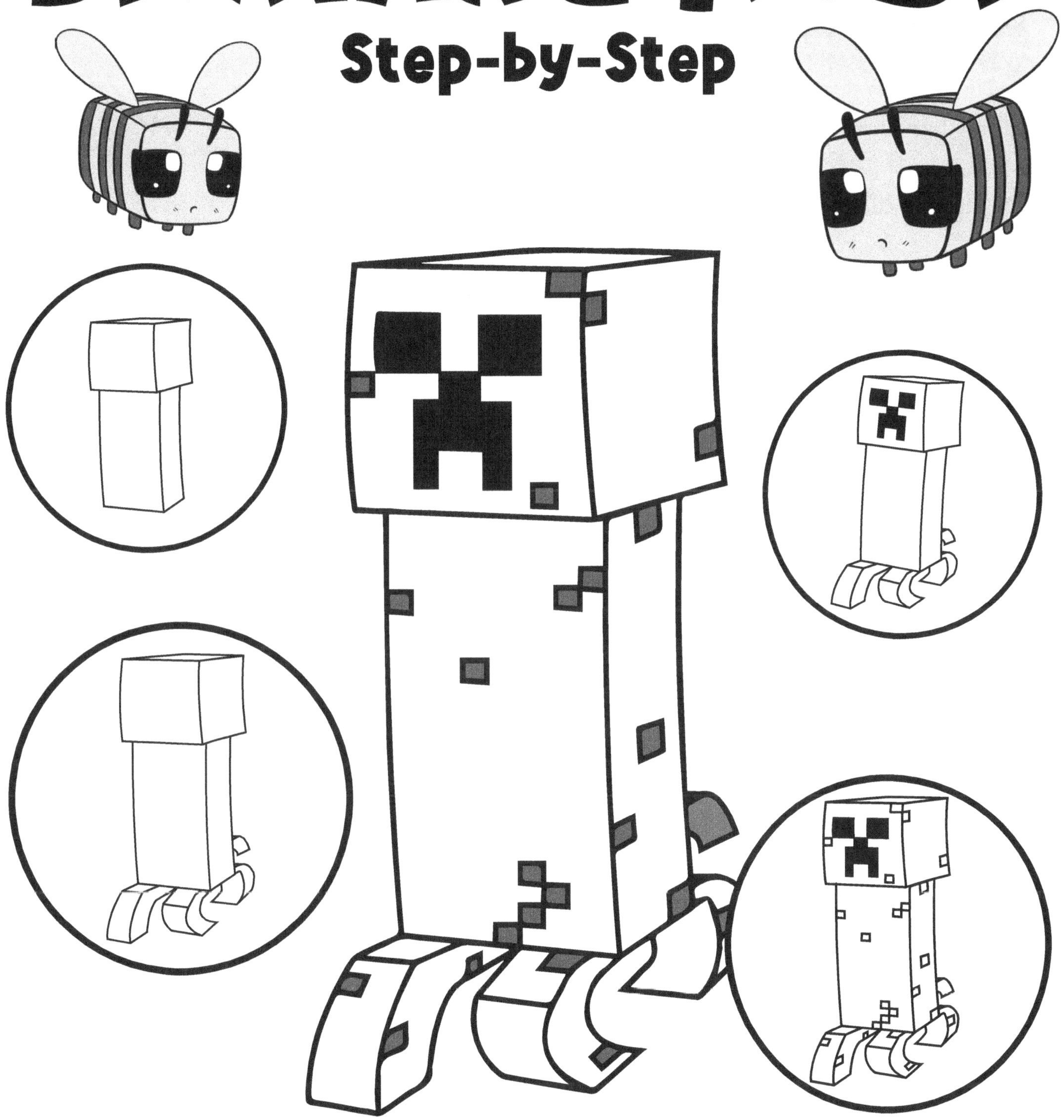

WWW.CUBEHUNTER.NET

Copyright © 2024 by Cube Hunter

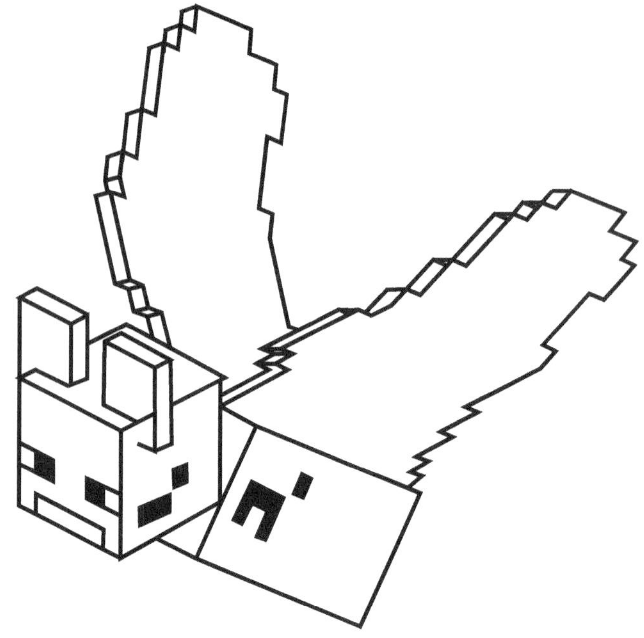

Rock Cooper

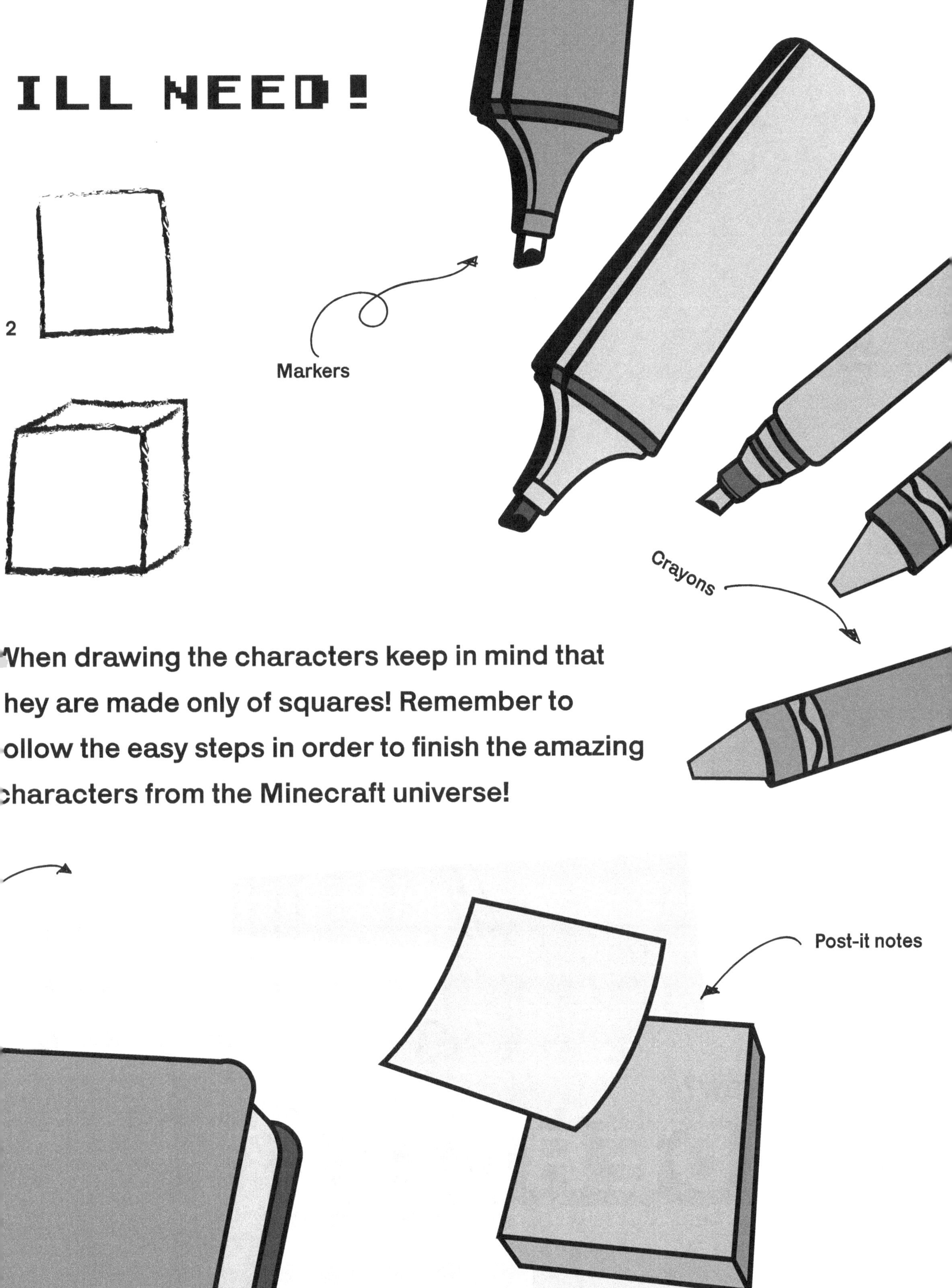

When drawing the characters keep in mind that they are made only of squares! Remember to follow the easy steps in order to finish the amazing characters from the Minecraft universe!

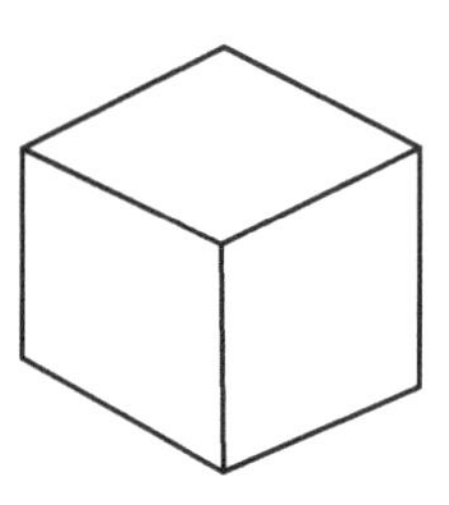

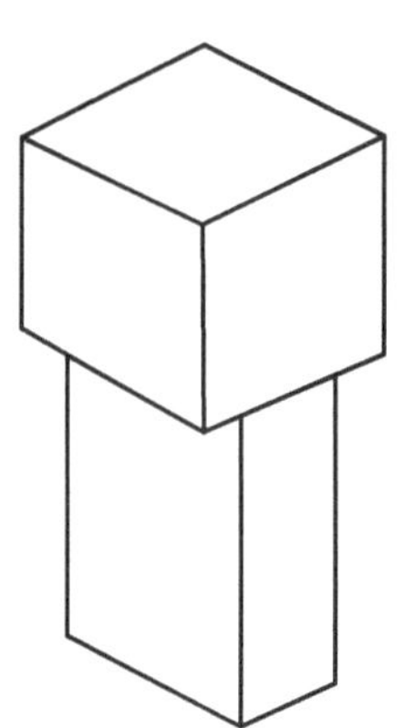

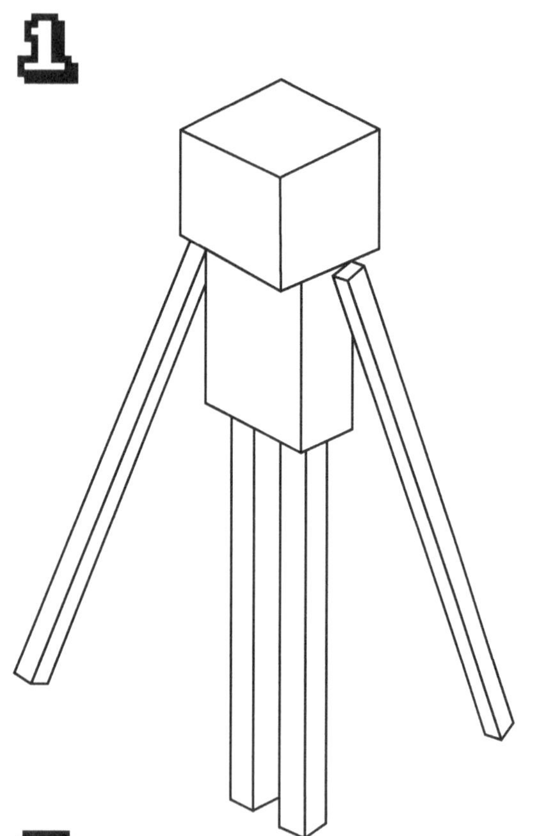

How to draw?

ENDERMAN

Difficulty

NOW, iT'S YOUR TURN

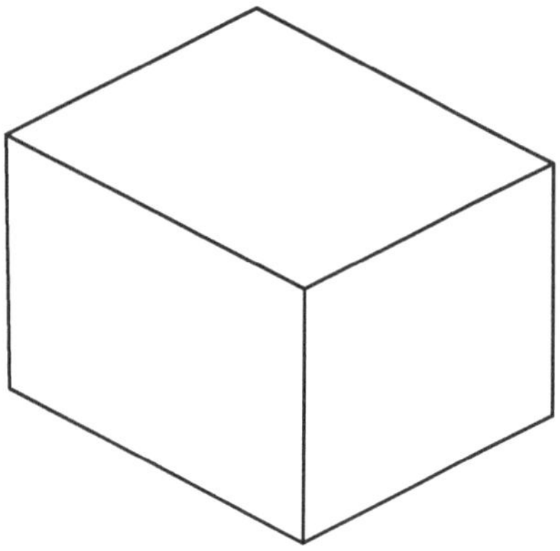

1

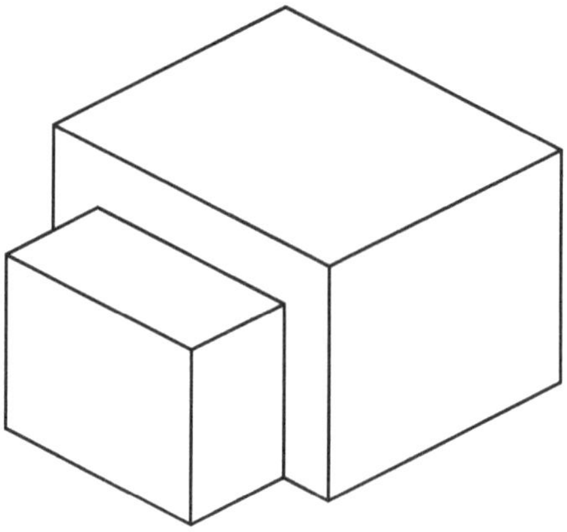

2

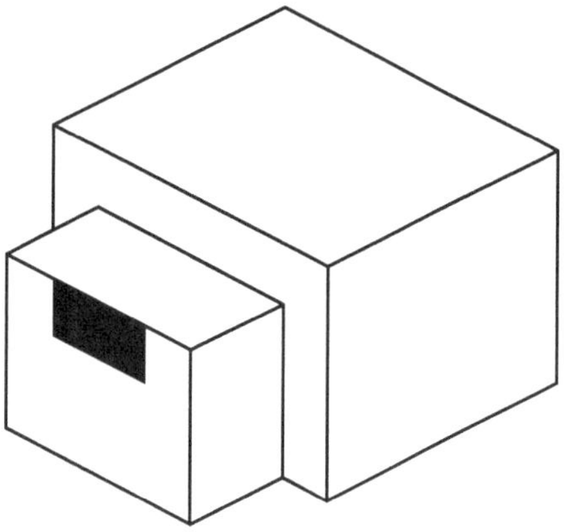

3

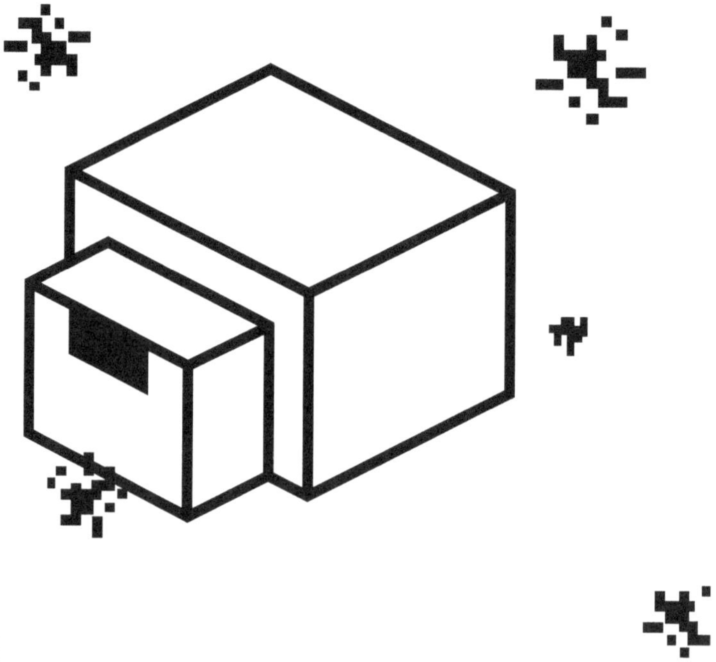

4

How to draw?

ENDERMITE

Difficulty 

NOW, iT'S YOUR TURN

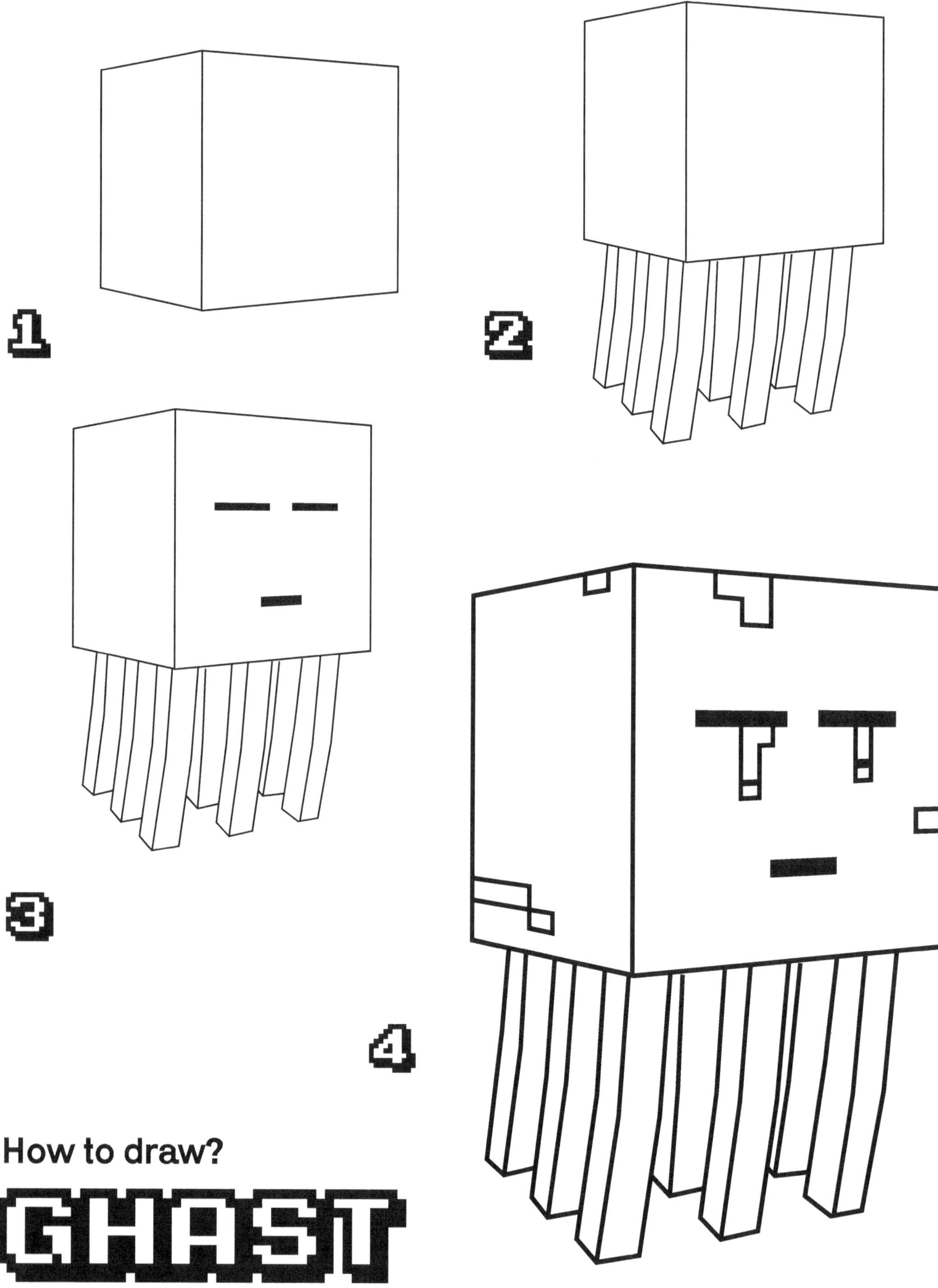

1

2

3

4

How to draw?

GHAST

Difficulty

NOW, IT'S YOUR TURN

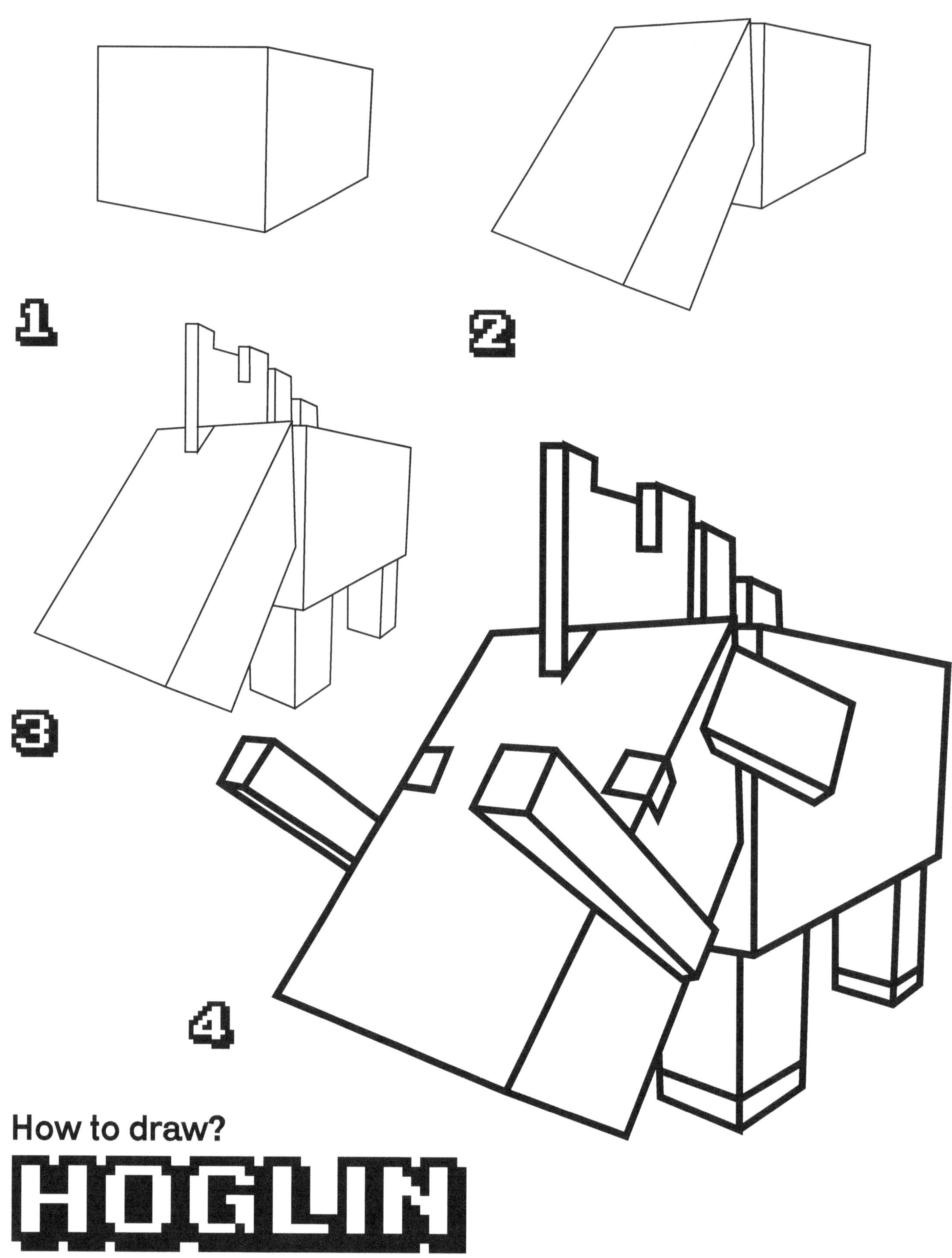

How to draw?

HOGLIN

Difficulty

NOW, IT'S YOUR TURN

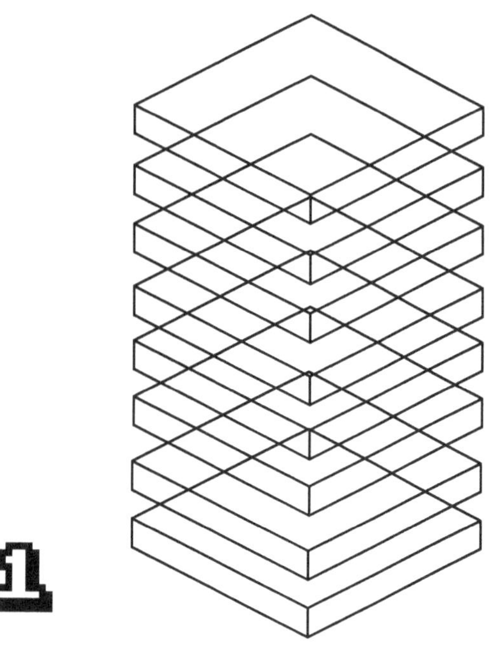

1

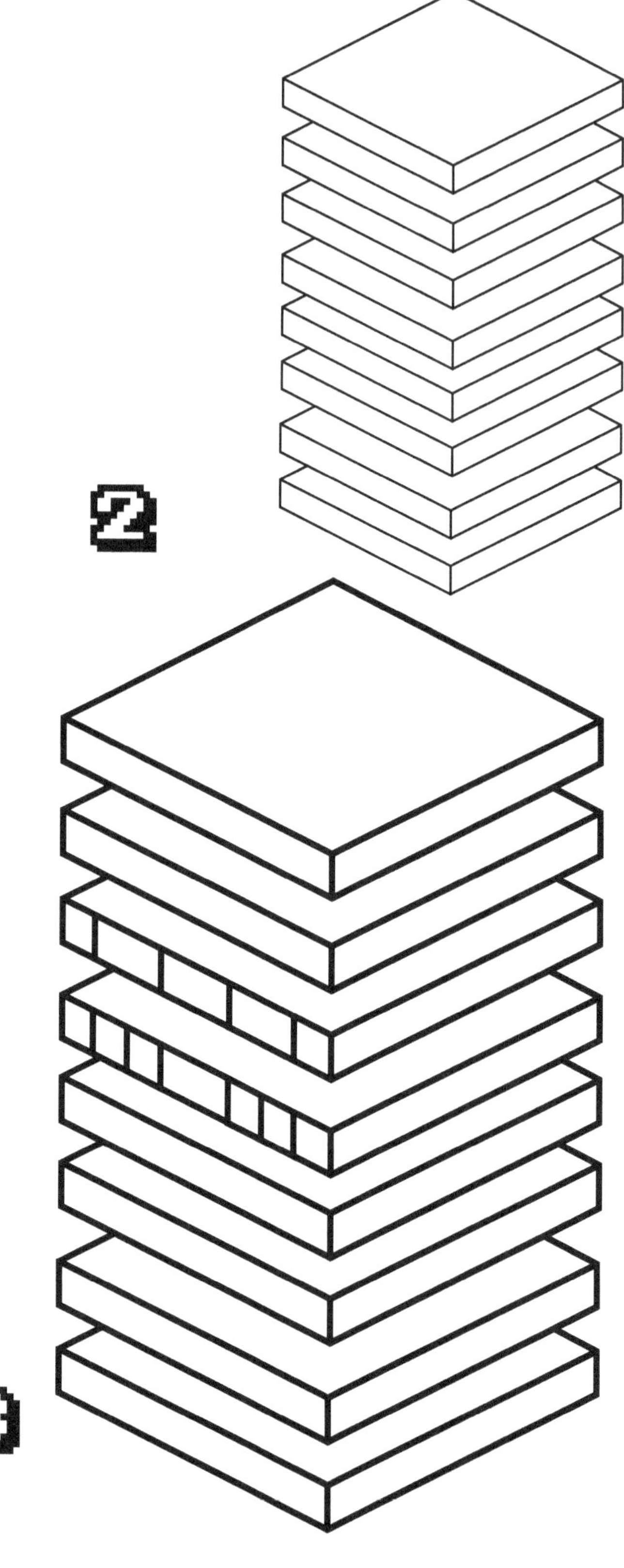

2

3

How to draw?

MAGMA CUBE

Difficulty 

NOW, IT'S YOUR TURN

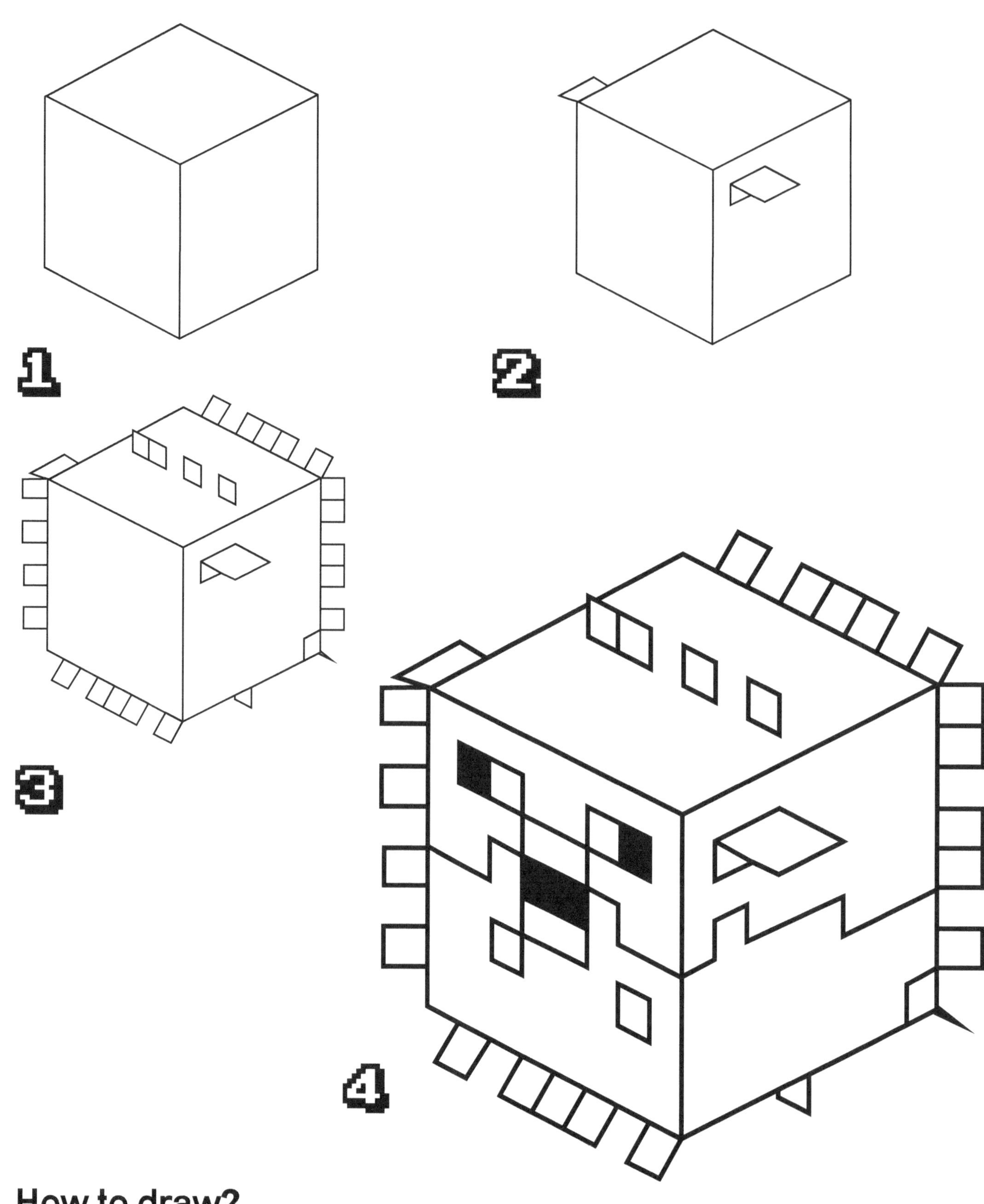

How to draw?

PUFFER FISH

Difficulty

NOW, iT'S YOUR TURN

NOW, iT'S YOUR TURN

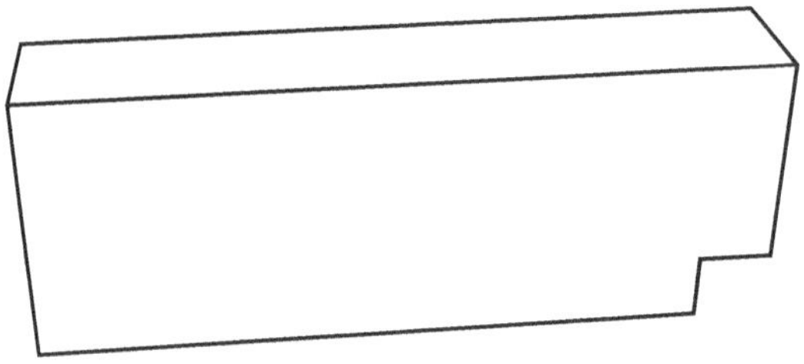

1

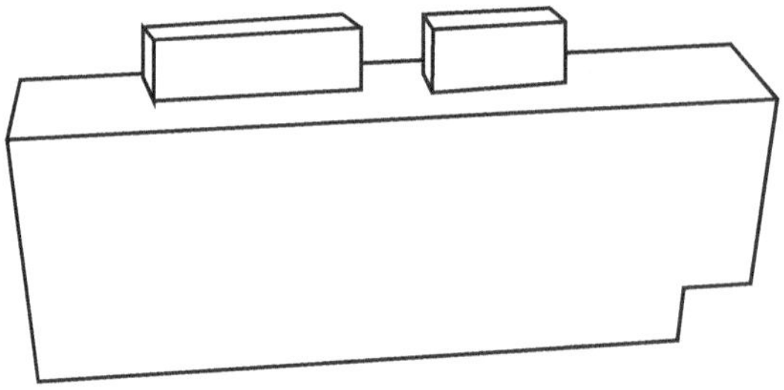

2

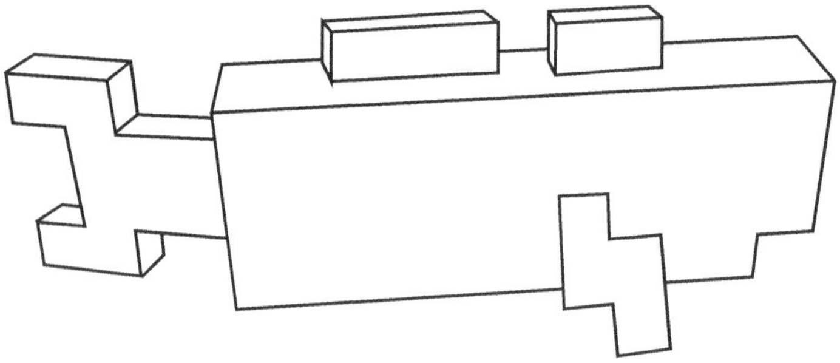

3

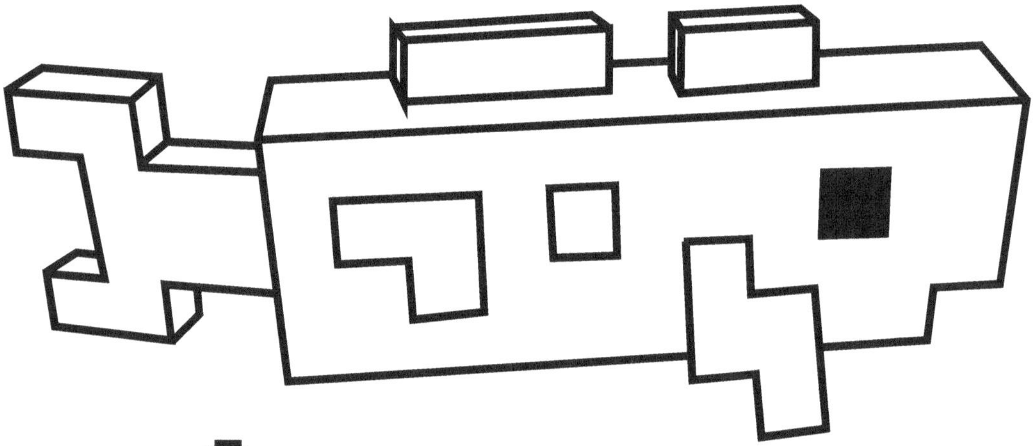

4

How to draw?

COD

Difficulty 

NOW, IT'S YOUR TURN

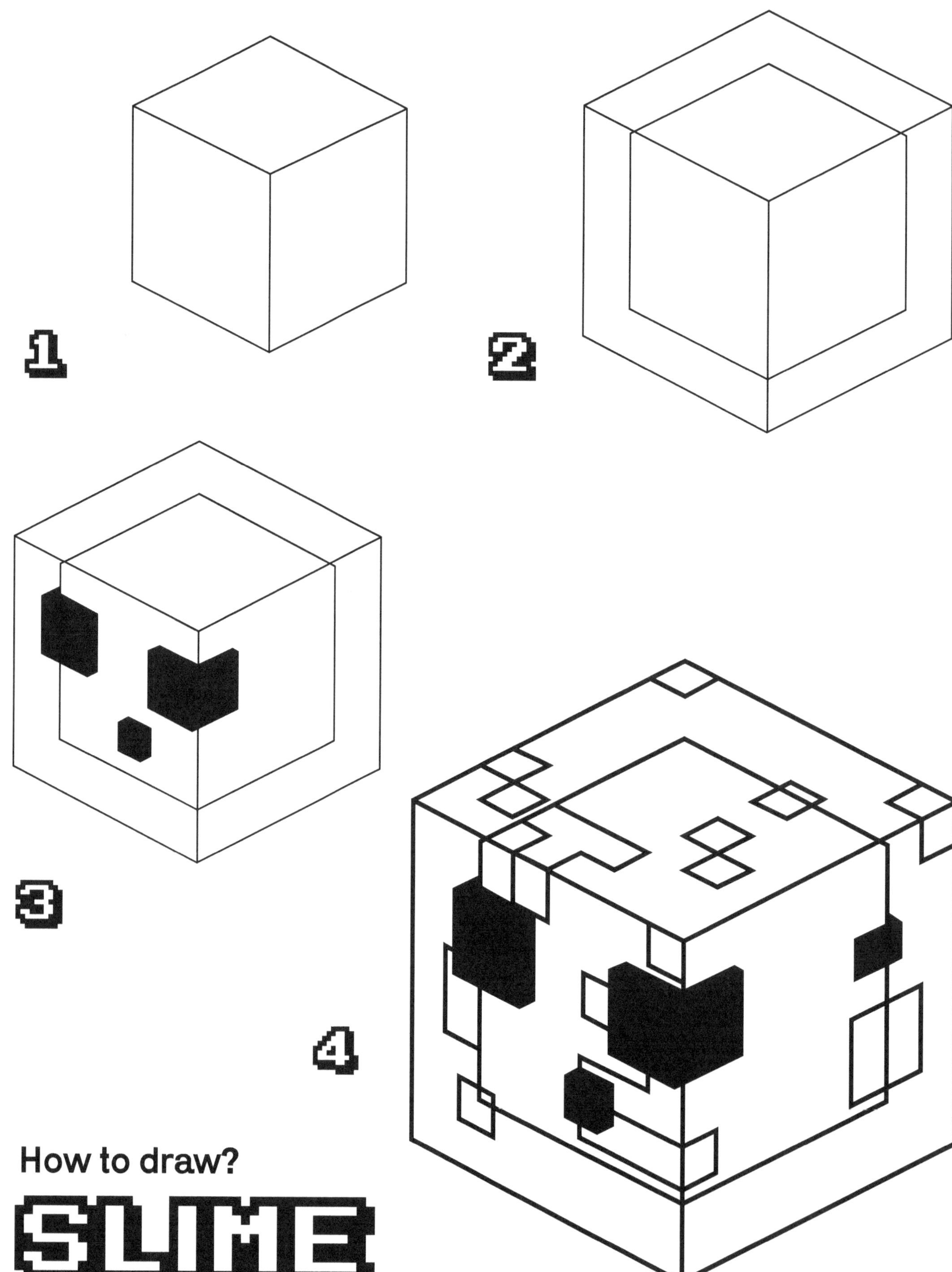

1

2

3

4

How to draw?

SLIME

Difficulty

NOW, iT'S YOUR TURN

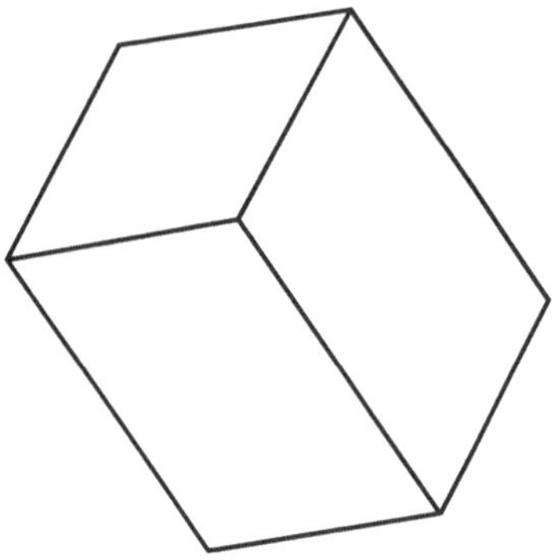

1

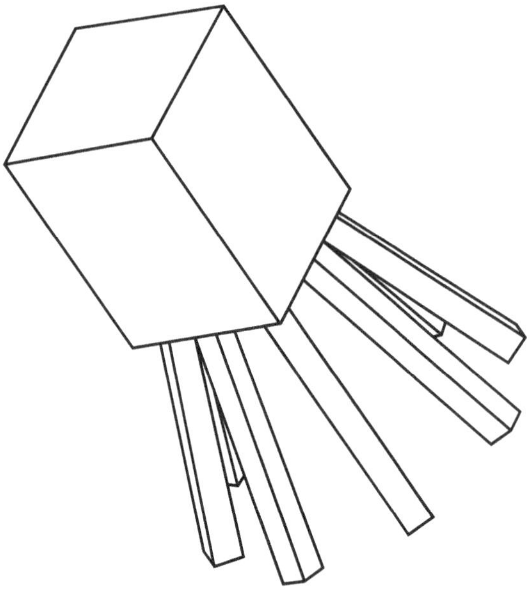

2

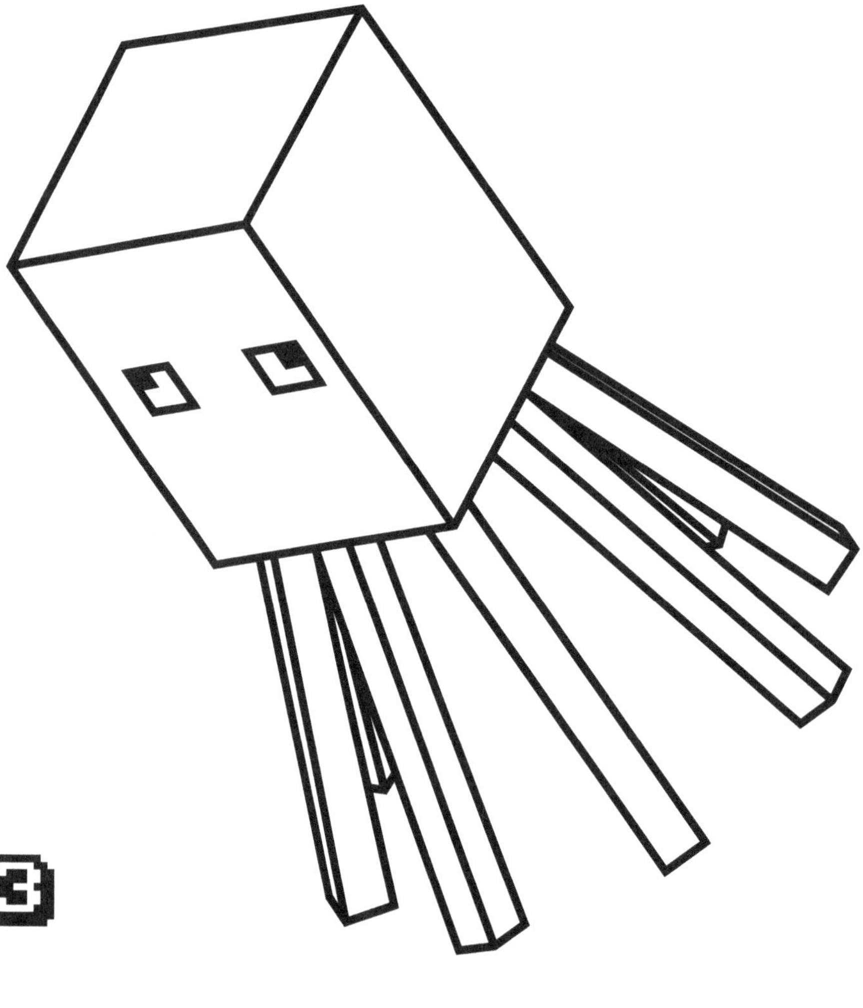

3

How to draw?

SQUID

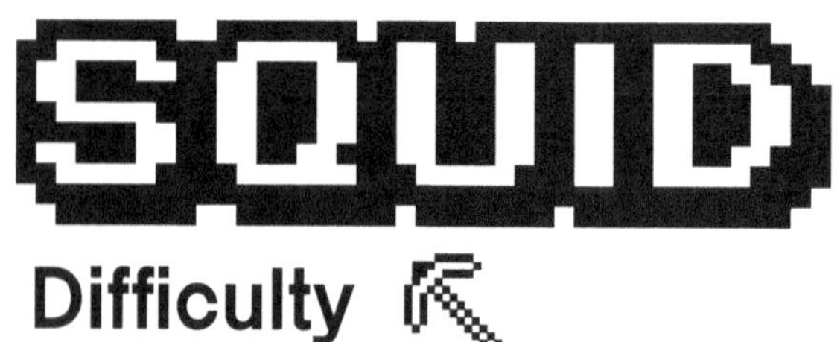

Difficulty

NOW, IT'S YOUR TURN

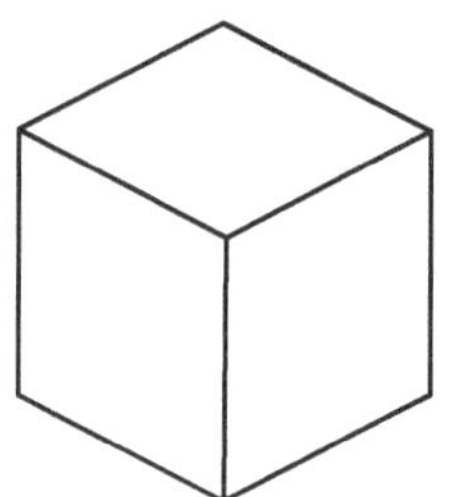

1

2

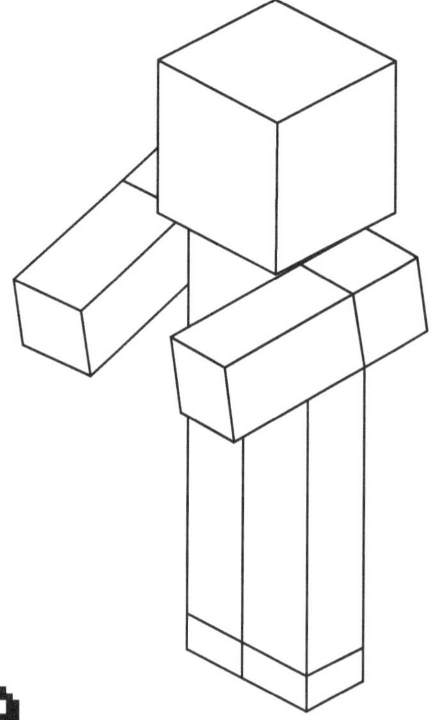

3

4

How to draw?

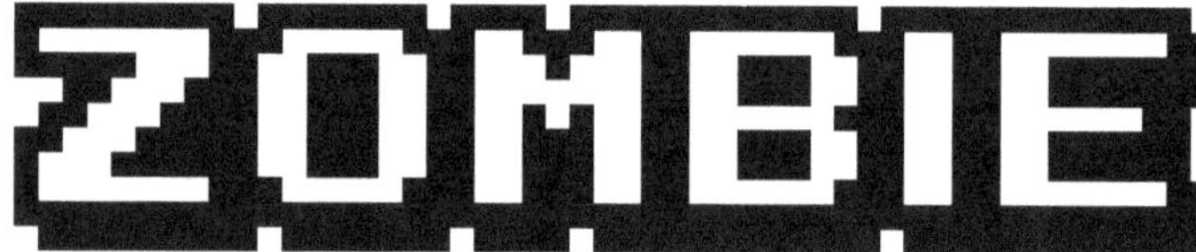

ZOMBIE

Difficulty

NOW, IT'S YOUR TURN

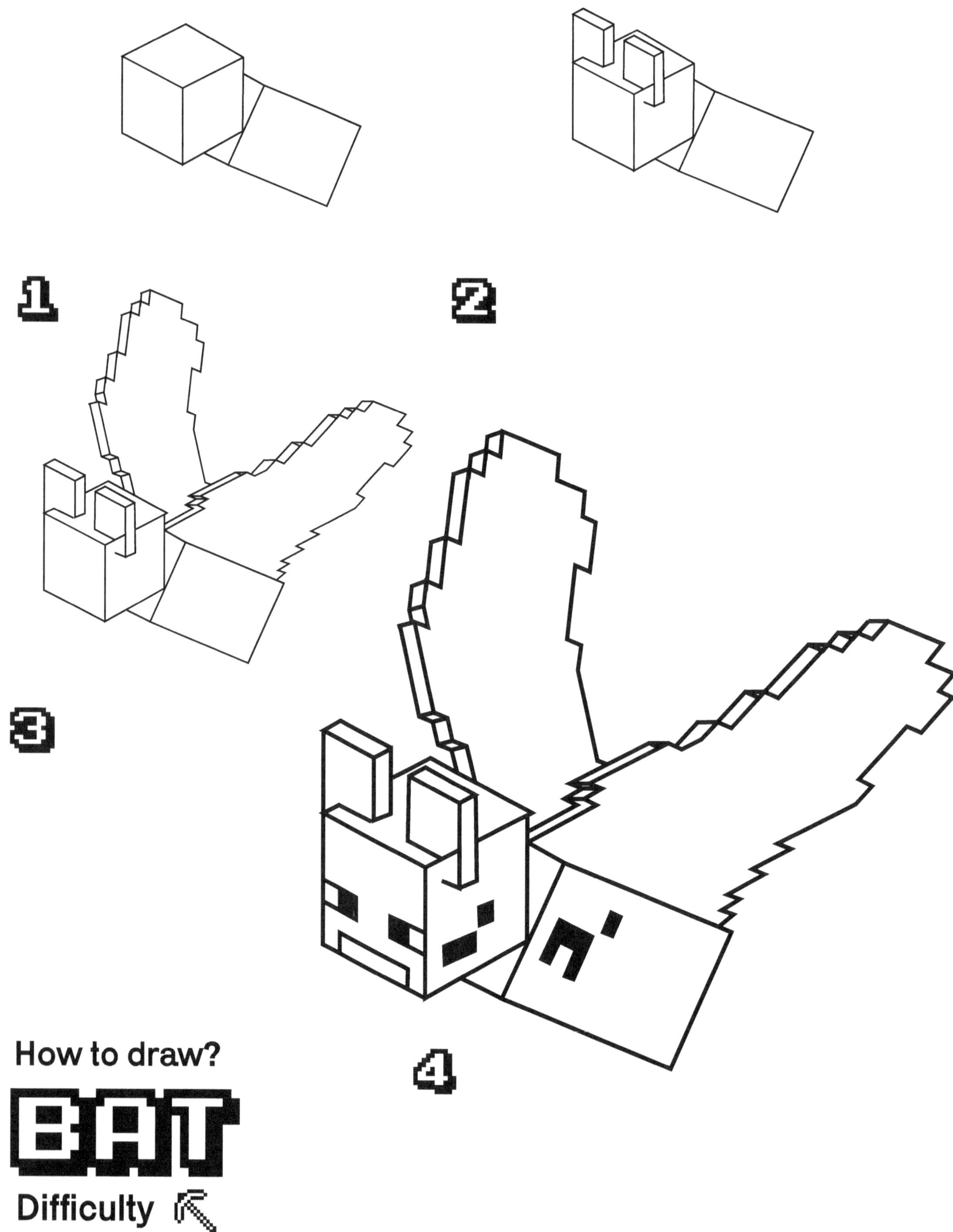

1
2
3
How to draw?
BAT
Difficulty
4

NOW, IT'S YOUR TURN

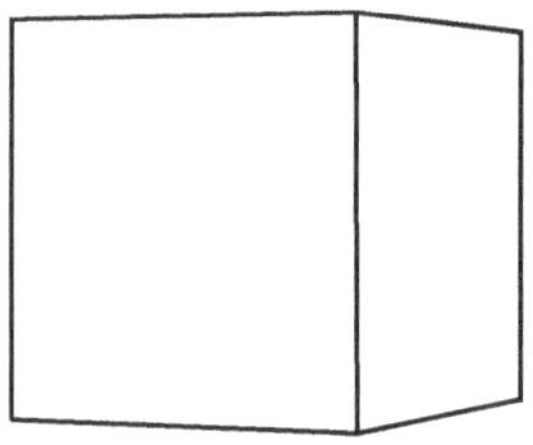

How to draw?

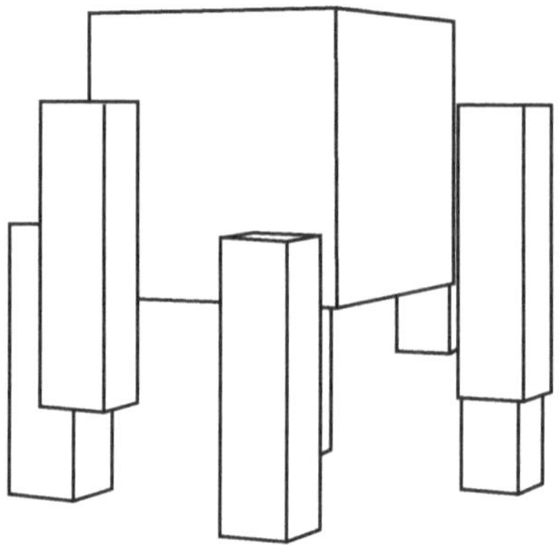

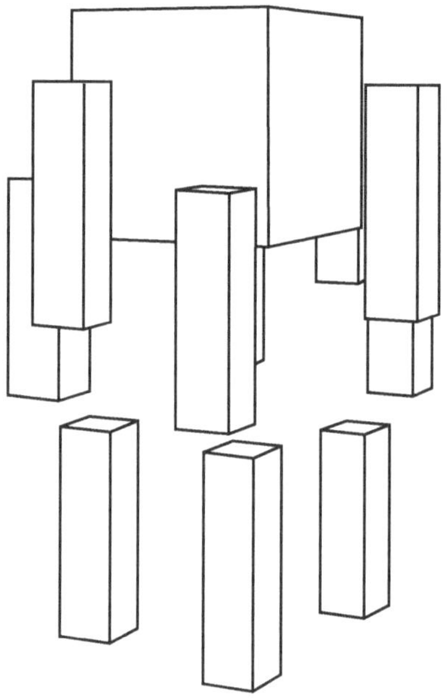

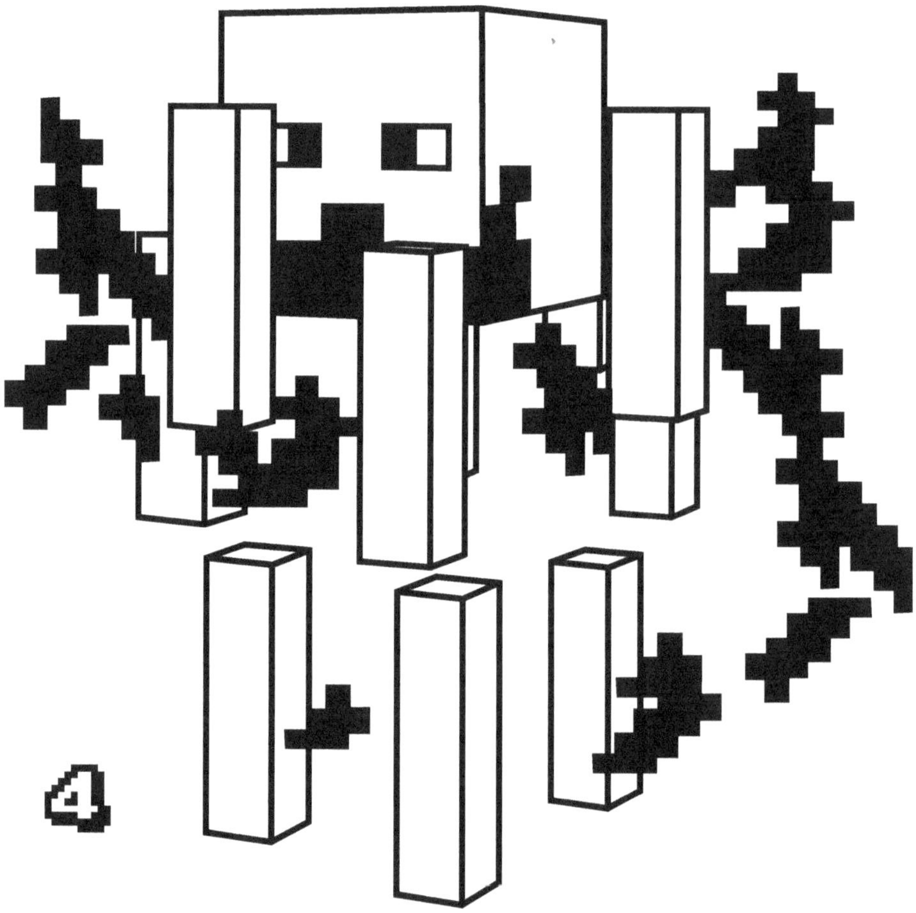

BLAZE

Difficulty

NOW, iT'S YOUR TURN

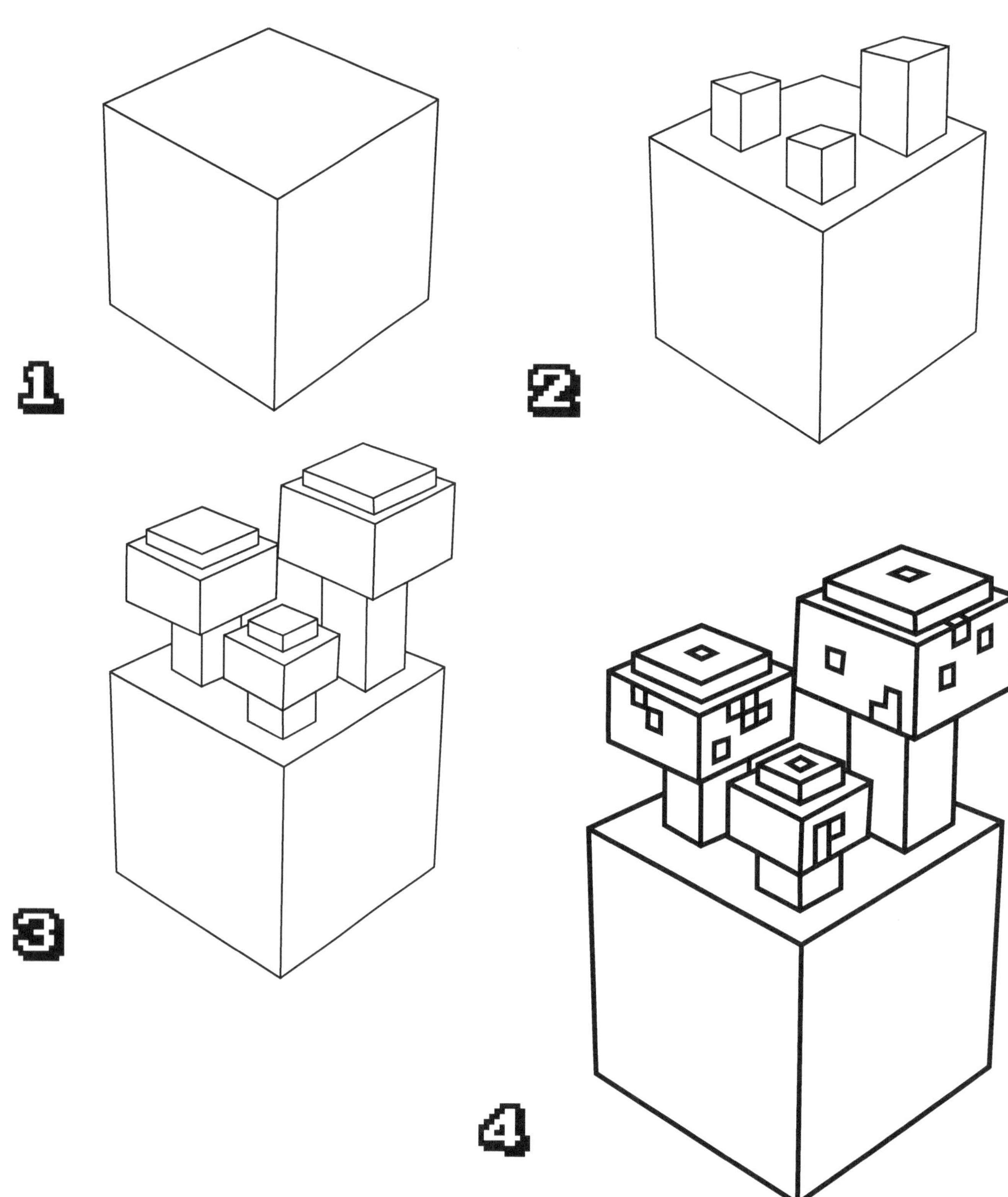

How to draw?

MUSHROOMS

Difficulty

NOW, IT'S YOUR TURN

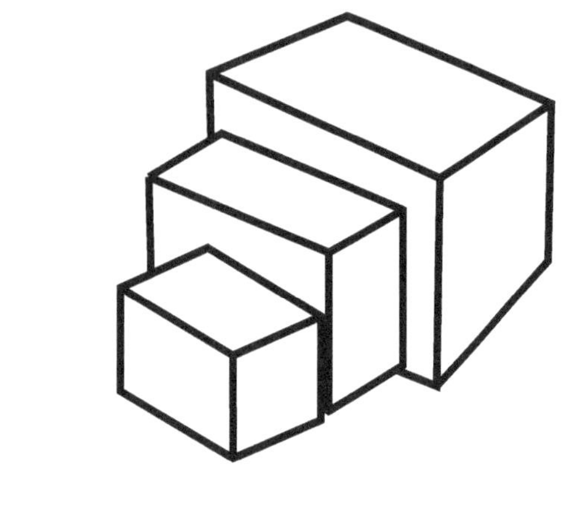

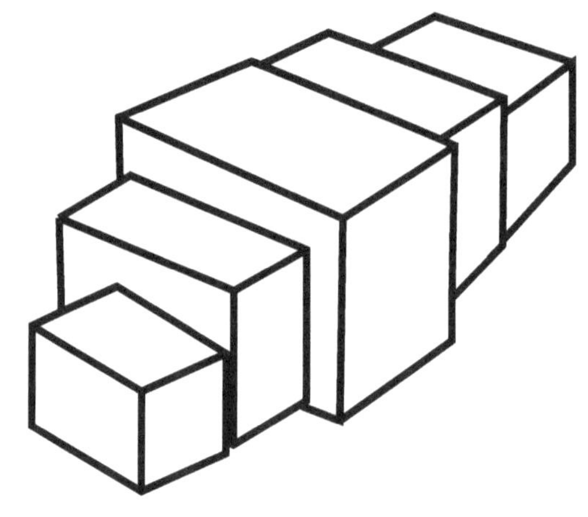

How to draw?

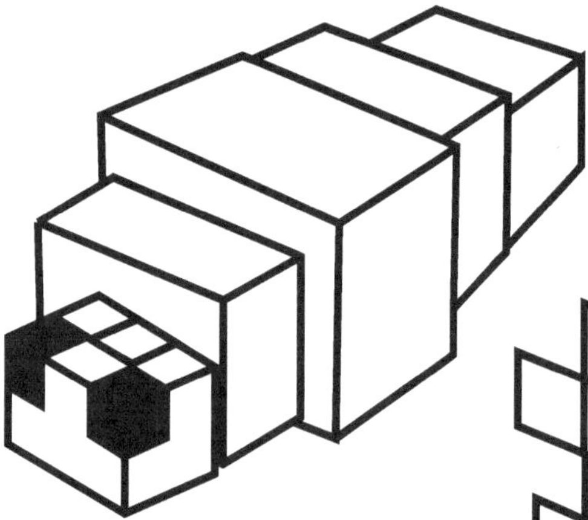

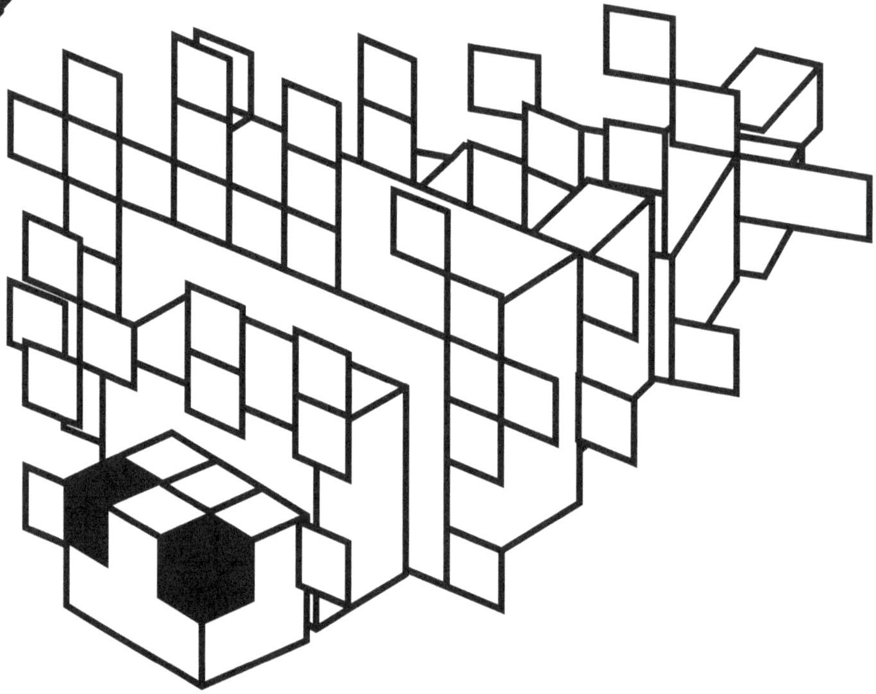

SILVER FISH

Difficulty

NOW, IT'S YOUR TURN

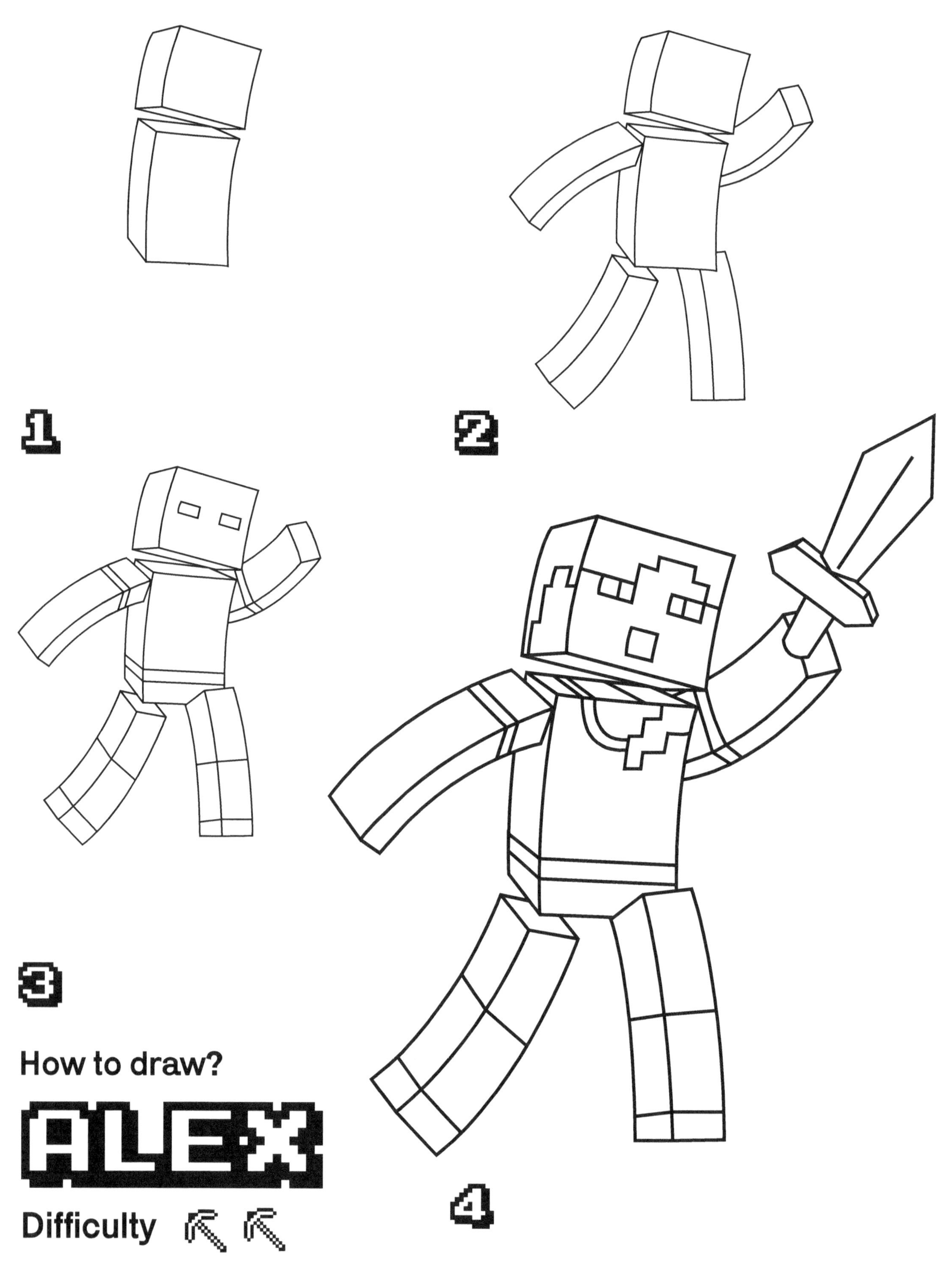

1
2
3
4
How to draw?
ALEX
Difficulty

NOW, IT'S YOUR TURN

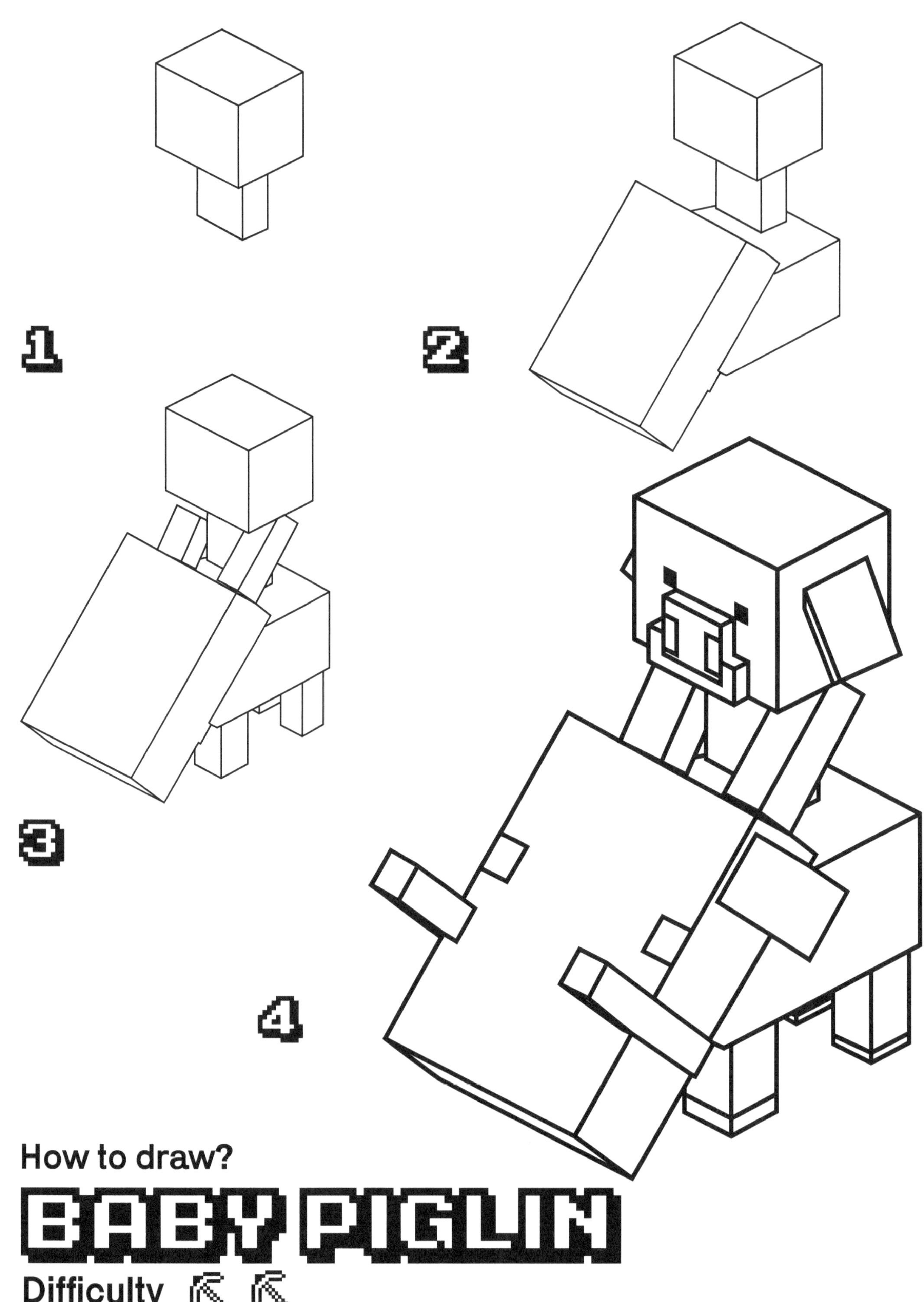

1
2
3
4
How to draw?
BABY PIGLIN
Difficulty

NOW, IT'S YOUR TURN

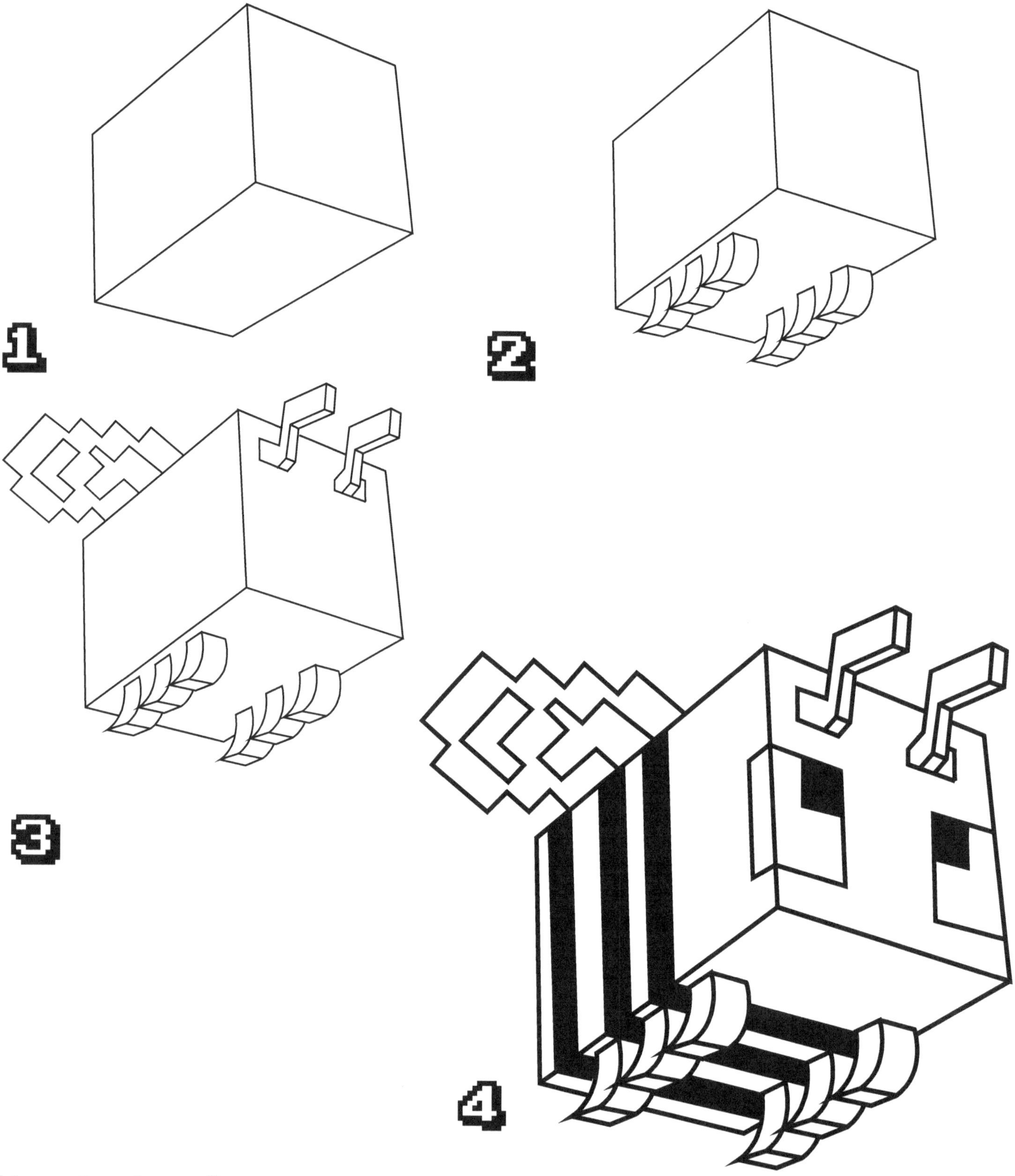

How to draw?

Difficulty

NOW, IT'S YOUR TURN

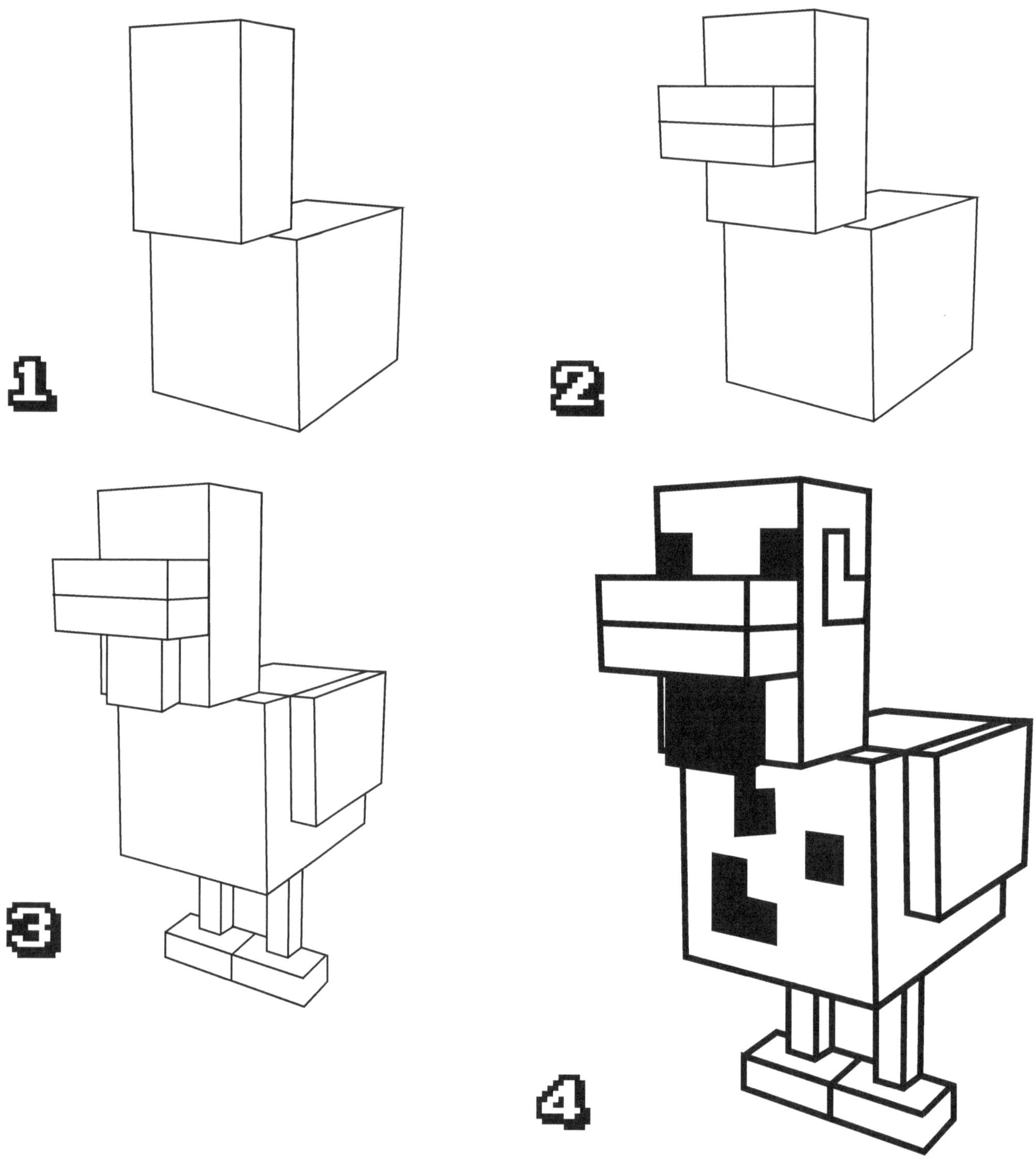

How to draw?

CHICKEN

Difficulty

NOW, IT'S YOUR TURN

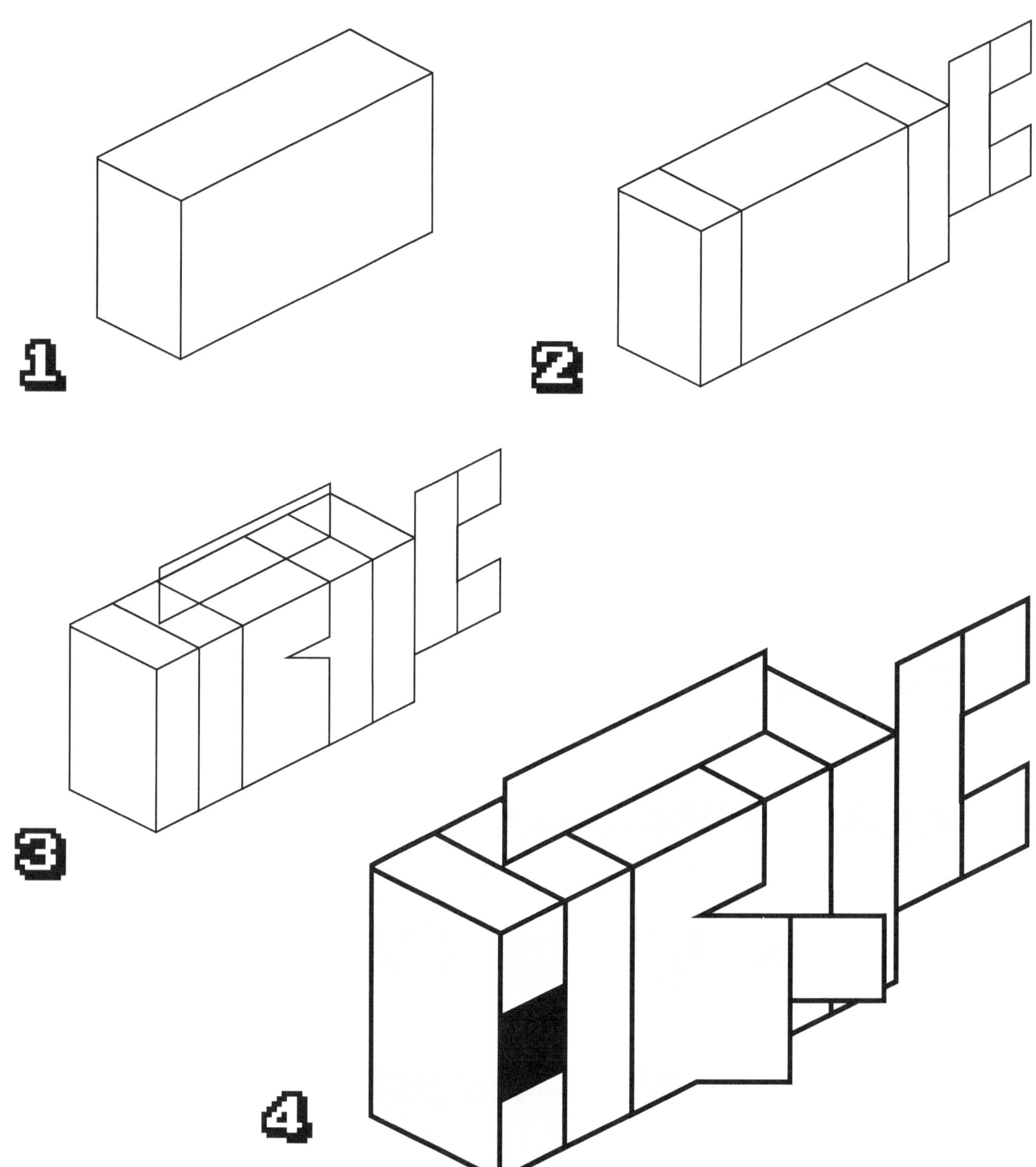

How to draw?

CLOWNFISH

Difficulty

NOW, IT'S YOUR TURN

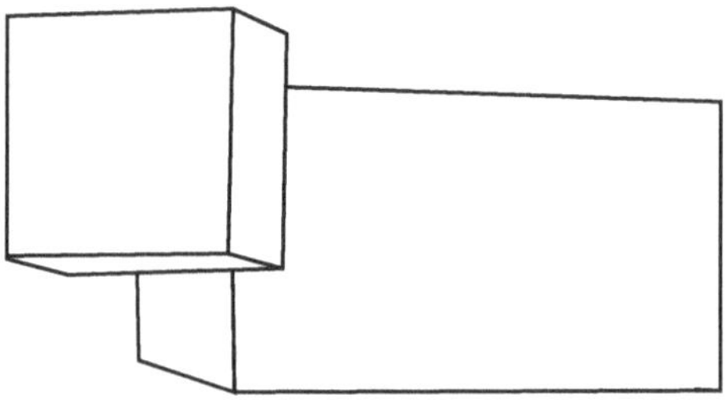

1

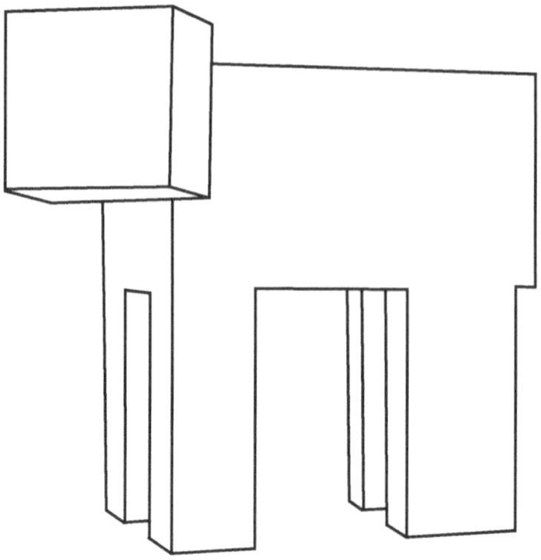

2

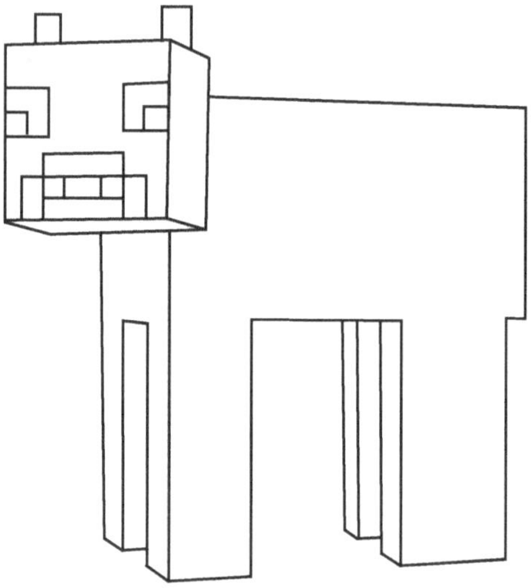

3

4

How to draw?

COW

Difficulty 

NOW, iT'S YOUR TURN

How to draw?

CREEPER

Difficulty

NOW, IT'S YOUR TURN

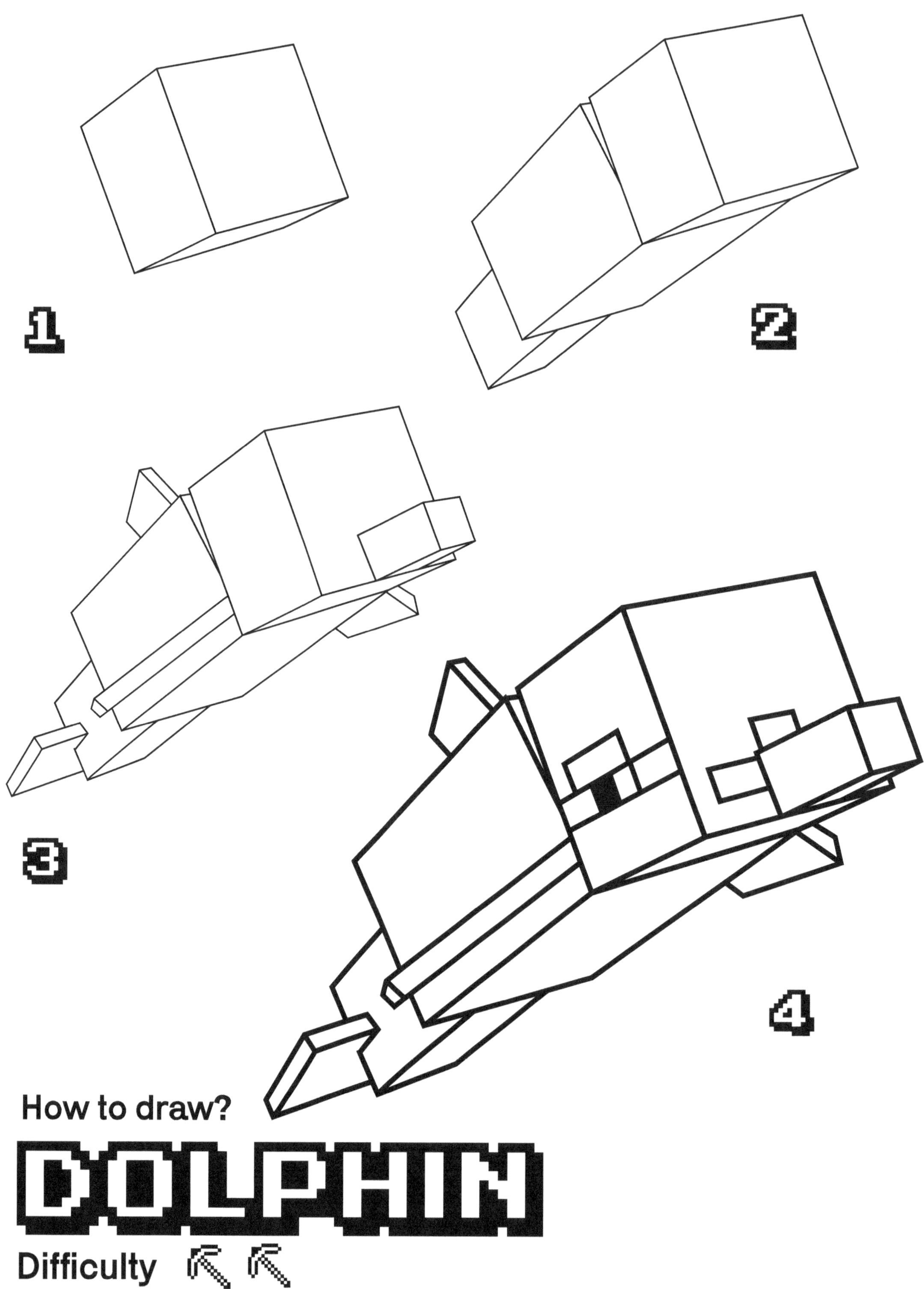

1
2
3
4
How to draw?
DOLPHIN
Difficulty

NOW, IT'S YOUR TURN

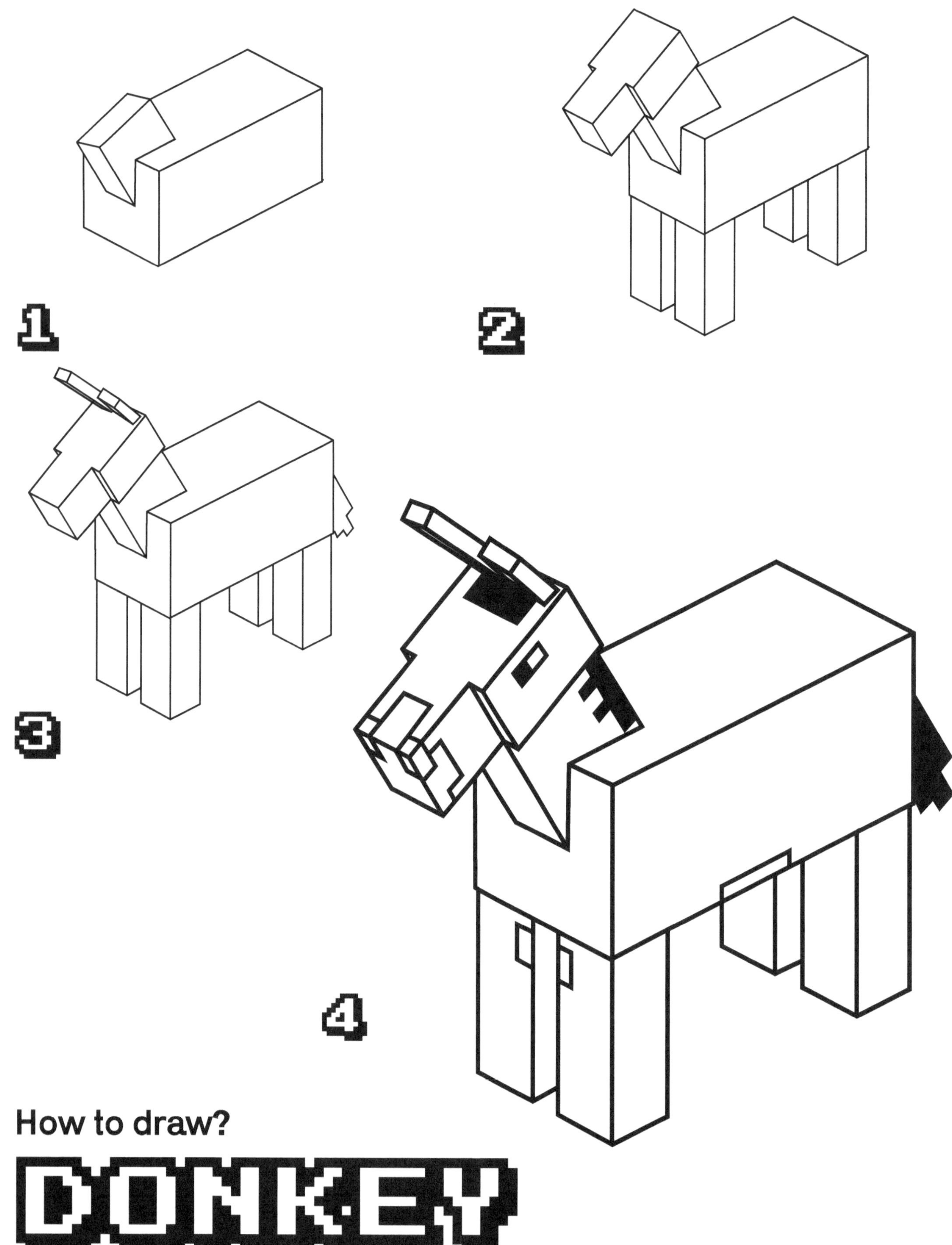

1

2

3

4

How to draw?

DONKEY

Difficulty

NOW, IT'S YOUR TURN

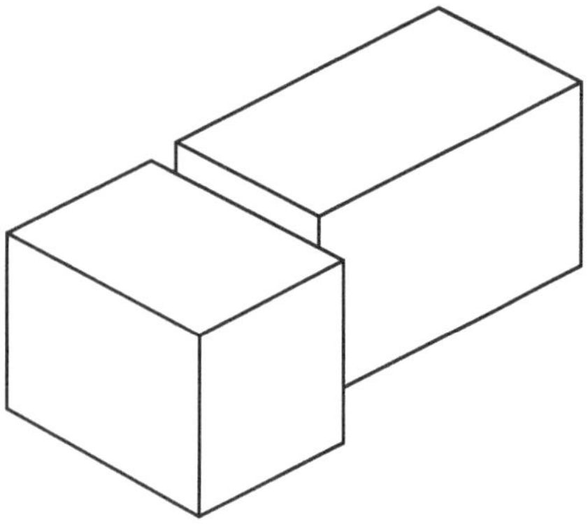

How to draw?

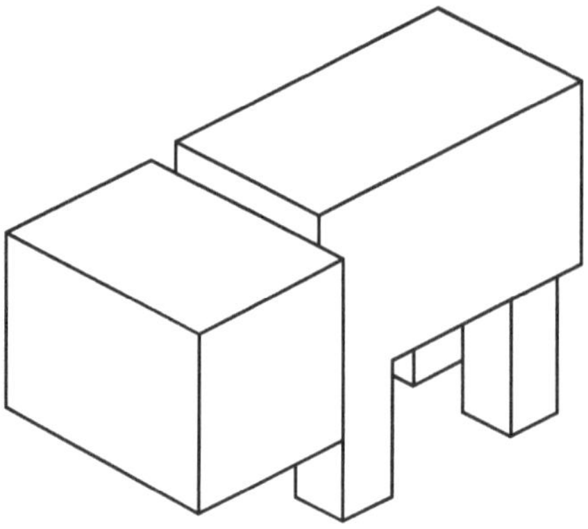

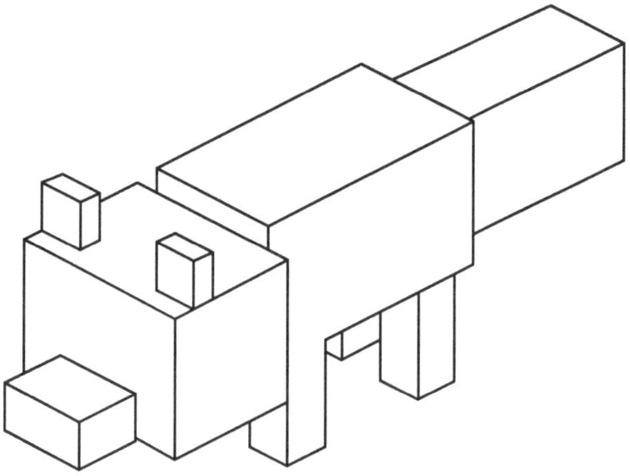

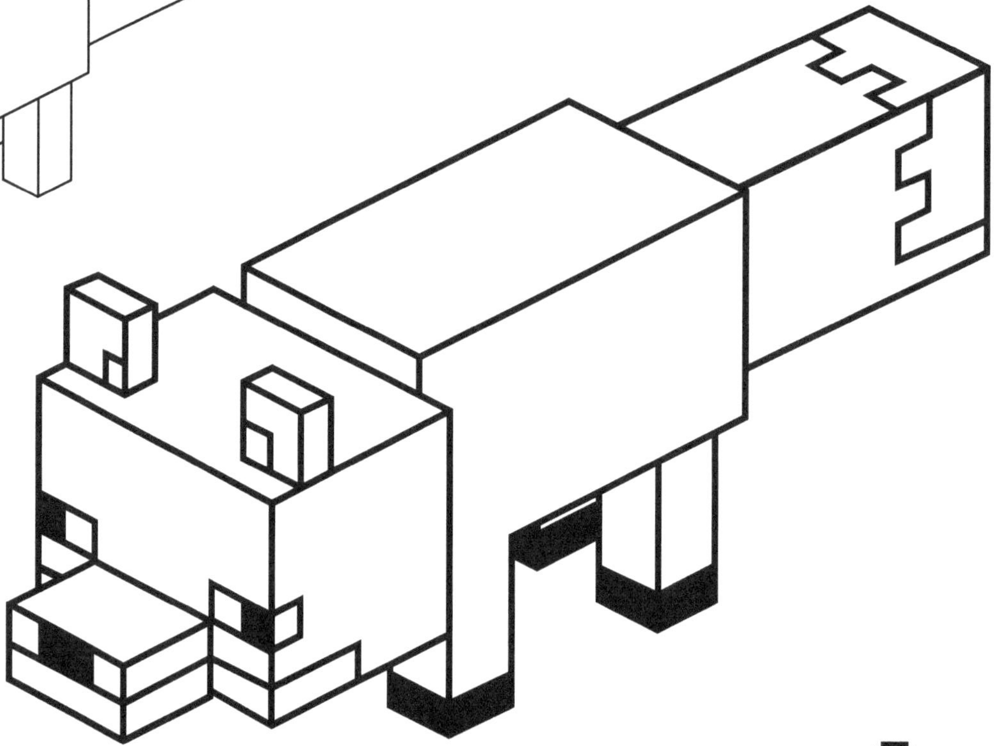

FOX

Difficulty

NOW, iT'S YOUR TURN

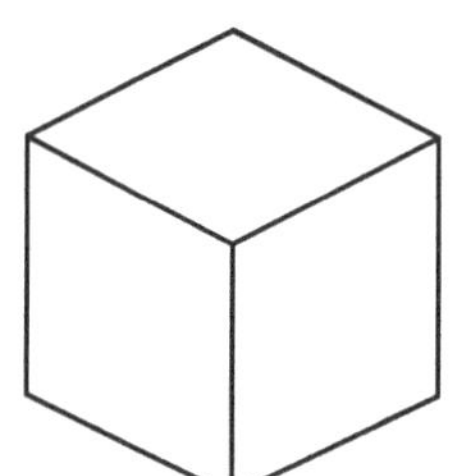

1

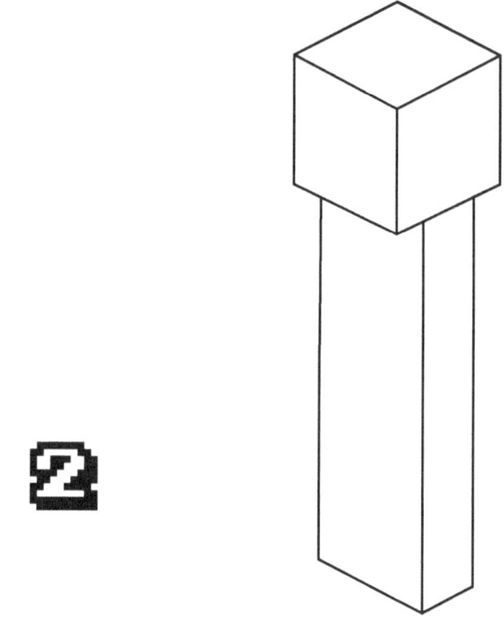

2

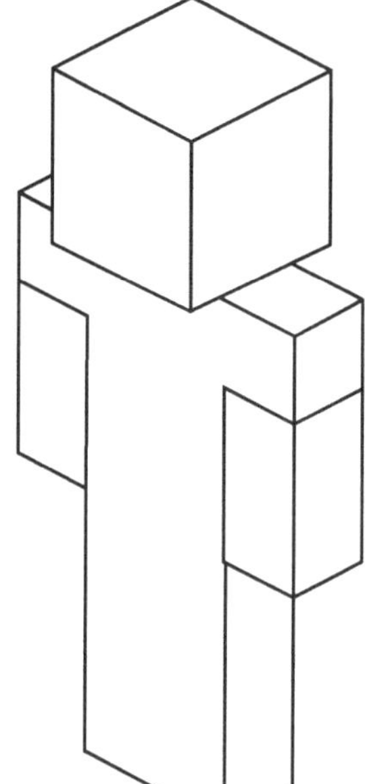

3

How to draw?

Difficulty 🔨 🔨

4

NOW, IT'S YOUR TURN

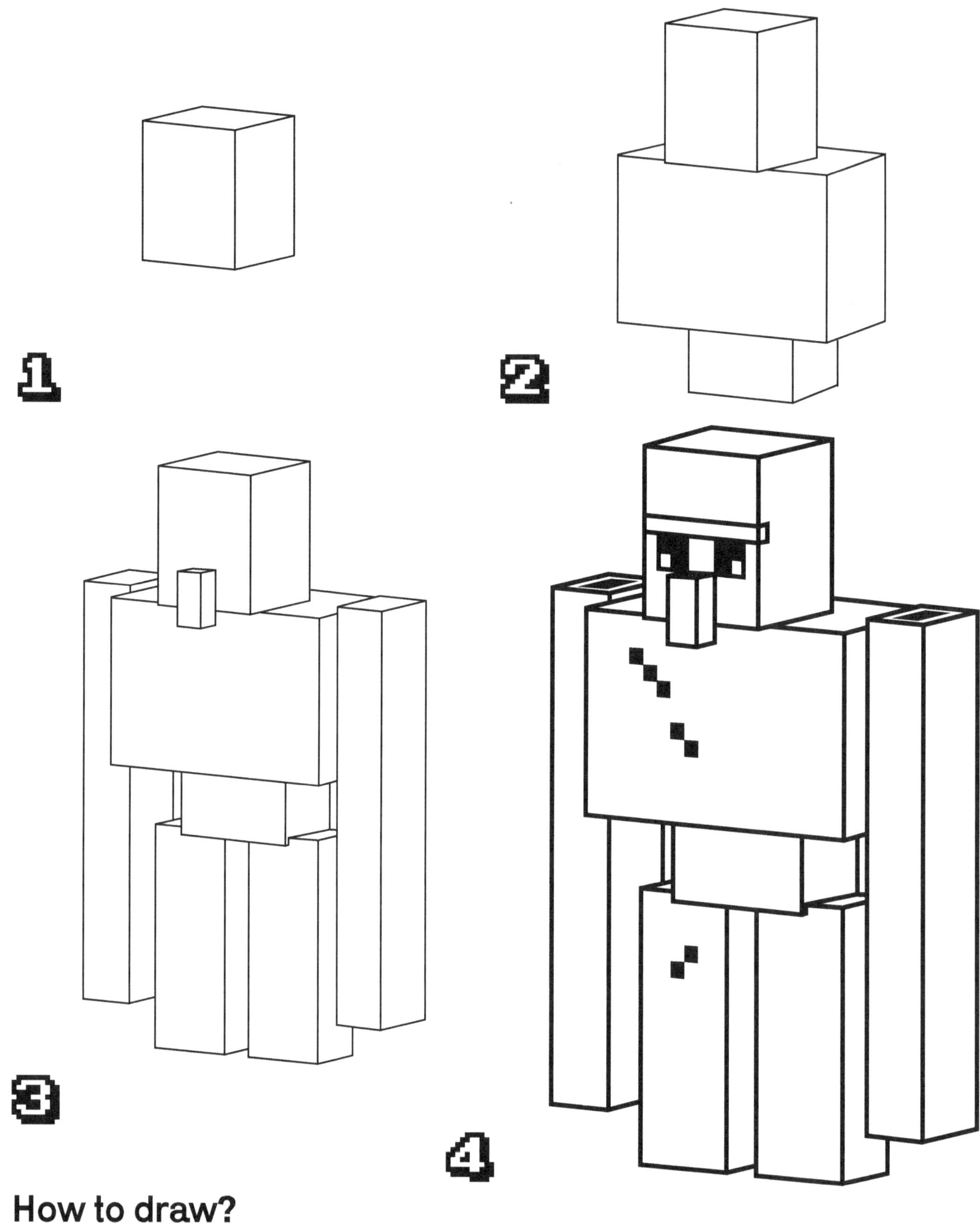

1

2

3

4

How to draw?

IRON GOLEM

Difficulty

NOW, IT'S YOUR TURN

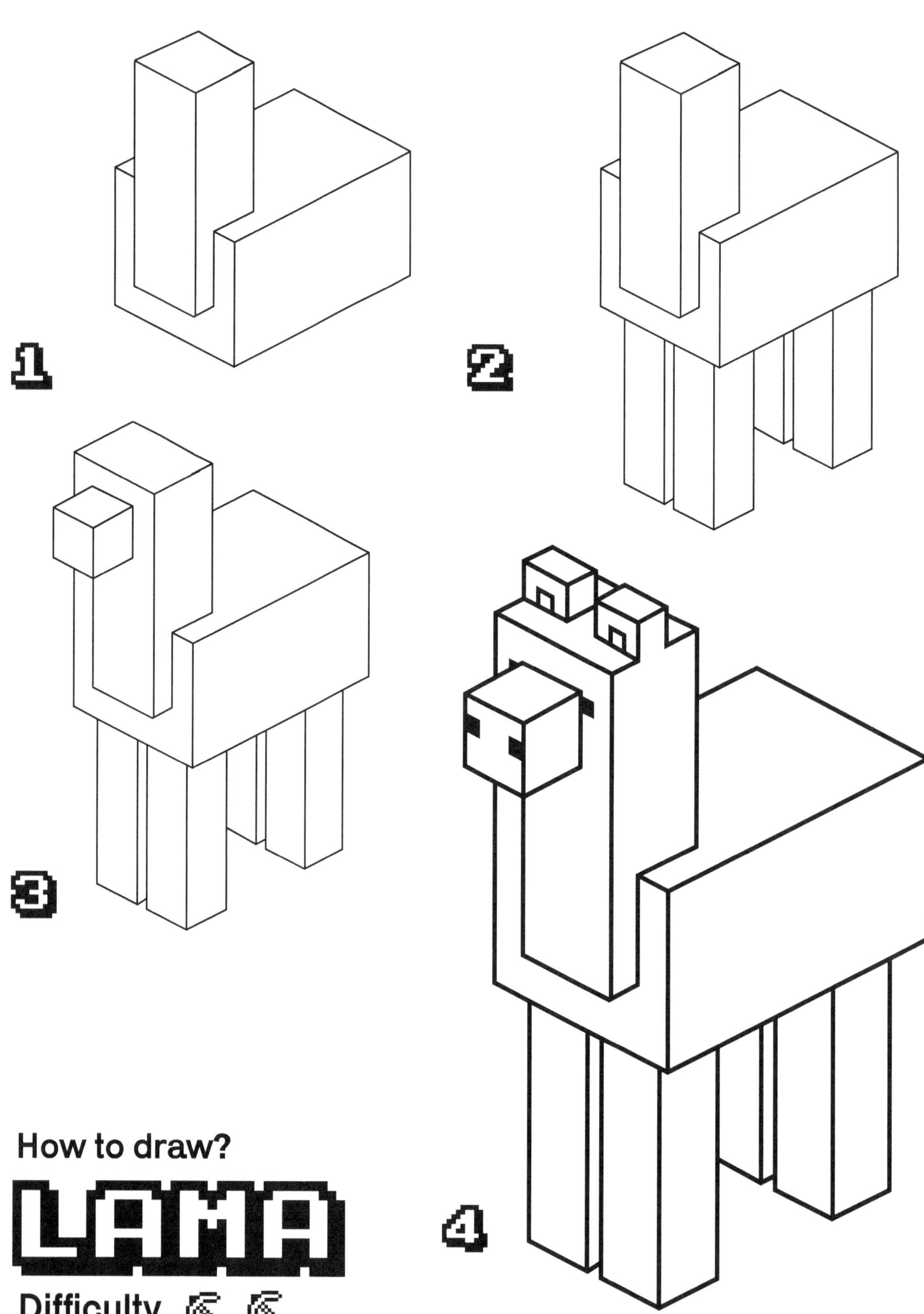

1
2
3
4
How to draw?
LAMA
Difficulty

NOW, iT'S YOUR TURN

NOW, iT'S YOUR TURN

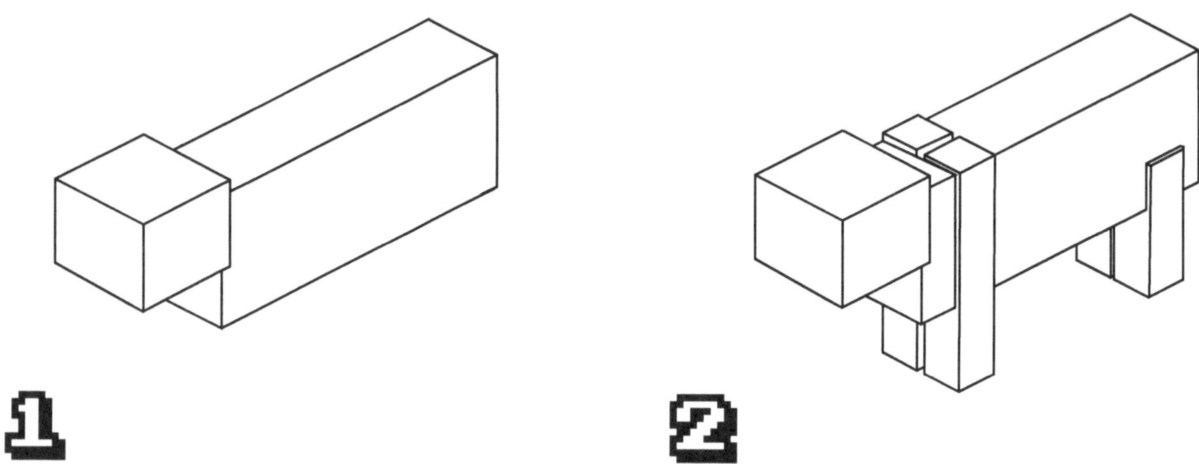

How to draw?

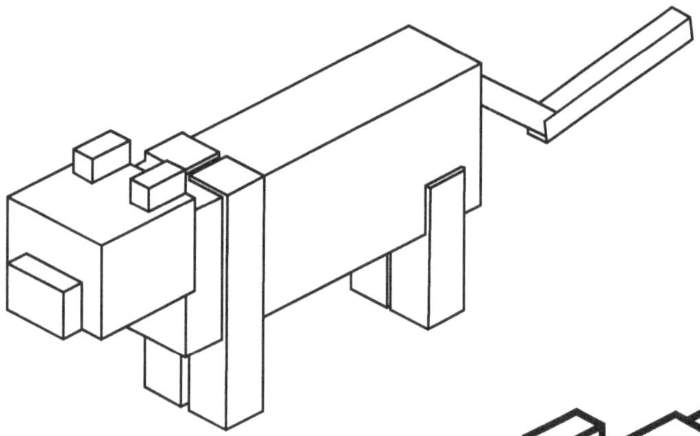

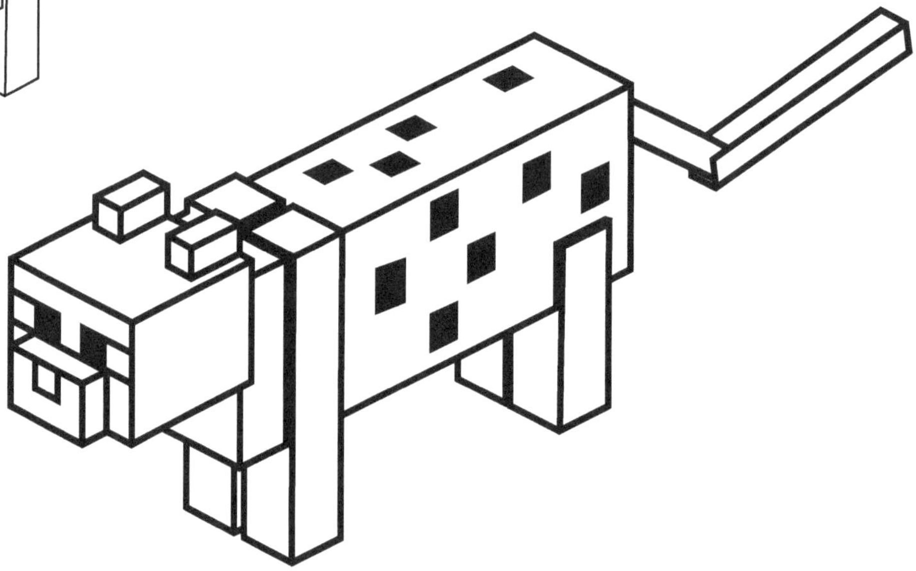

Difficulty 🔨 🔨

NOW, IT'S YOUR TURN

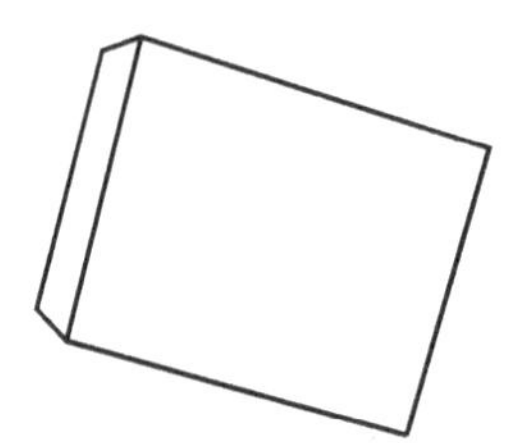

1

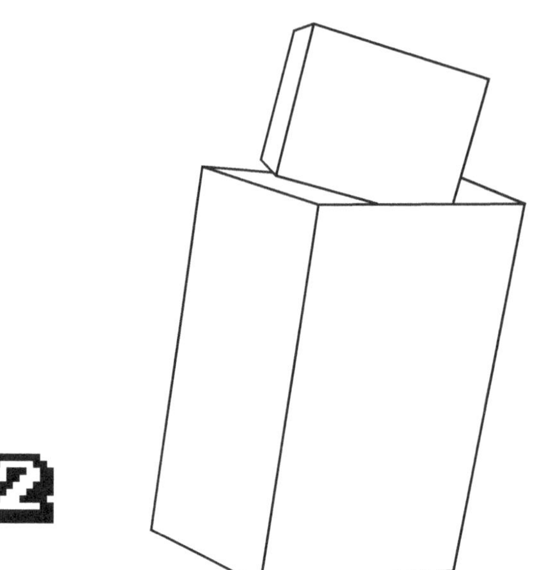

2

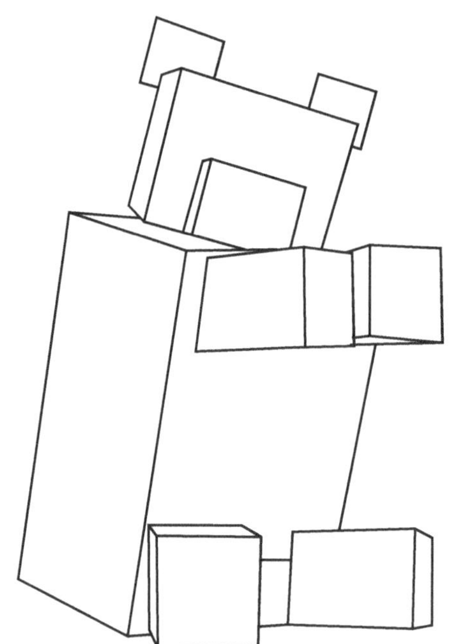

3

4

How to draw?

Difficulty 🔨🔨

NOW, IT'S YOUR TURN

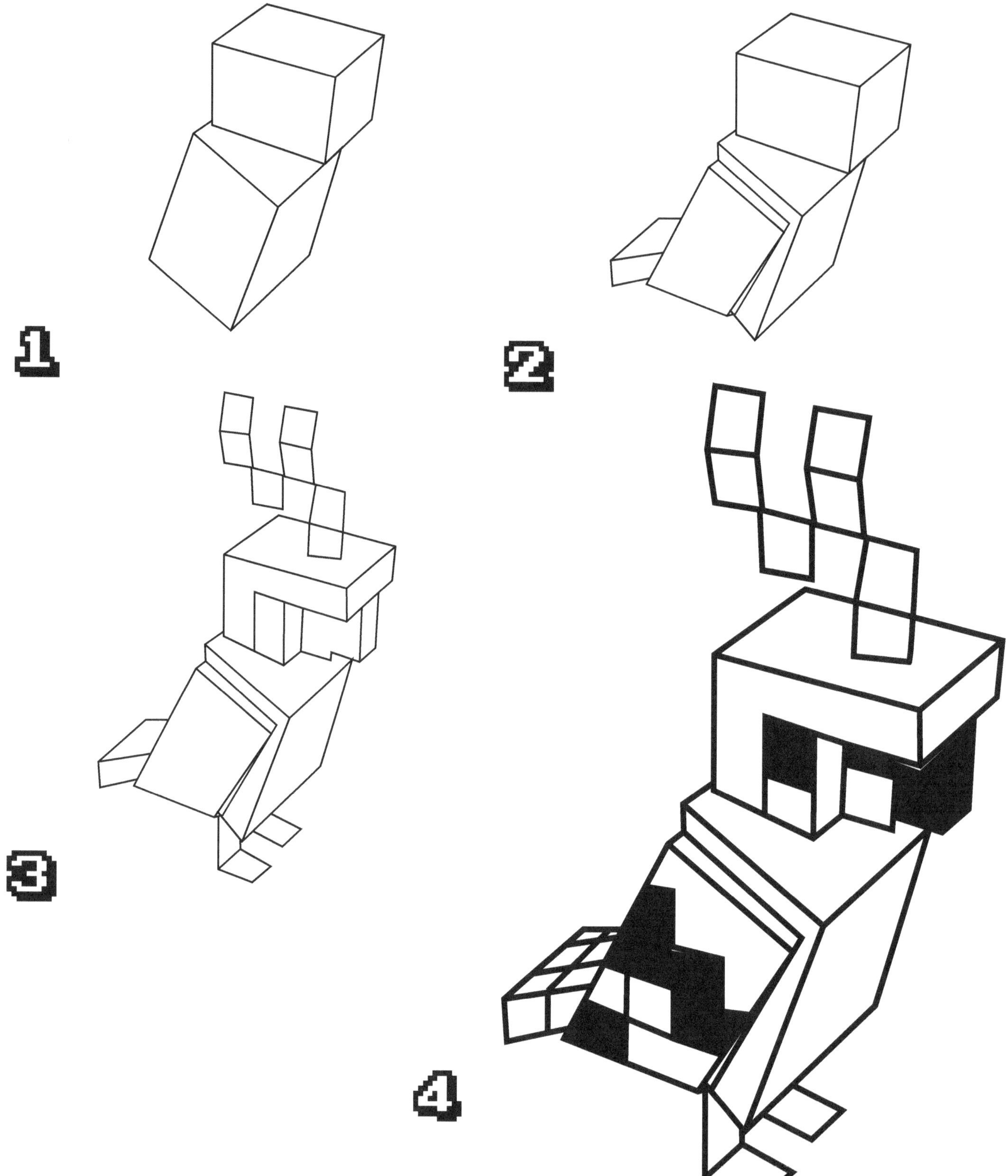

How to draw?

PARROT

Difficulty 

NOW, iT'S YOUR TURN

NOW, iT'S YOUR TURN

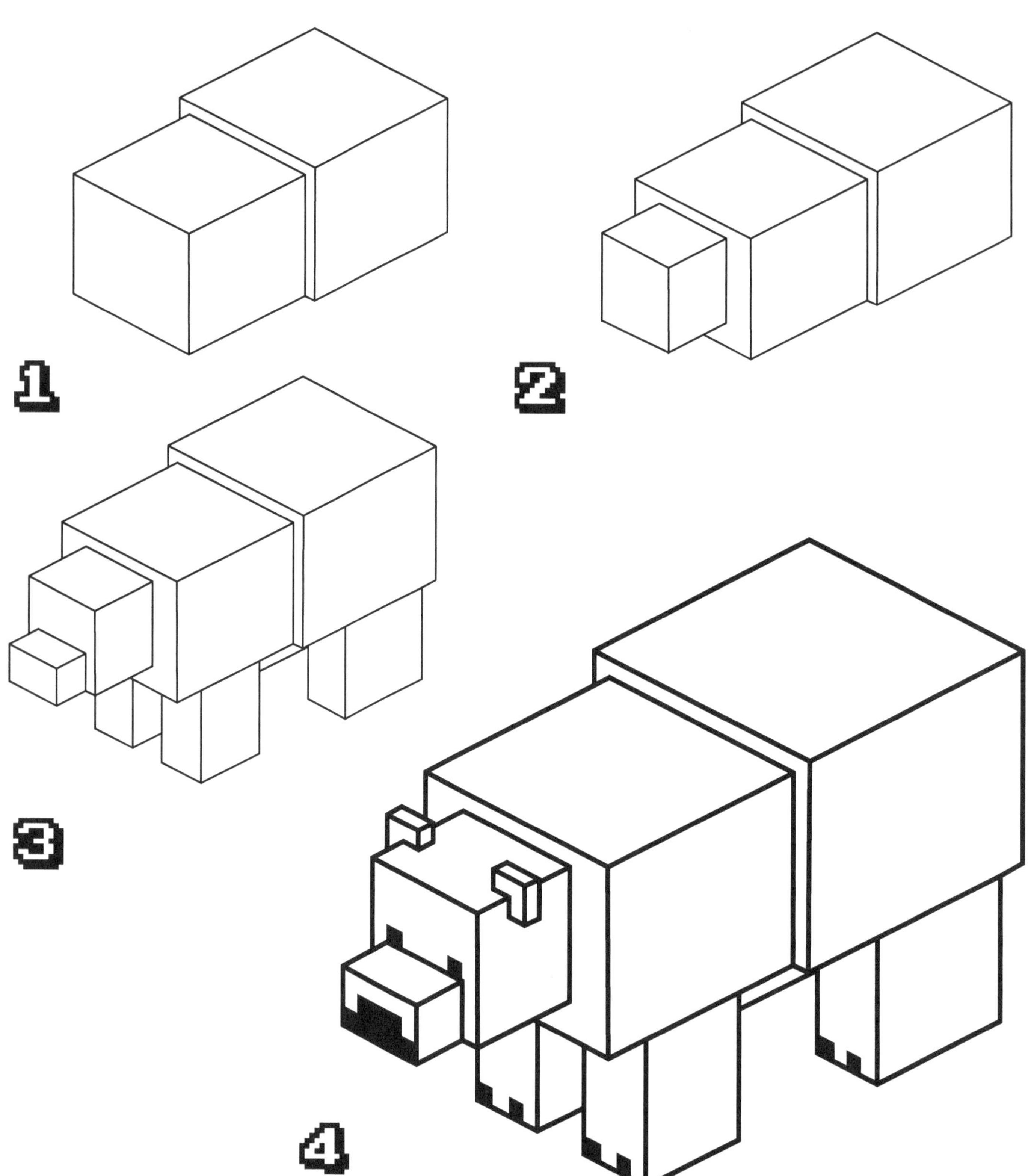

1
2
3
4
How to draw?
POLAR BEAR
Difficulty

NOW, iT'S YOUR TURN

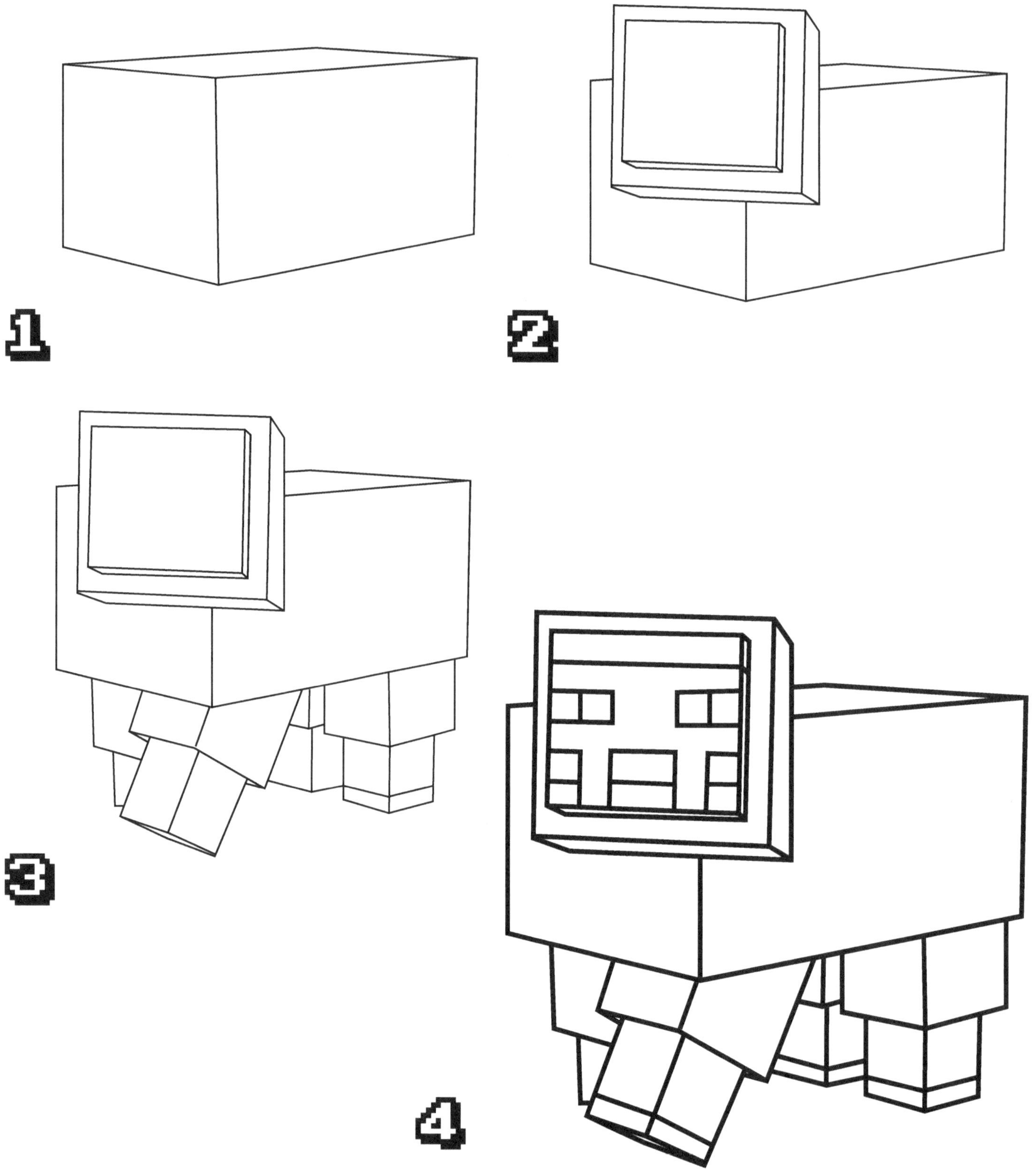

How to draw?

Difficulty

NOW, IT'S YOUR TURN

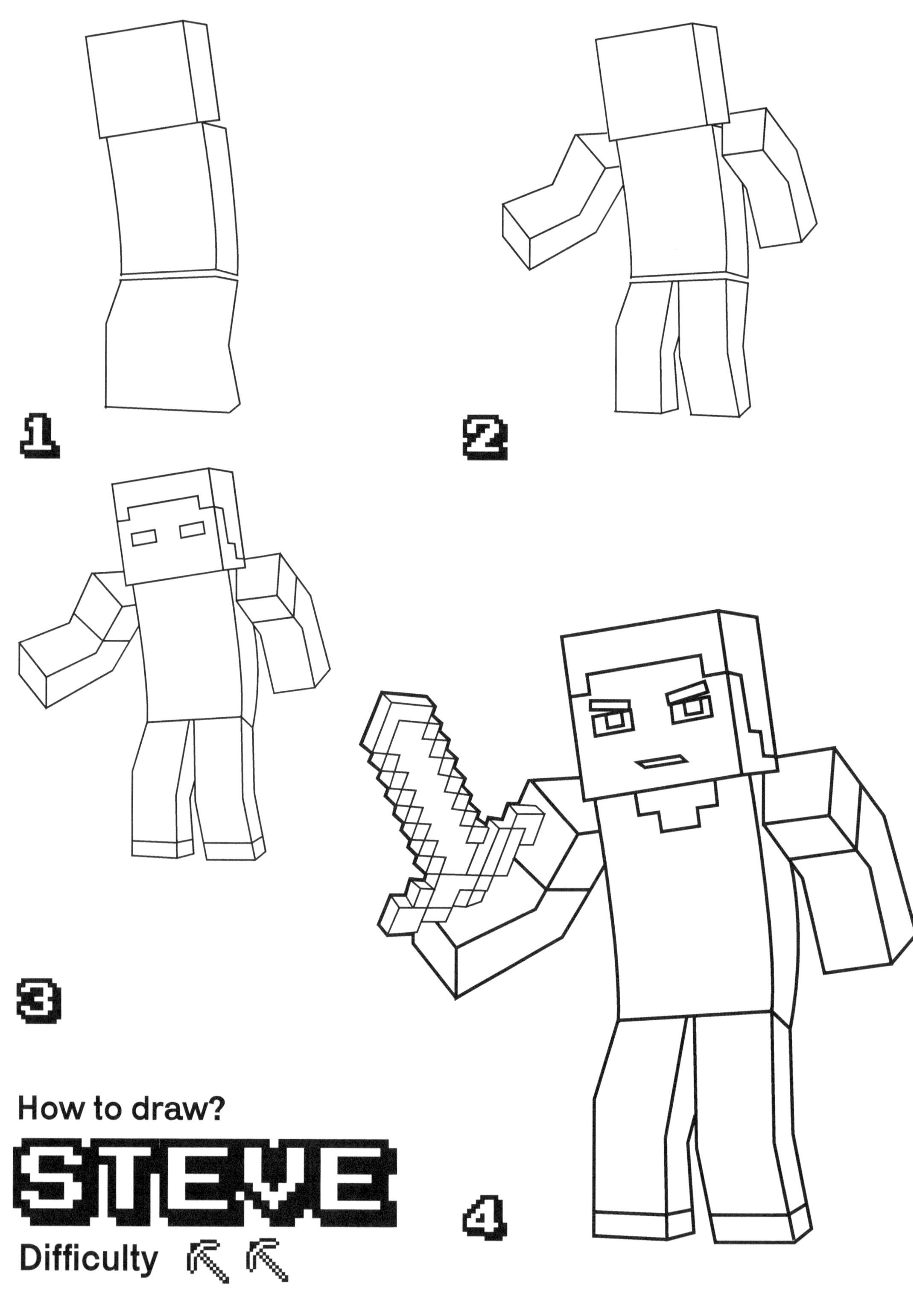

1
2
3
How to draw?
STEVE
Difficulty
4

NOW, iT'S YOUR TURN

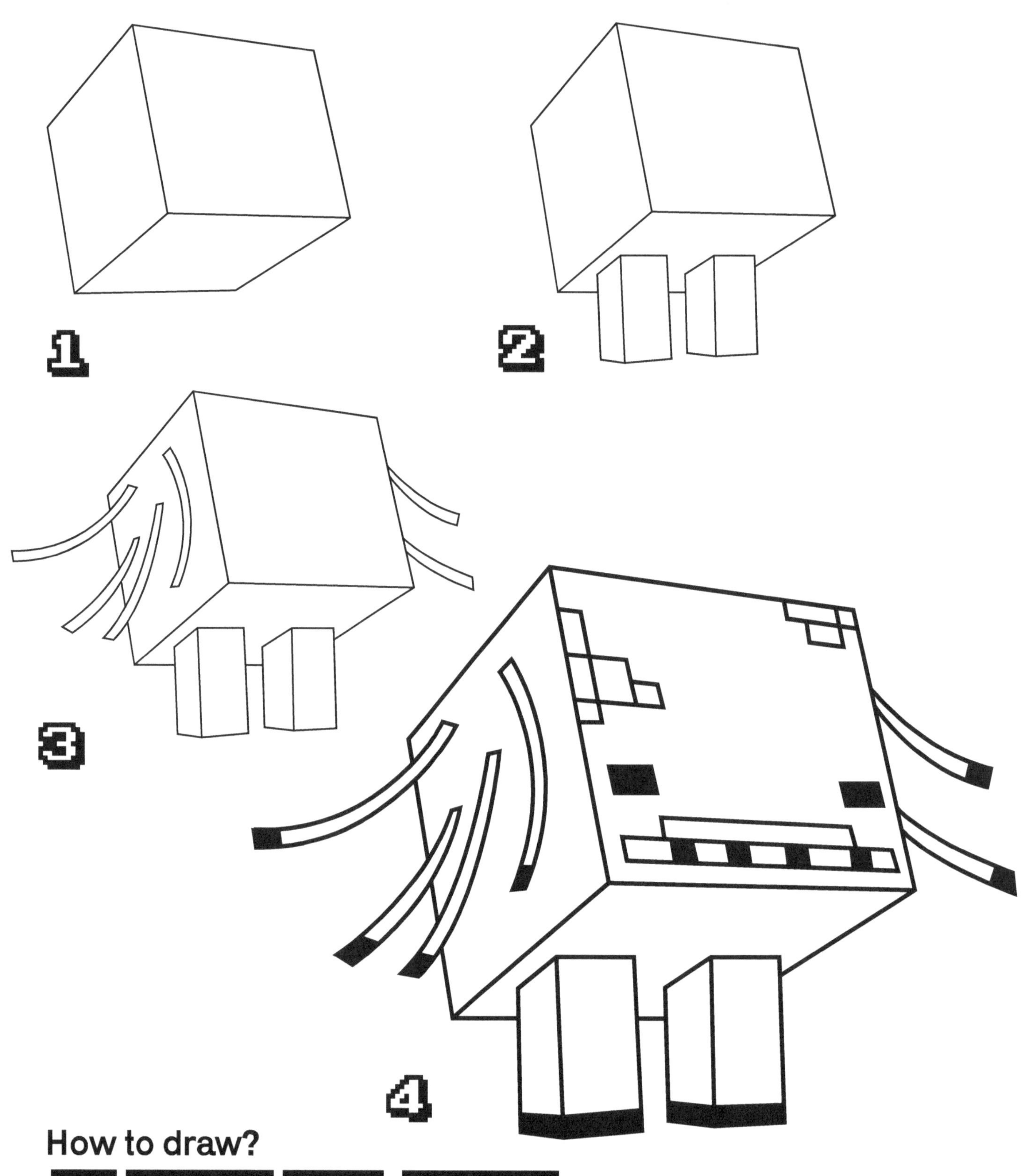

How to draw?

STRIDER

Difficulty

NOW, IT'S YOUR TURN

1

2

3

4

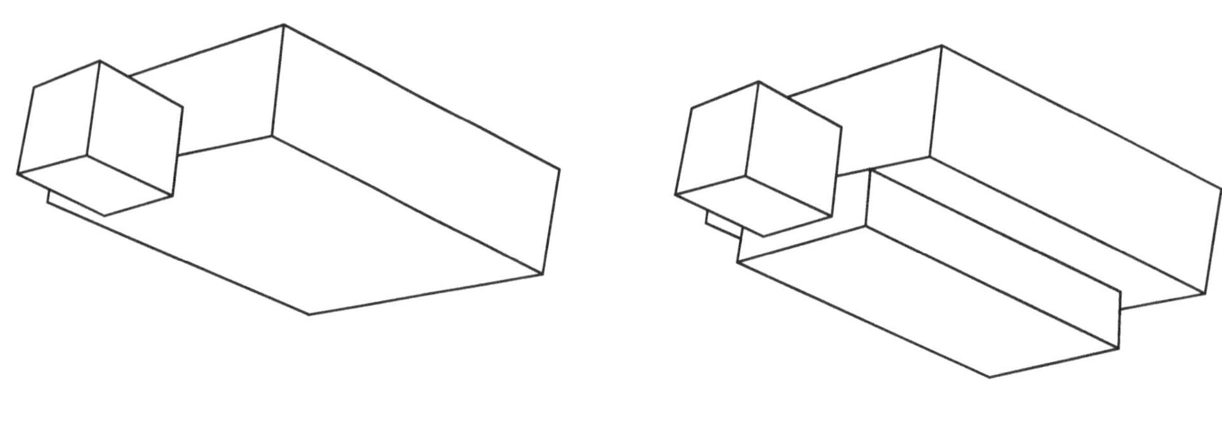

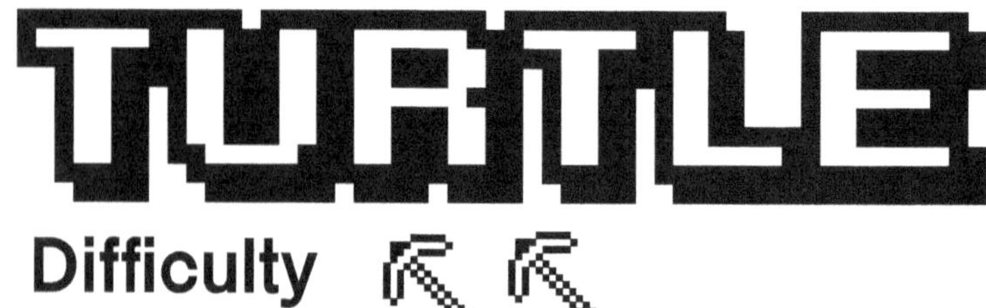

How to draw?

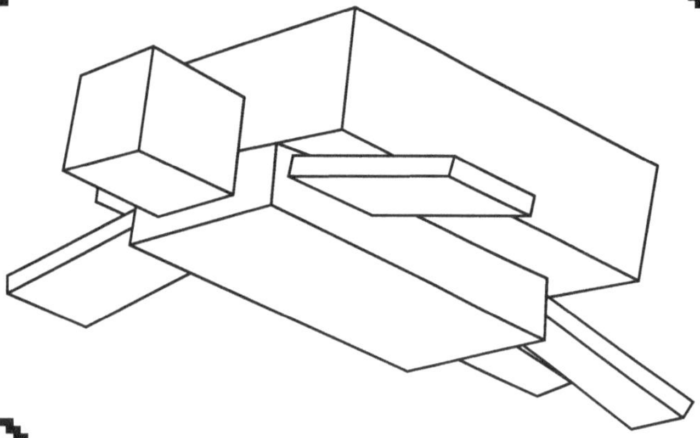

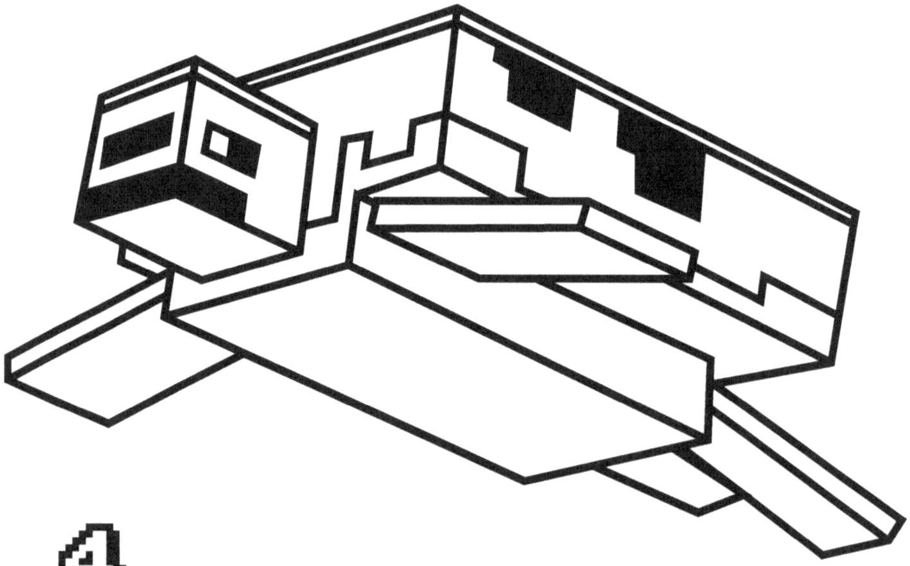

TURTLE

Difficulty

NOW, IT'S YOUR TURN

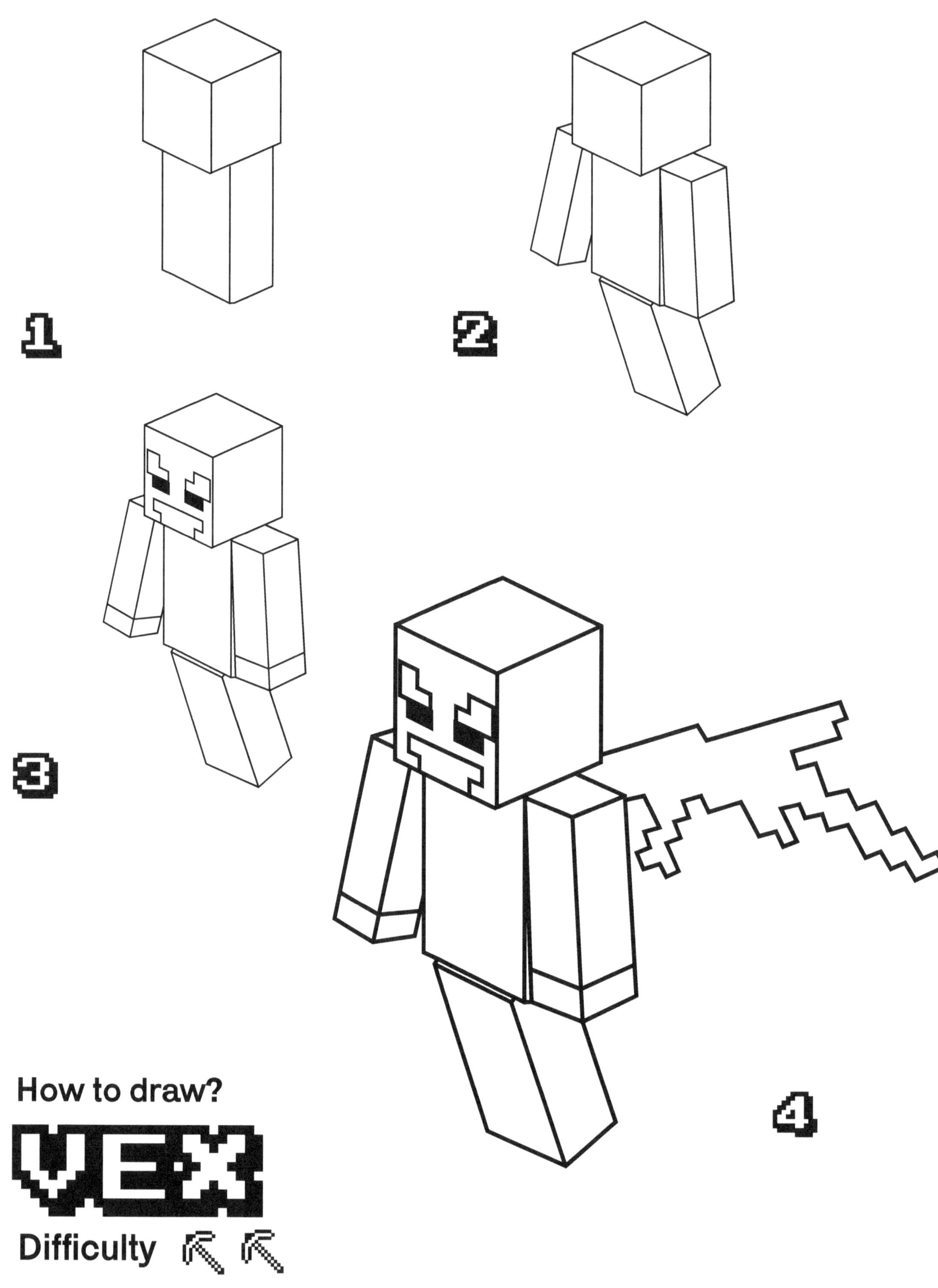

1
2
3
4
How to draw?
VEX
Difficulty

NOW, IT'S YOUR TURN

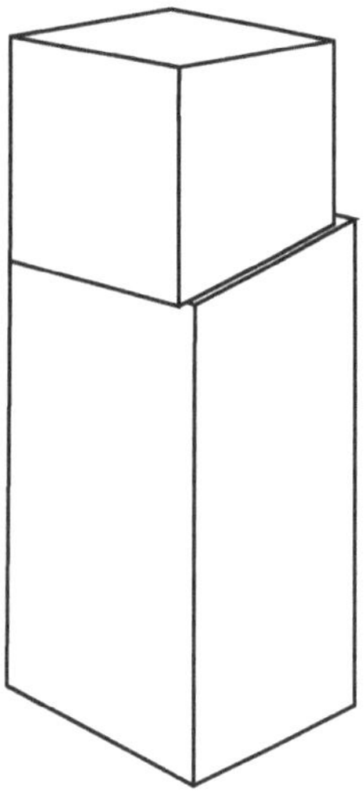

1

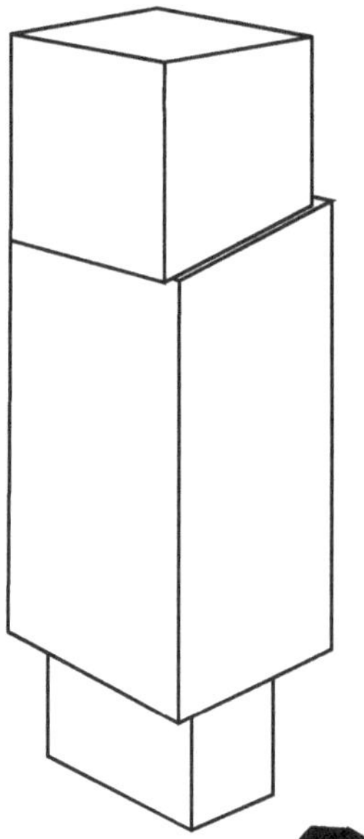

2

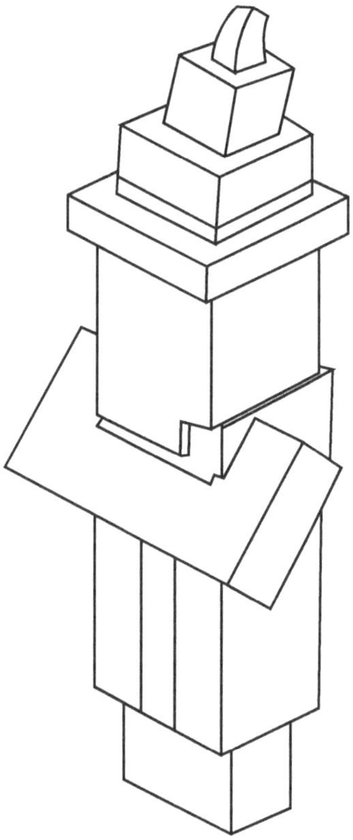

3

4

How to draw?

WITCH

Difficulty

NOW, IT'S YOUR TURN

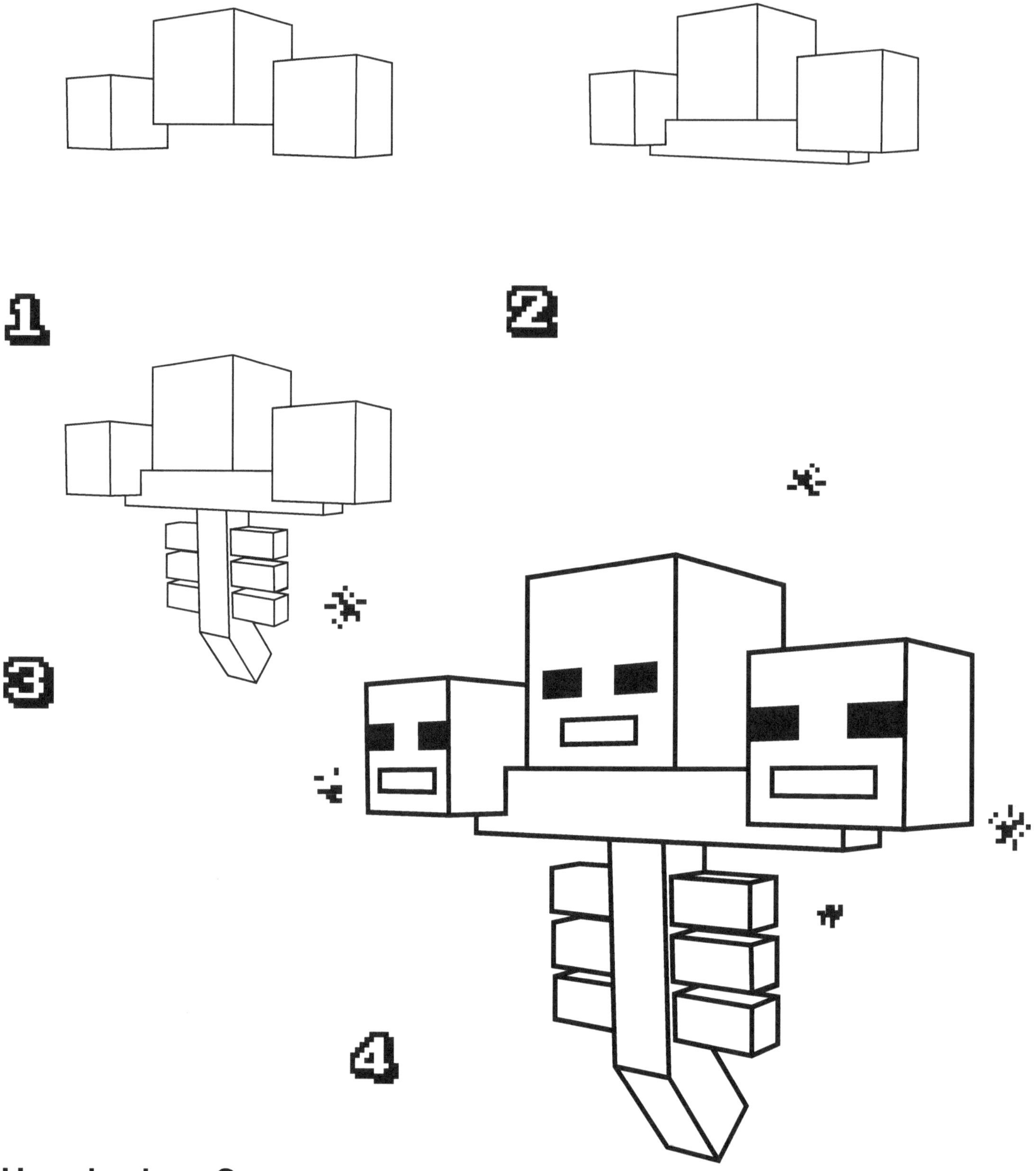

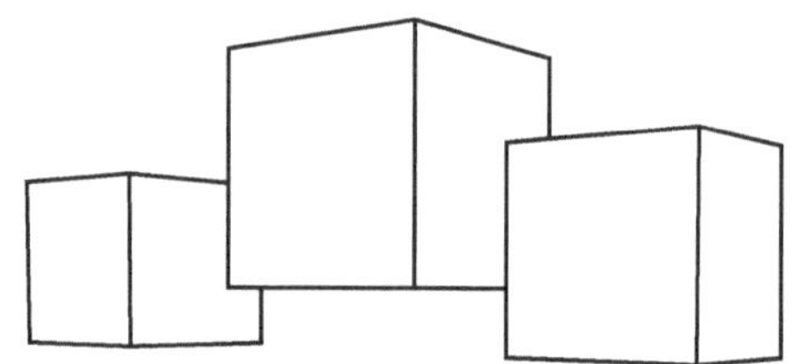

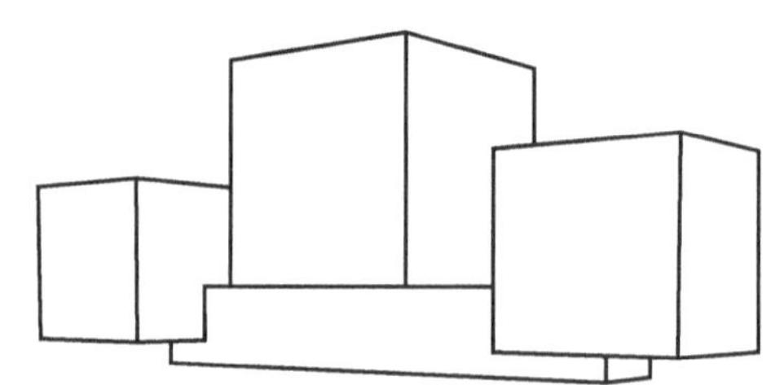

1

2

3

4

How to draw?

Difficulty

NOW, iT'S YOUR TURN

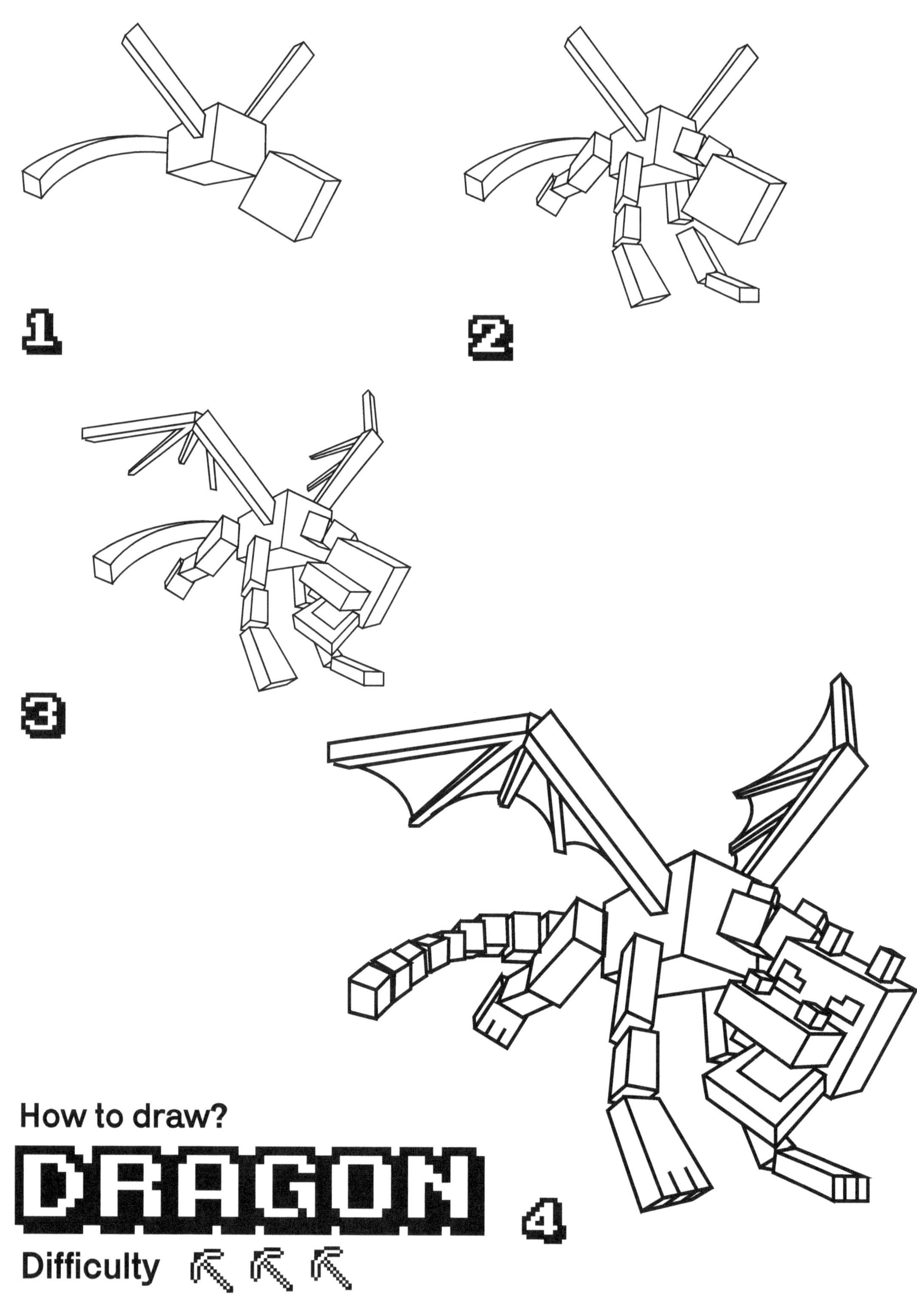

1
2
3
4
How to draw?
DRAGON
Difficulty

NOW, IT'S YOUR TURN

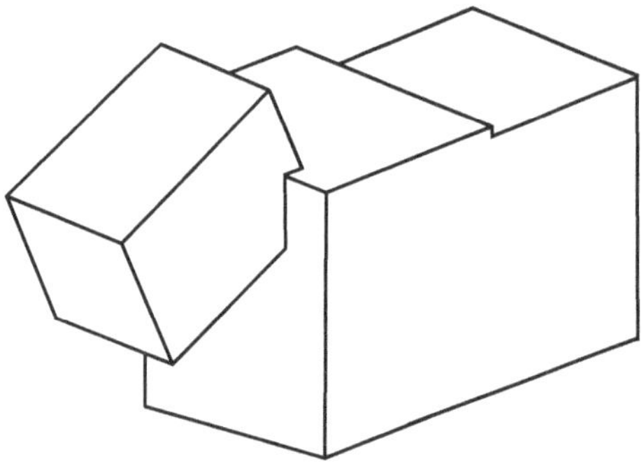

How to draw?

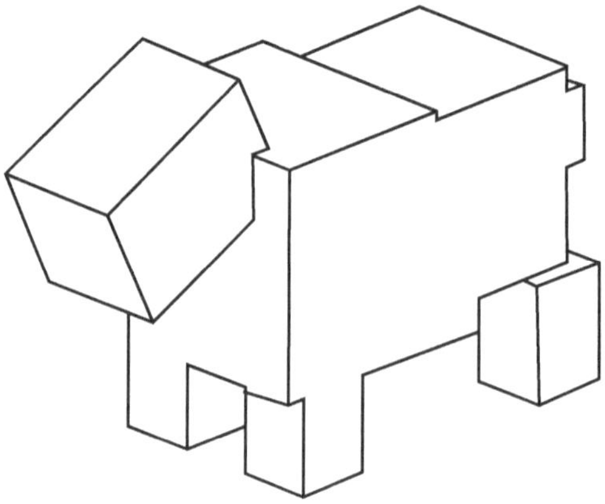

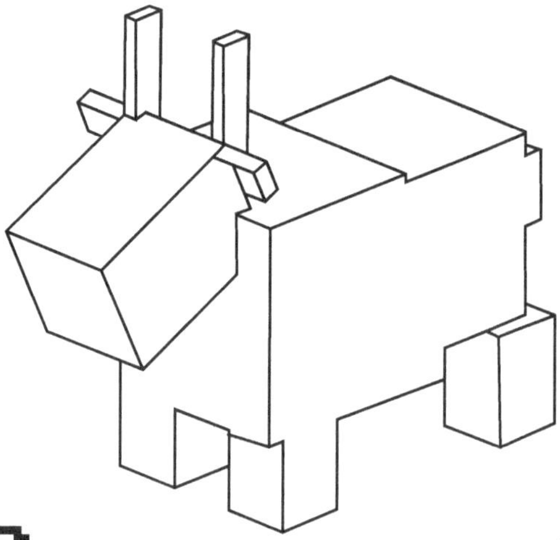

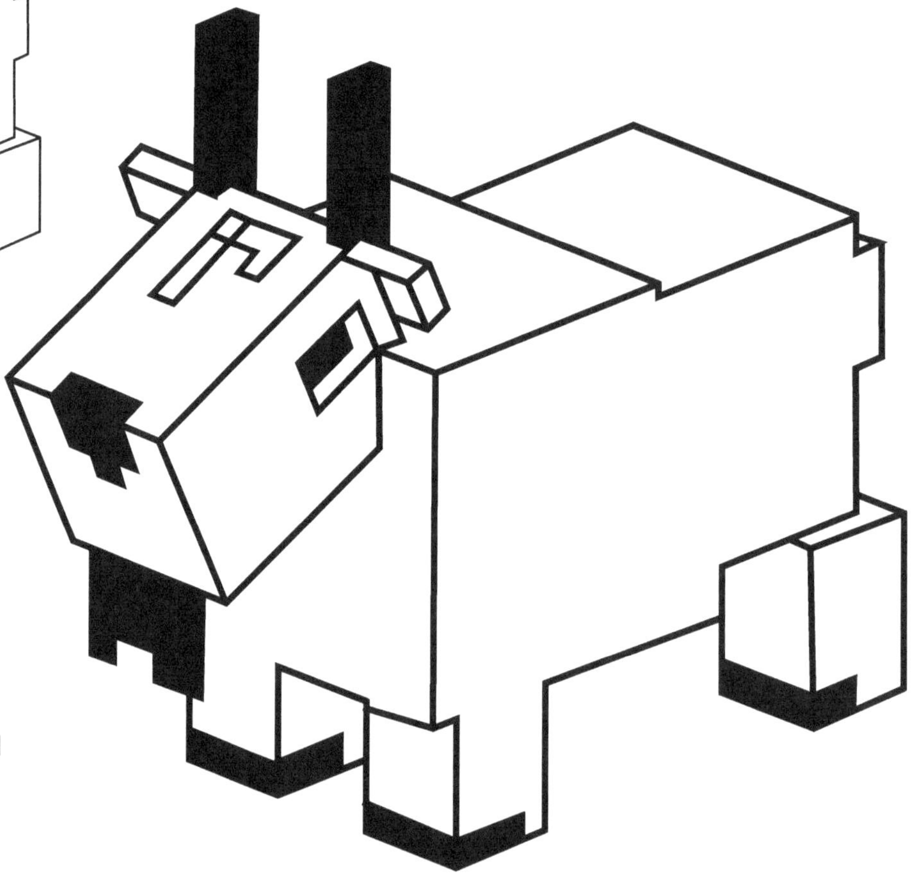

GOAT

Difficulty

NOW, IT'S YOUR TURN

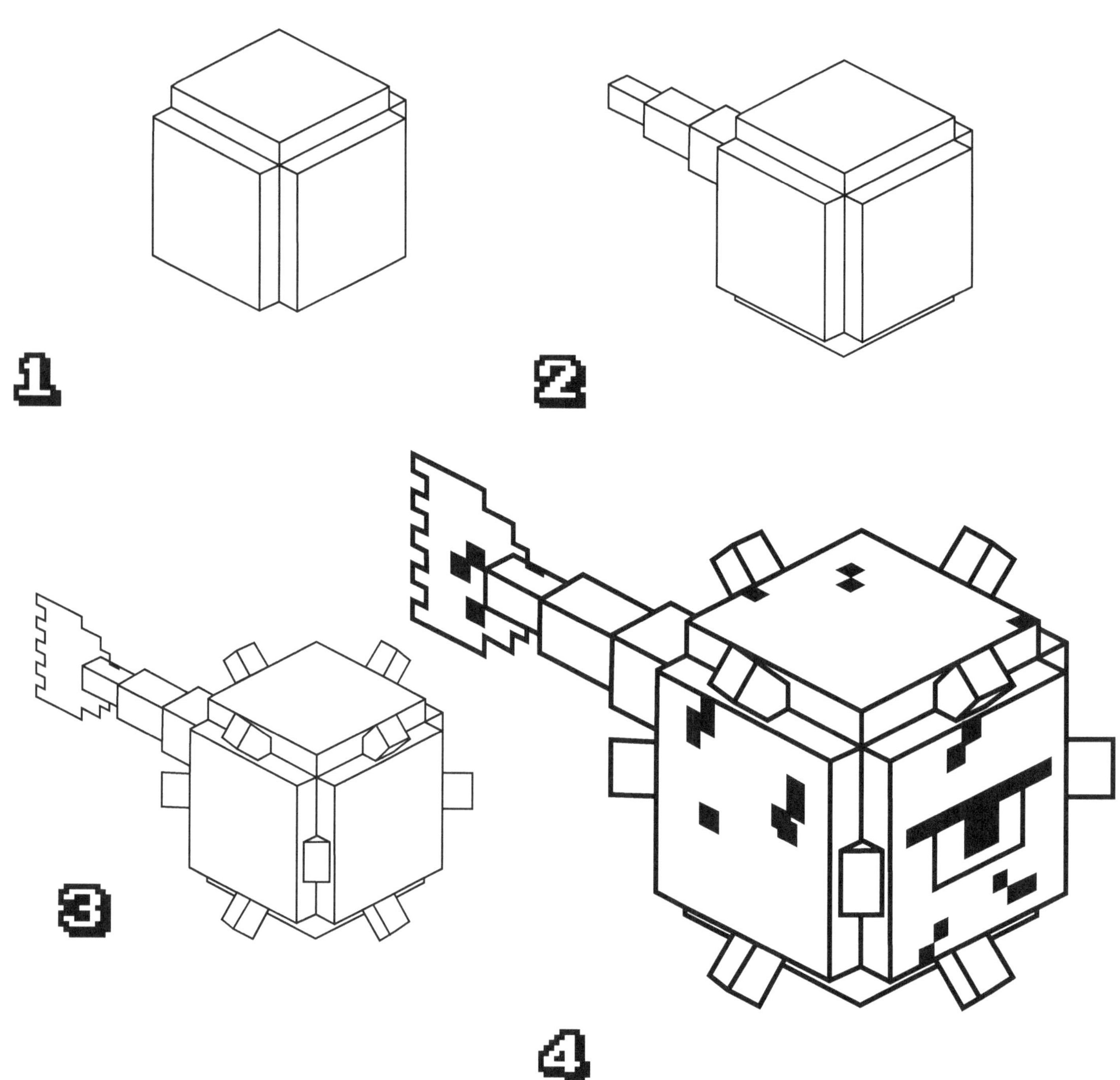

How to draw?

GUARDIAN

Difficulty

NOW, iT'S YOUR TURN

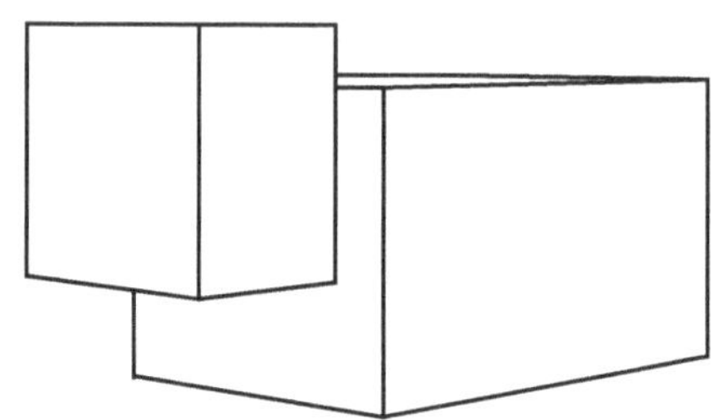

1

2

3

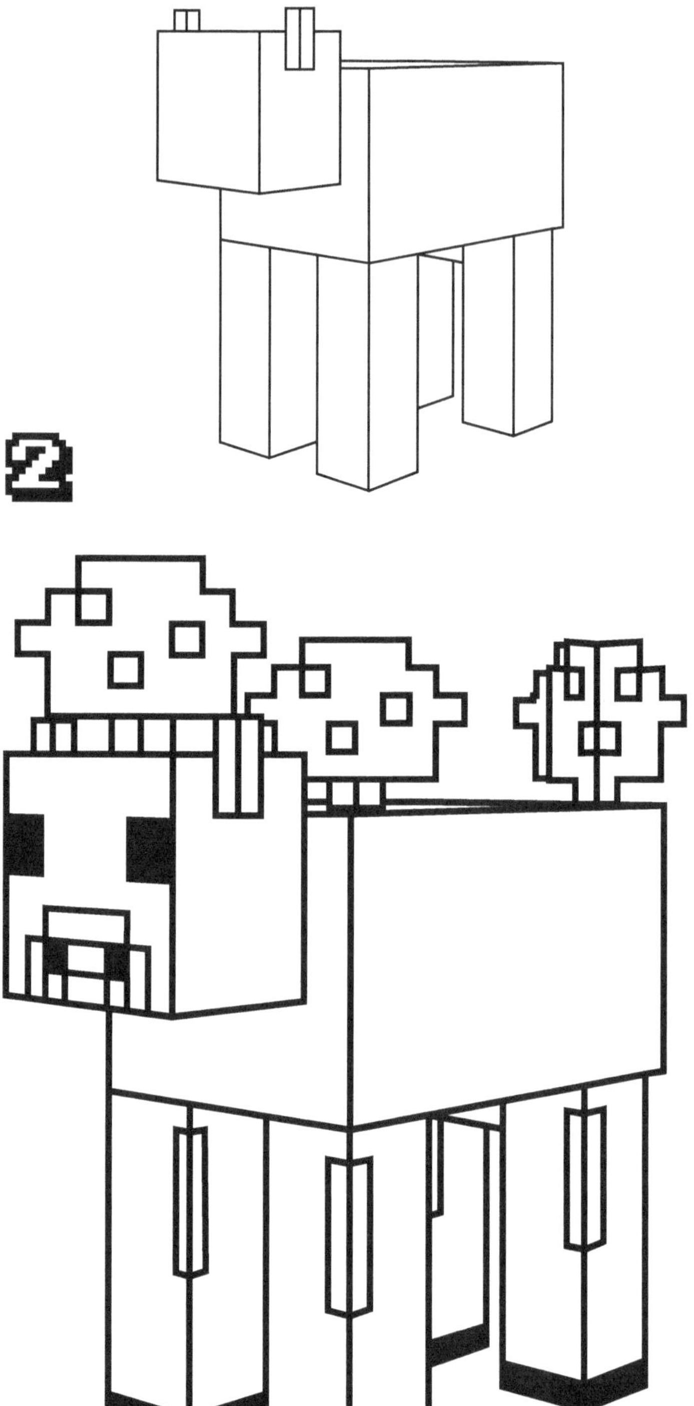

4

How to draw?

MUSHROOM COW

Difficulty ⛏ ⛏ ⛏

NOW, IT'S YOUR TURN

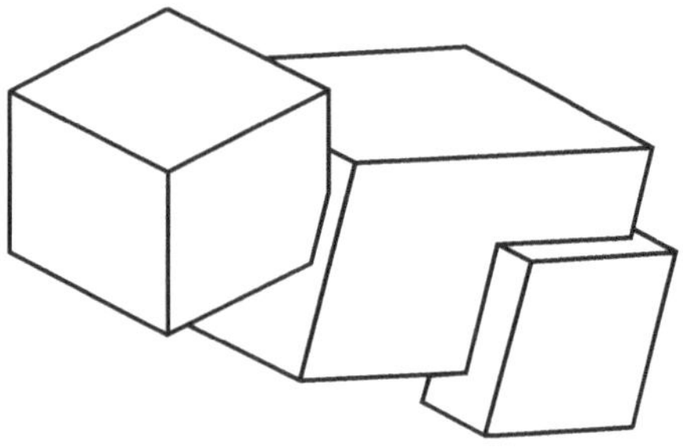

How to draw?

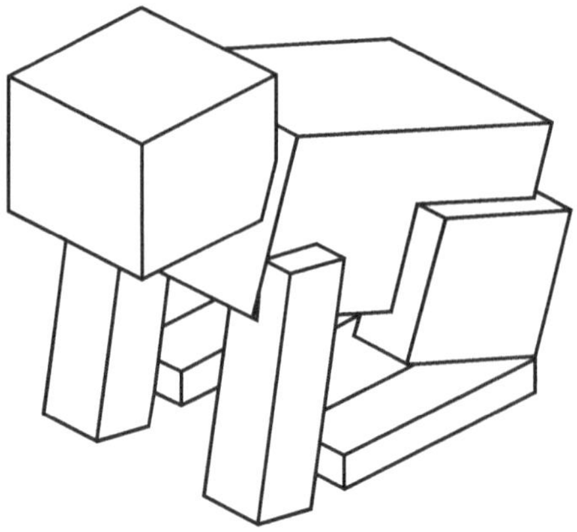

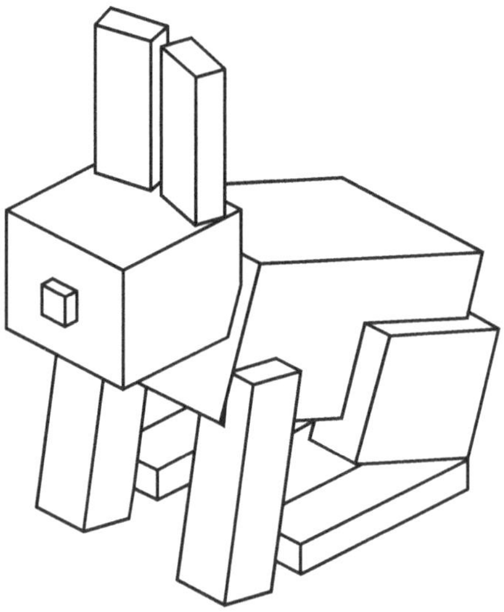

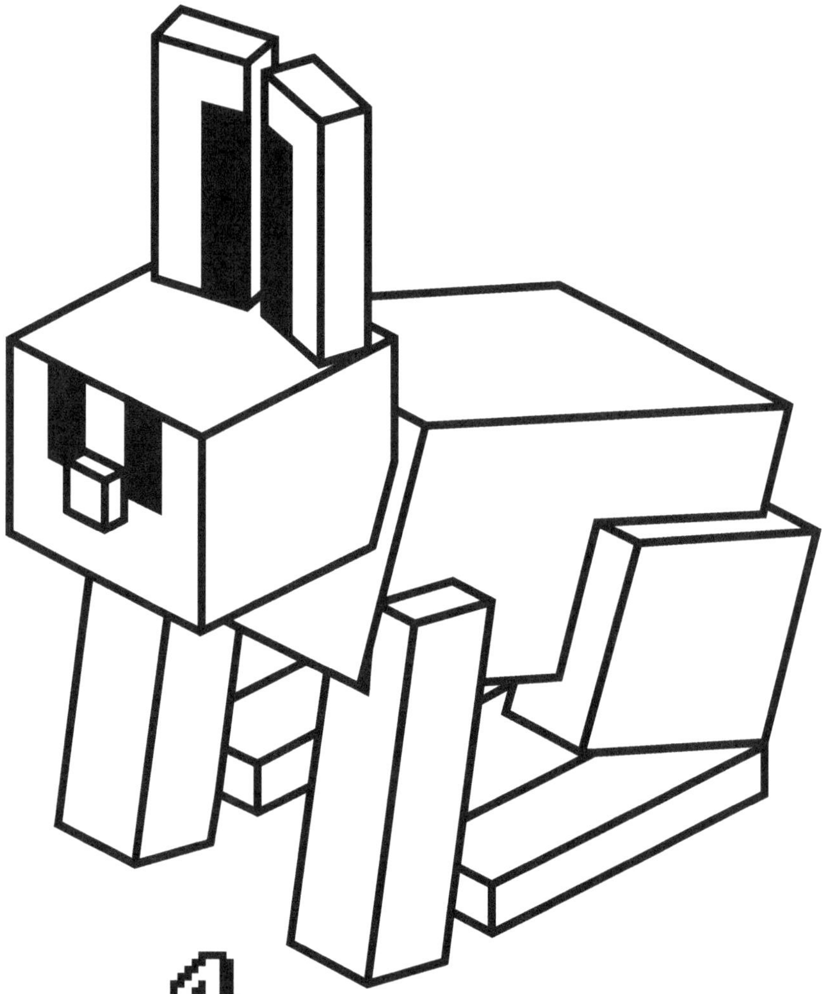

RABBIT

Difficulty

NOW, IT'S YOUR TURN

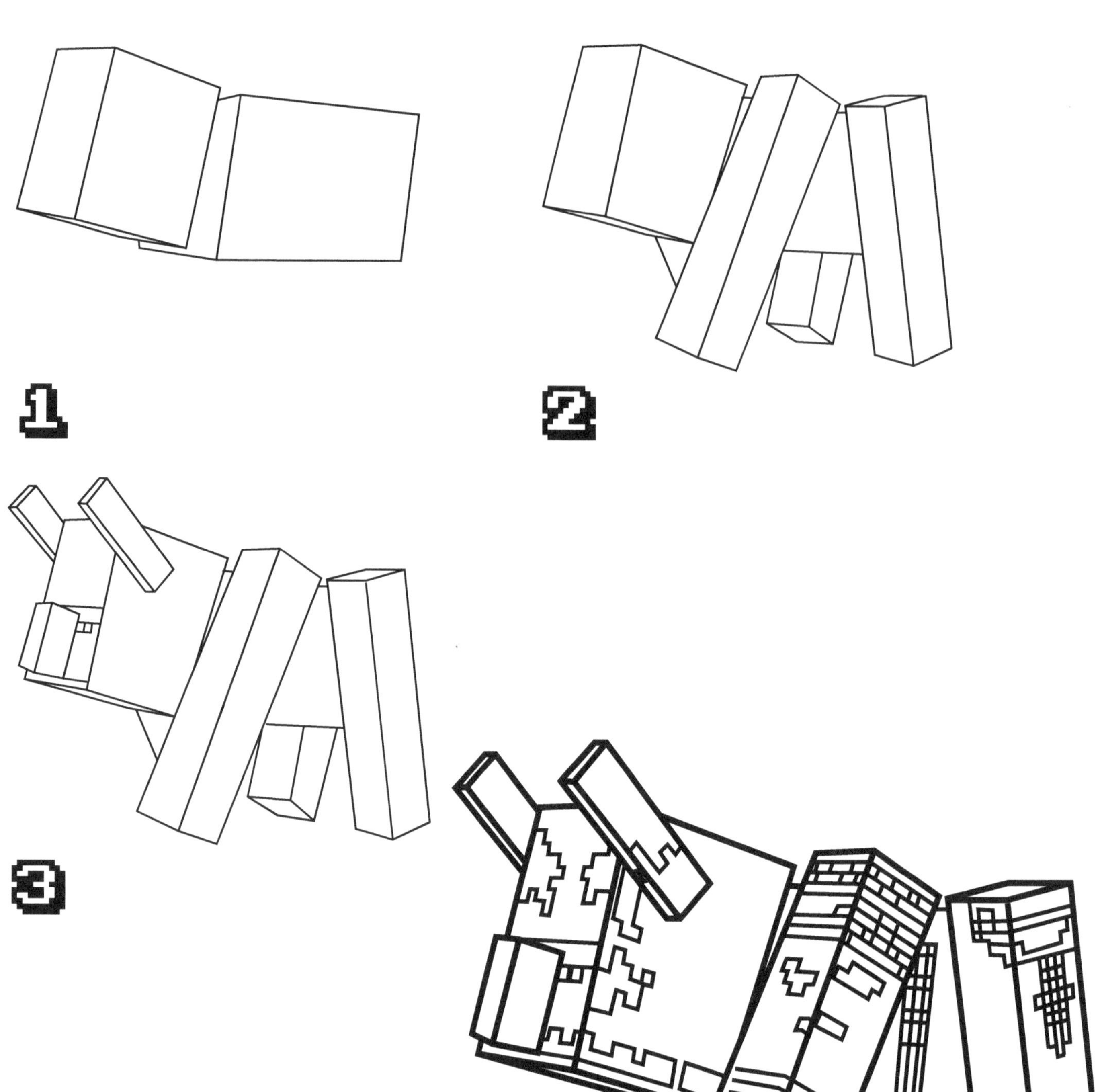

How to draw?

RAVAGER

Difficulty

NOW, iT'S YOUR TURN

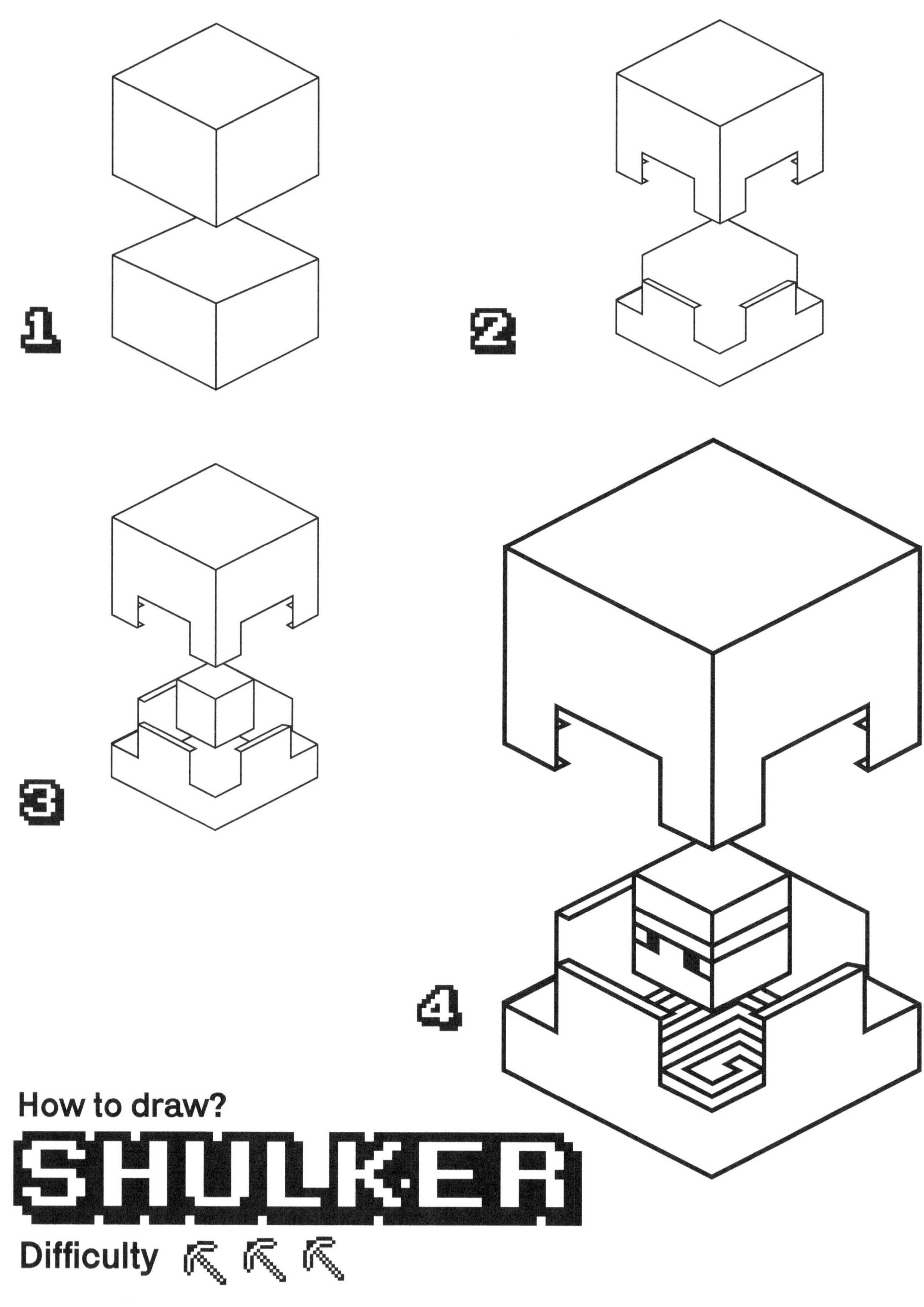
1
2
3
4
How to draw?
SHULKER
Difficulty

NOW, iT'S YOUR TURN

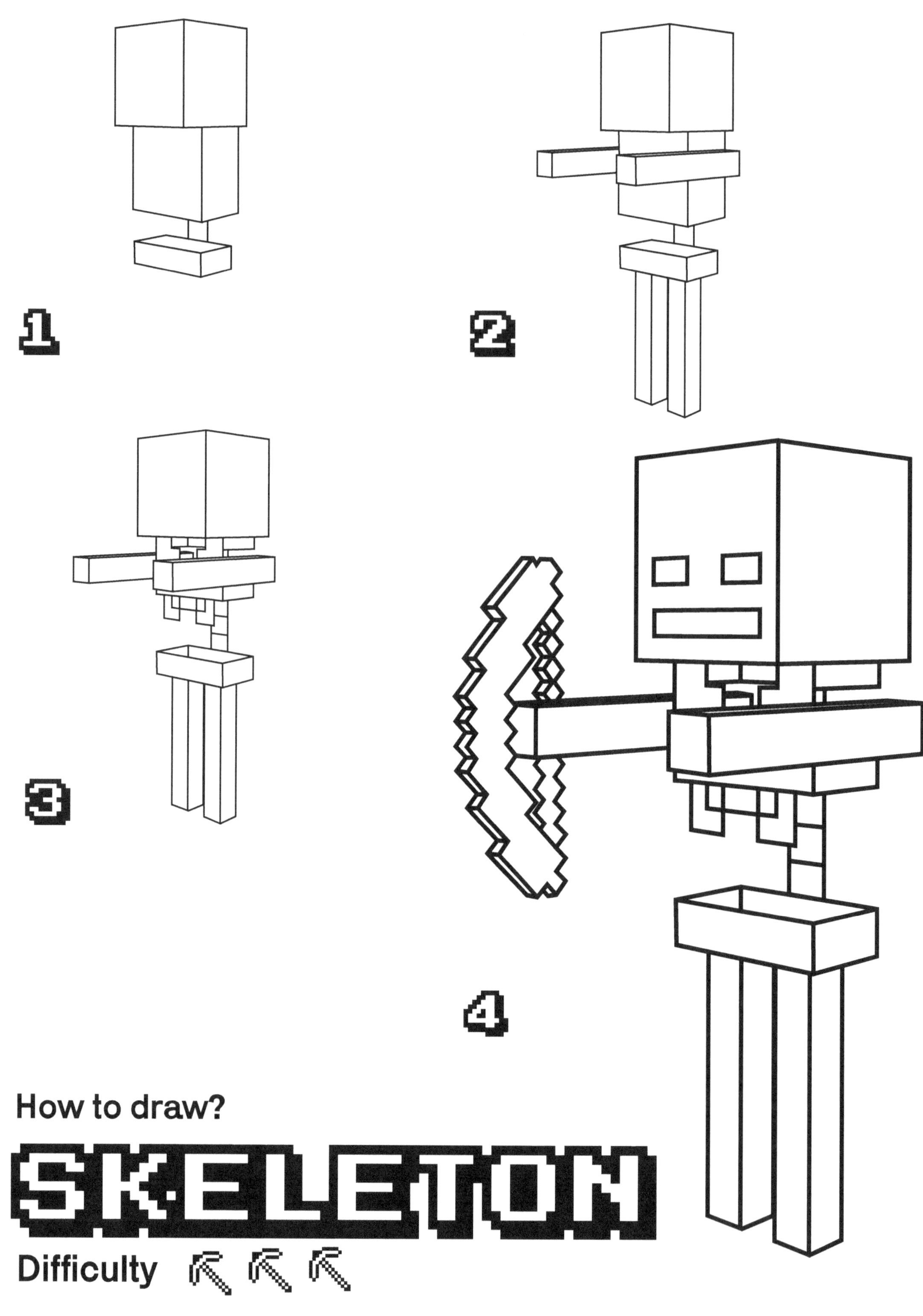

How to draw?

SKELETON

Difficulty

NOW, iT'S YOUR TURN

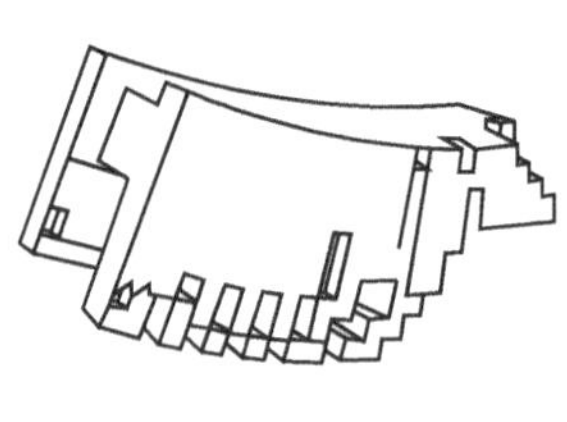

1

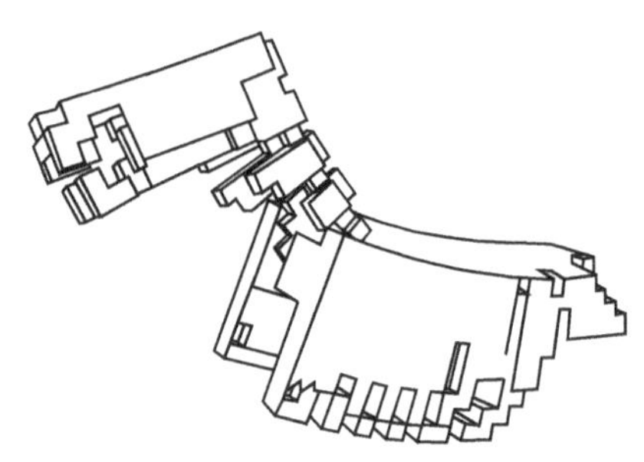

2

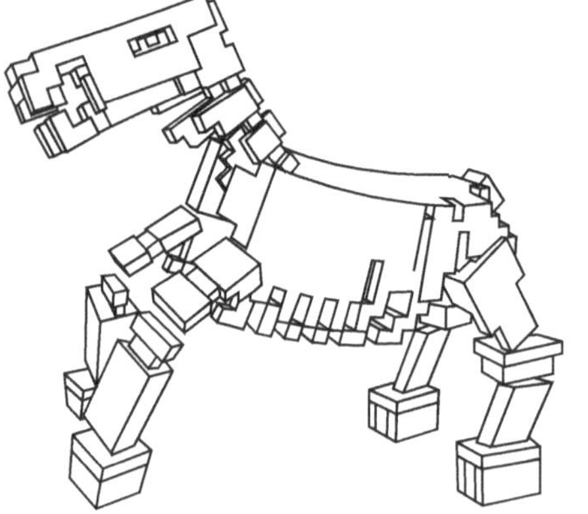

3

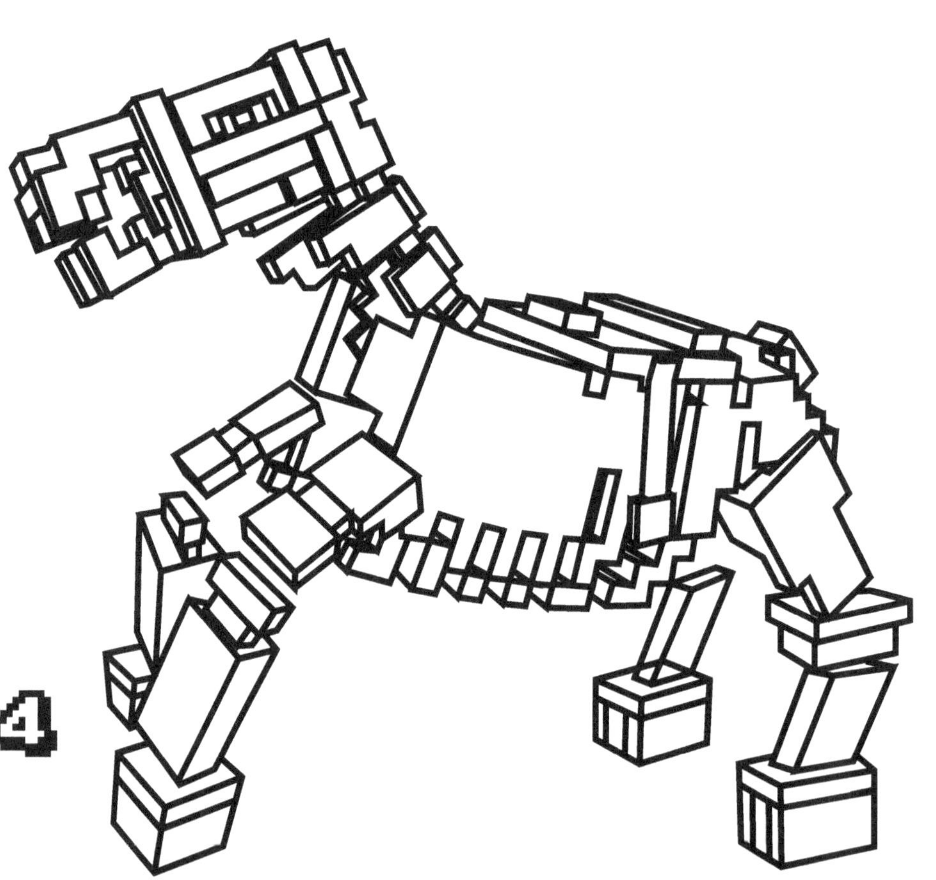

4

How to draw?

SKELETON HORSE

Difficulty

NOW, IT'S YOUR TURN

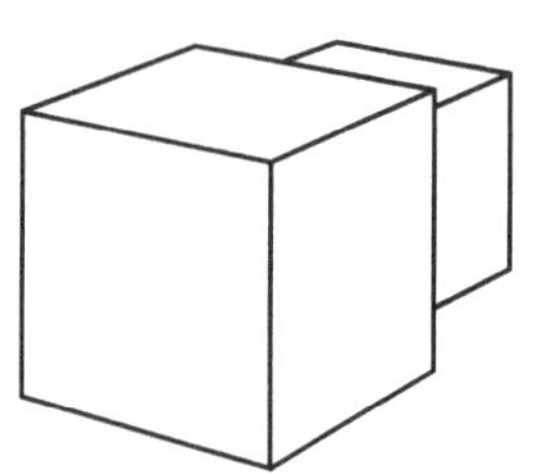

1

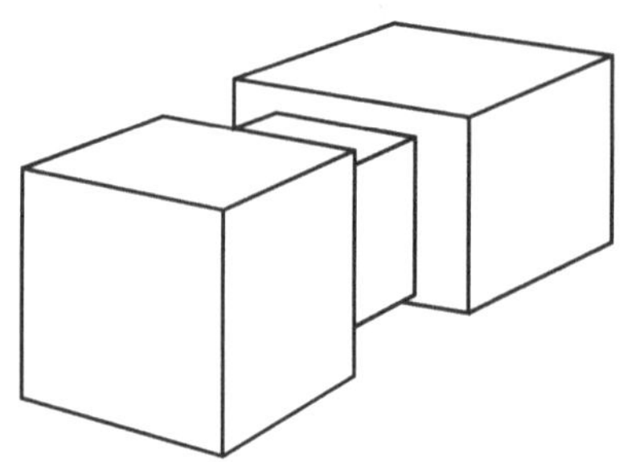

2

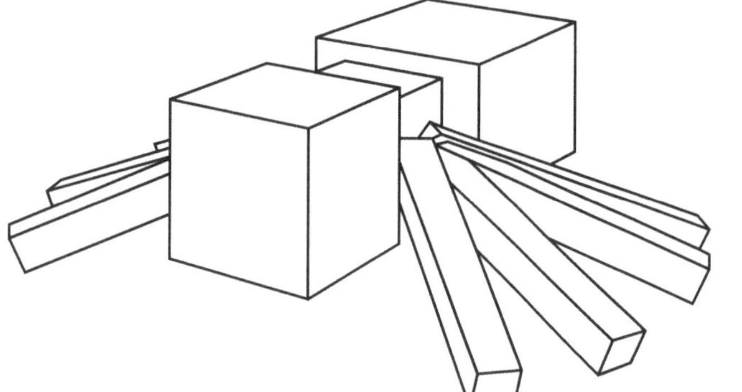

3

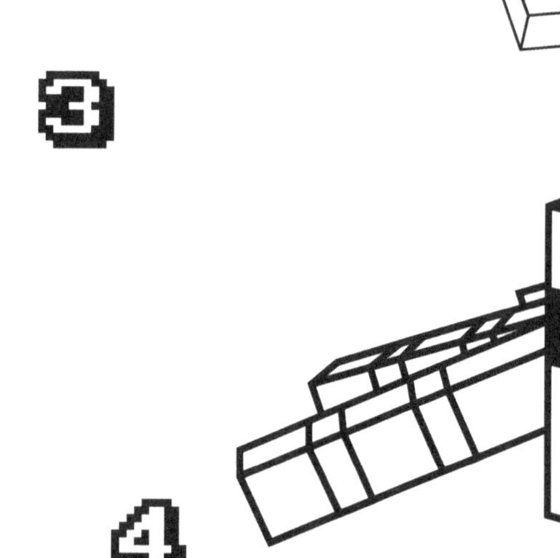

4

How to draw?

SPIDER

Difficulty 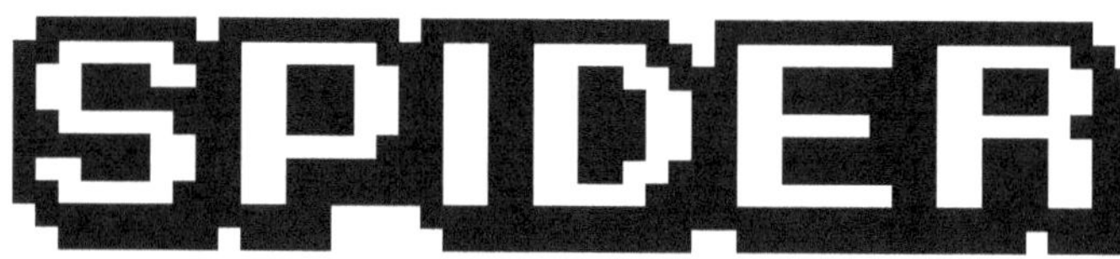

NOW, IT'S YOUR TURN

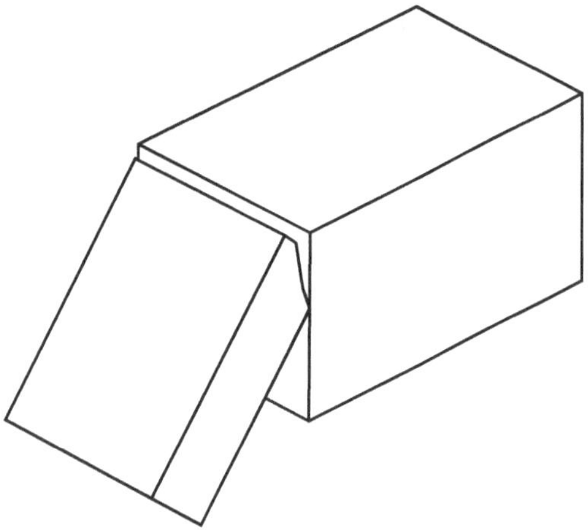

1

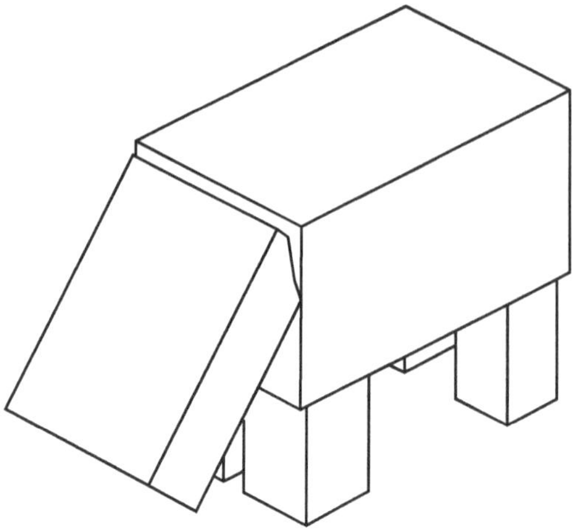

2

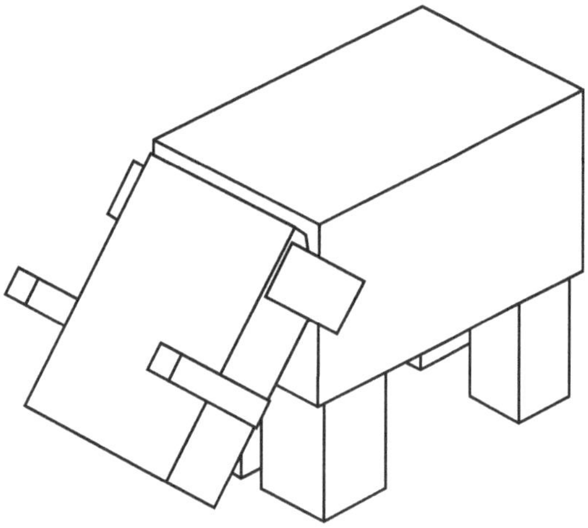

3

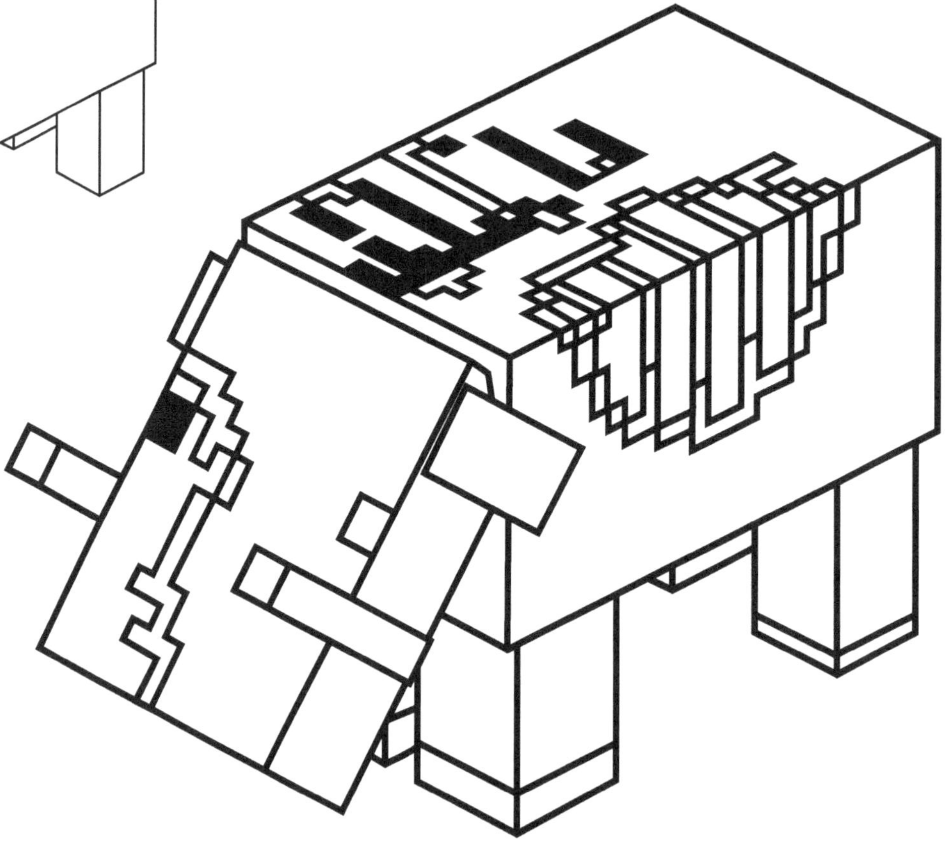

4

How to draw?

NOW, IT'S YOUR TURN

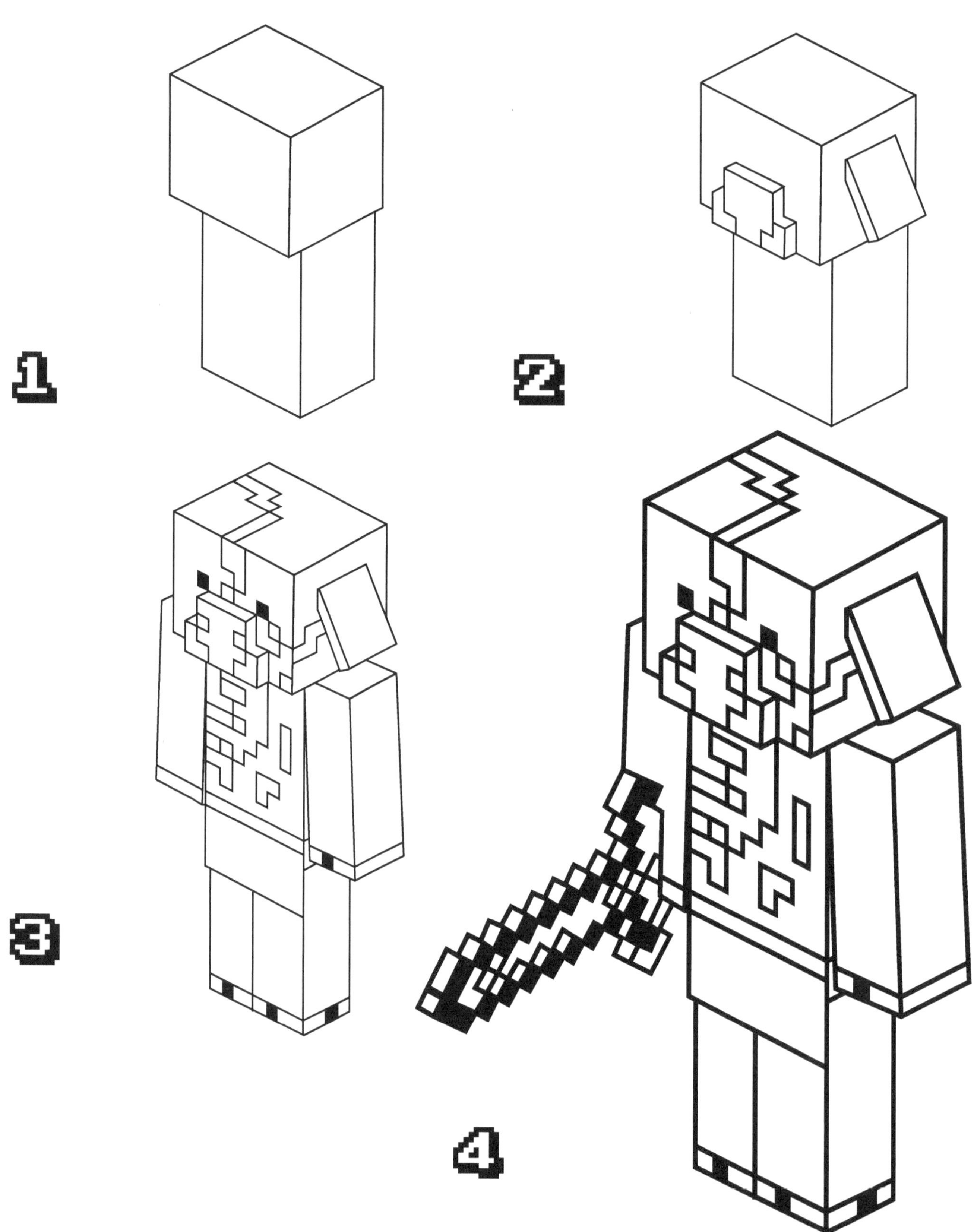

How to draw?

ZOMBIFIED PIGLIN

Difficulty

NOW, IT'S YOUR TURN

How to draw: Arch-Illager

NOW, IT'S YOUR TURN

How to draw: Axel

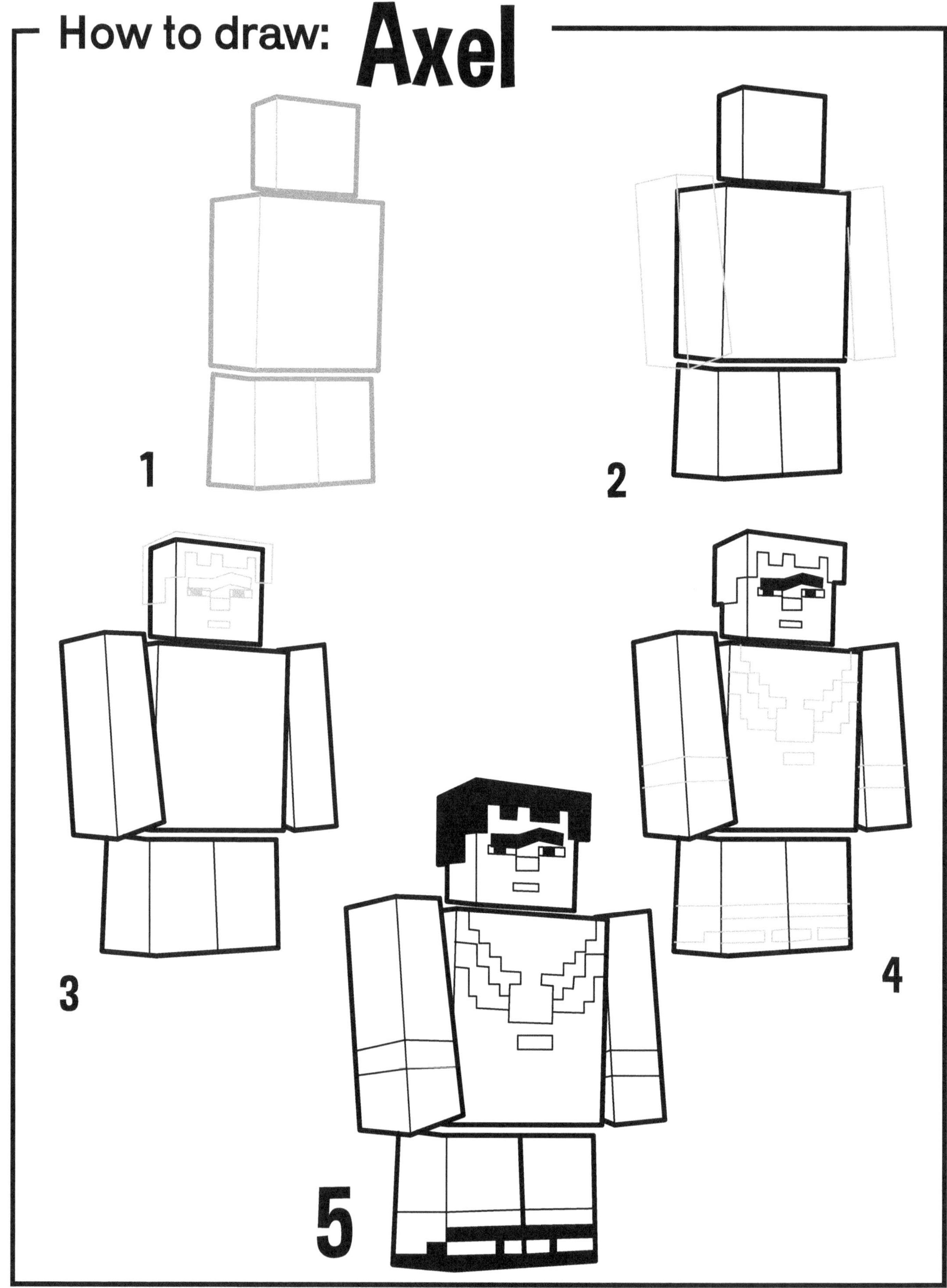

NOW, IT'S YOUR TURN

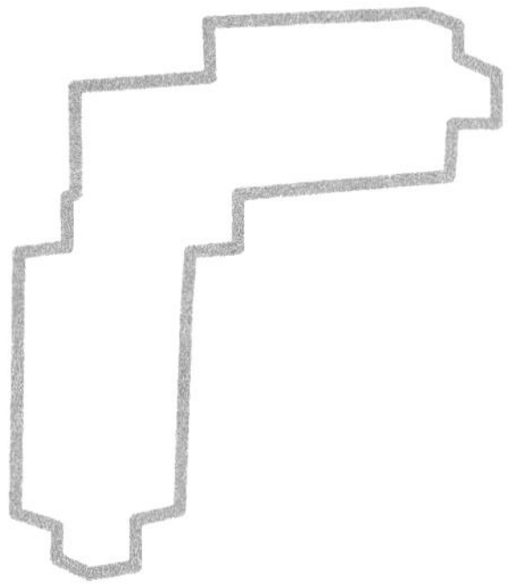

1

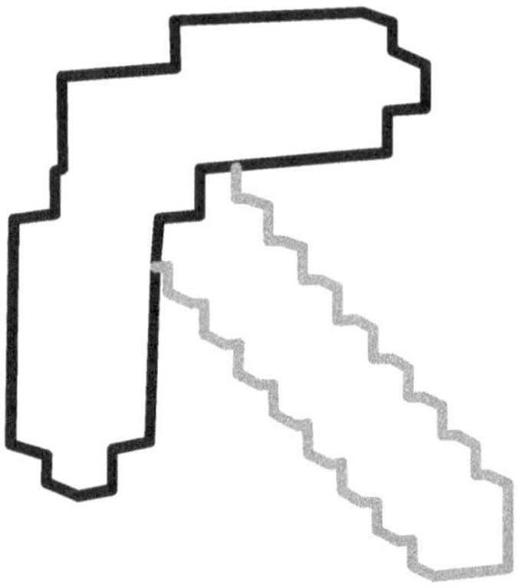

2

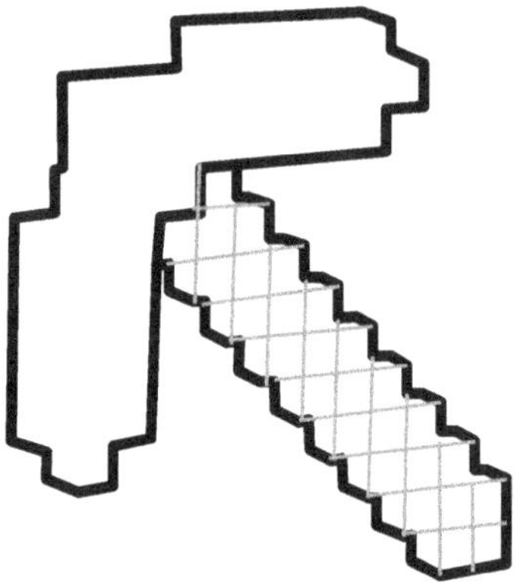

3

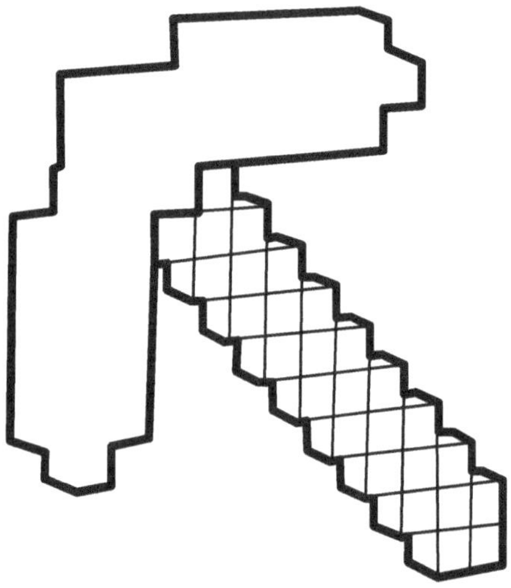

4

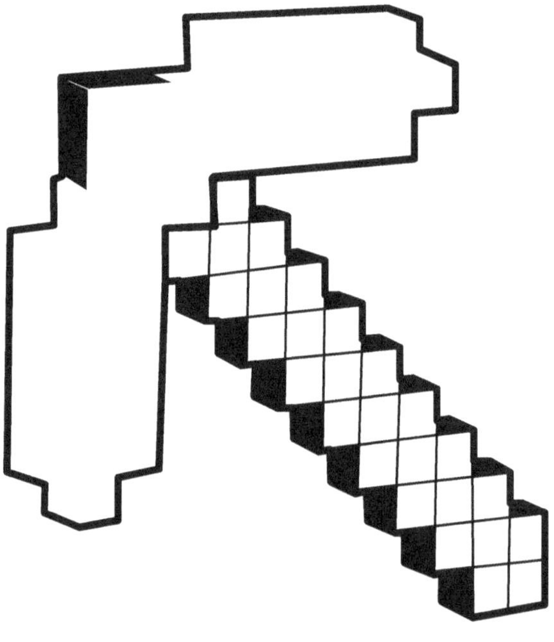

5

NOW, IT'S YOUR TURN

How to draw: **Blacksmith**

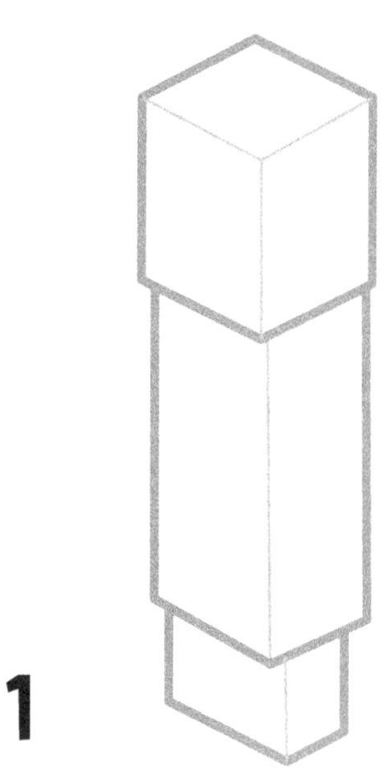

1

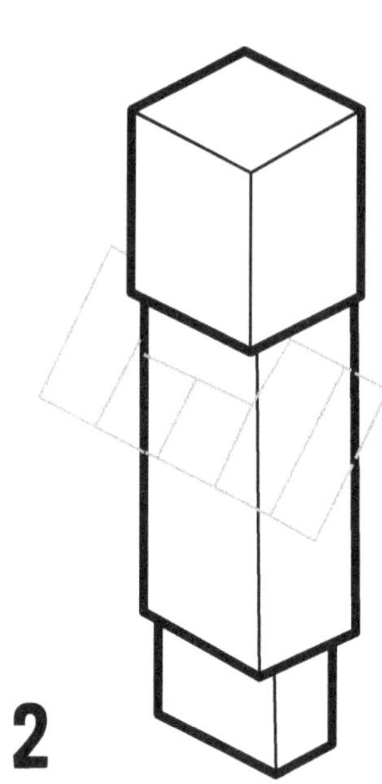

2

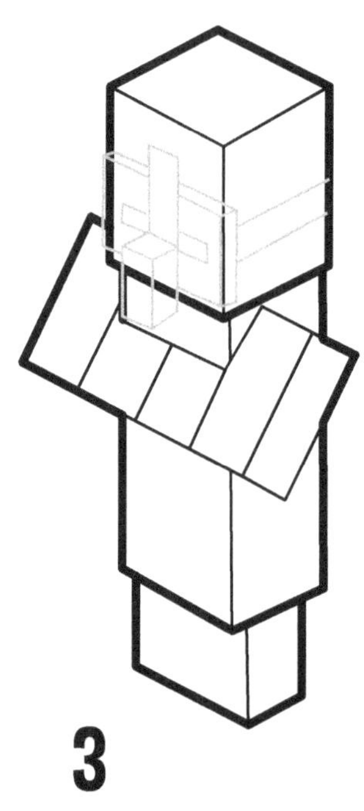

3

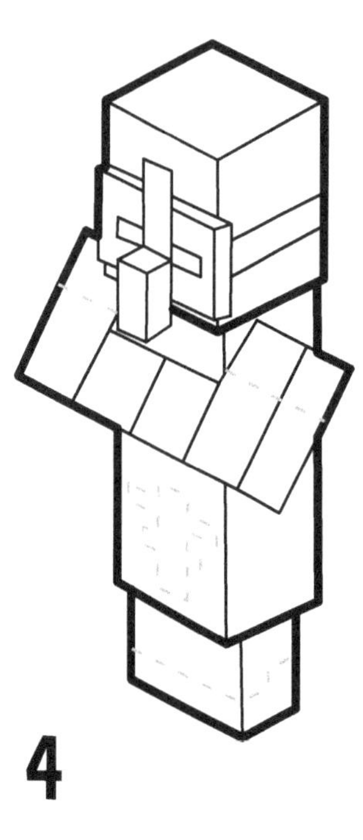

4

5

NOW, IT'S YOUR TURN

How to draw: **Bow**

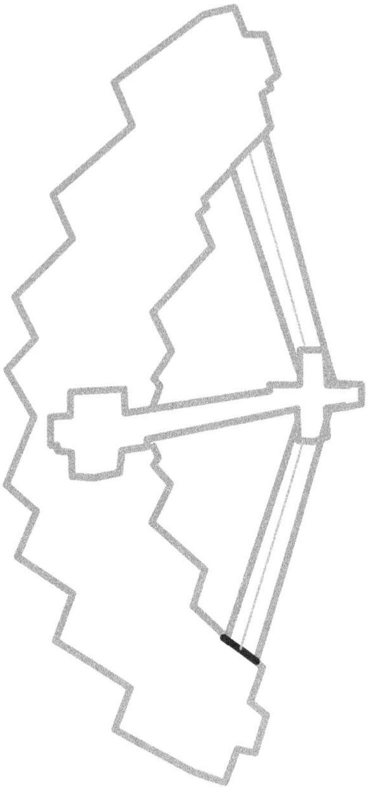

1

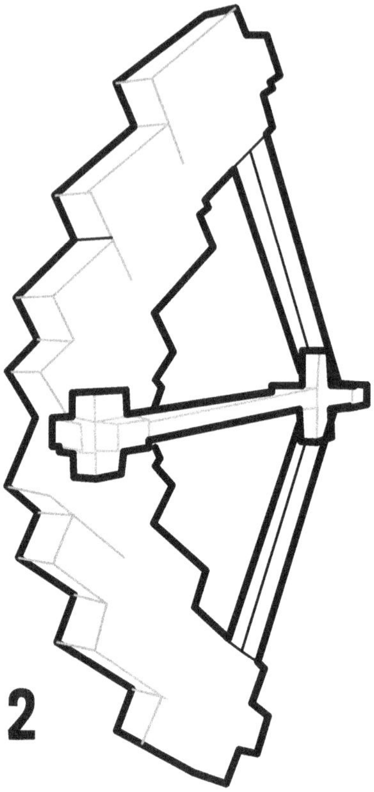

2

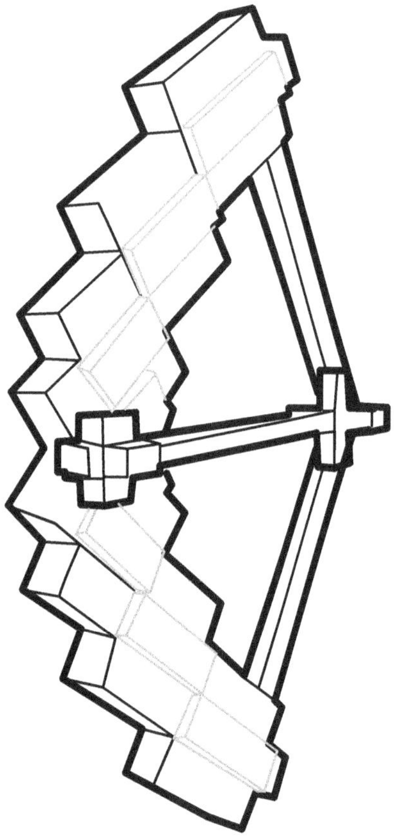

4

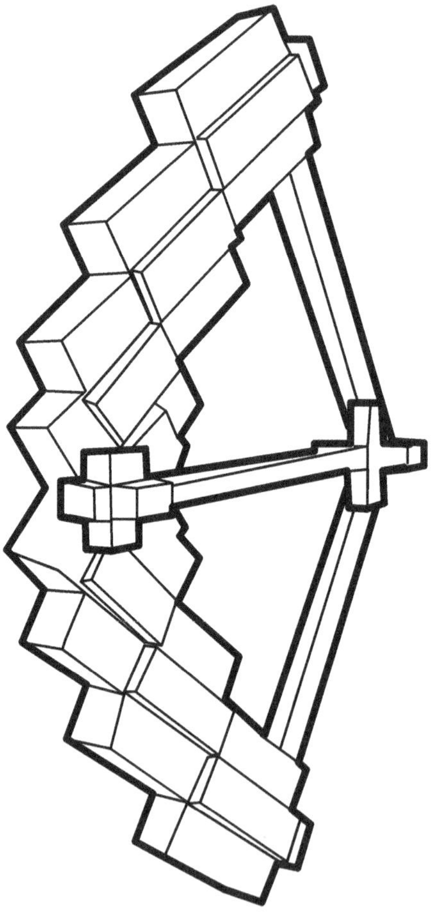

5

NOW, IT'S YOUR TURN

How to draw: Broadsword 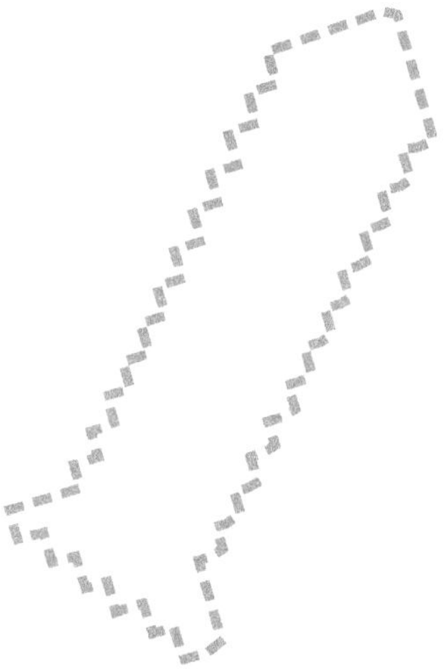
1 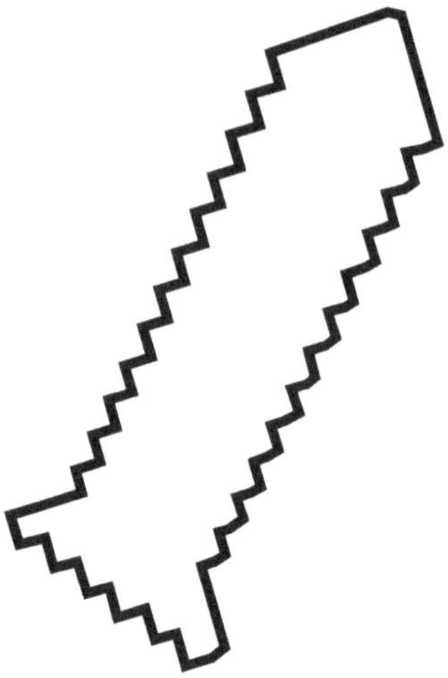
2 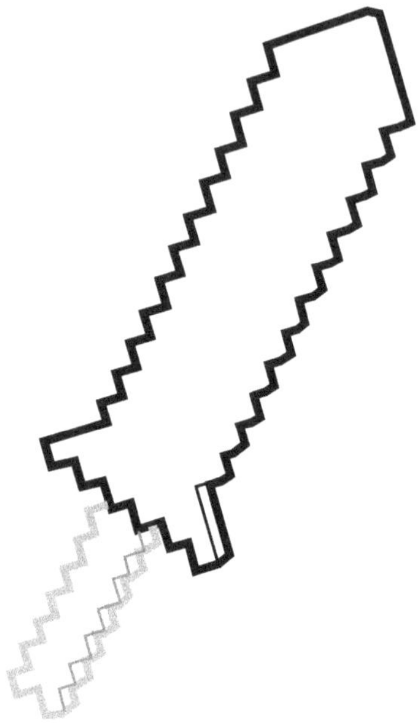
3 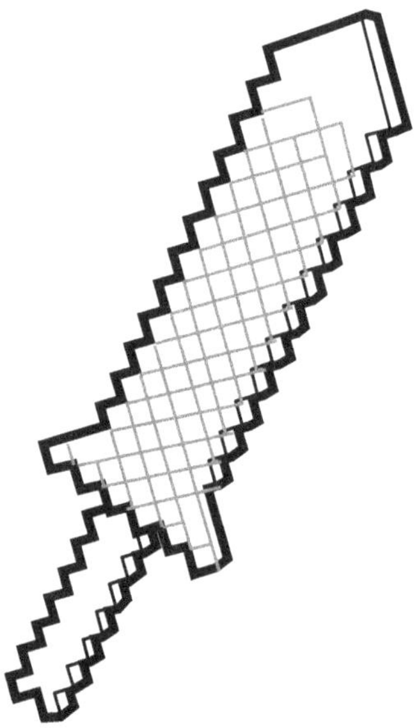
4 
5

NOW, iT'S YOUR TURN

How to draw: Corrupted Cauldron

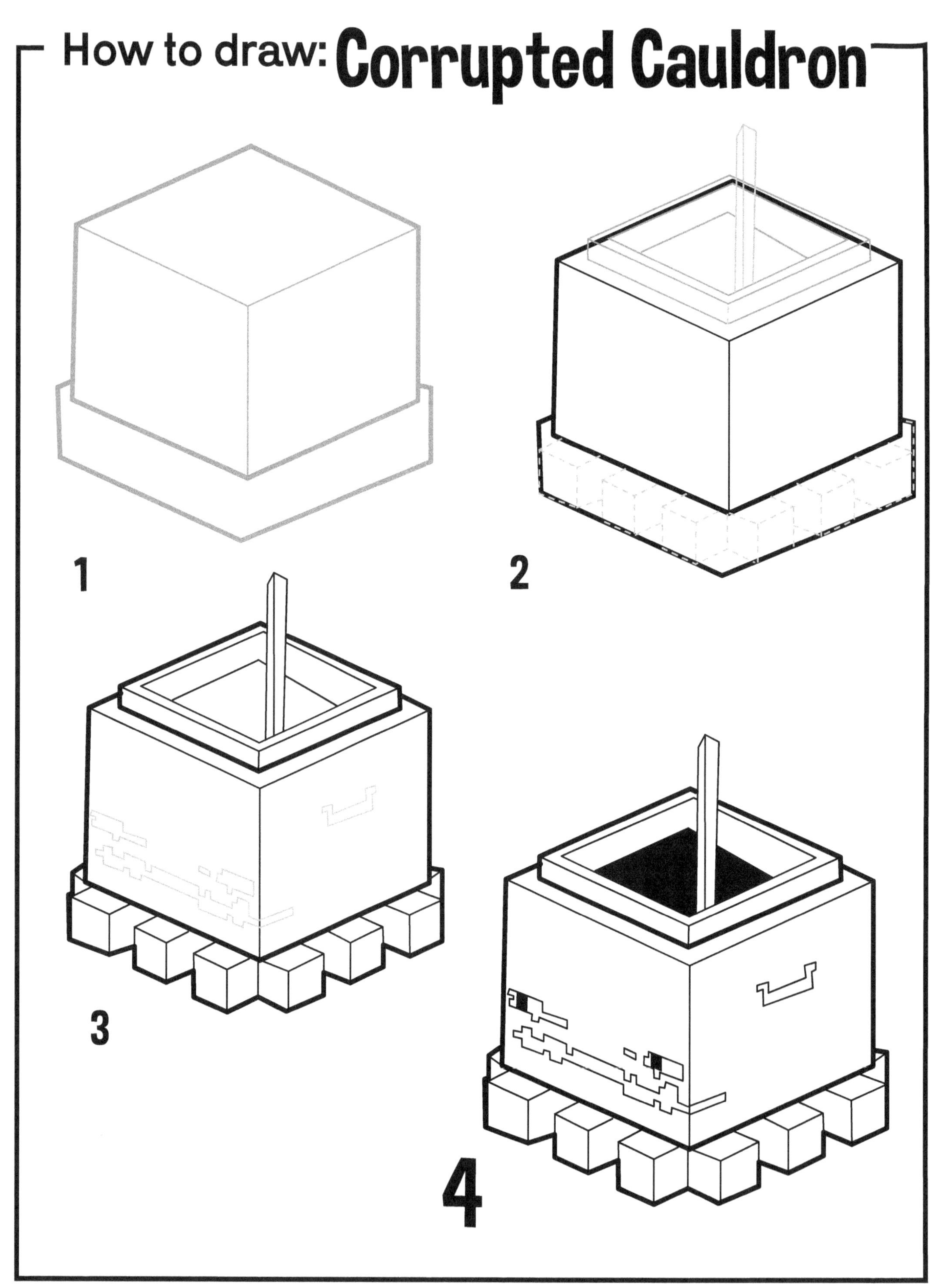

NOW, iT'S YOUR TURN

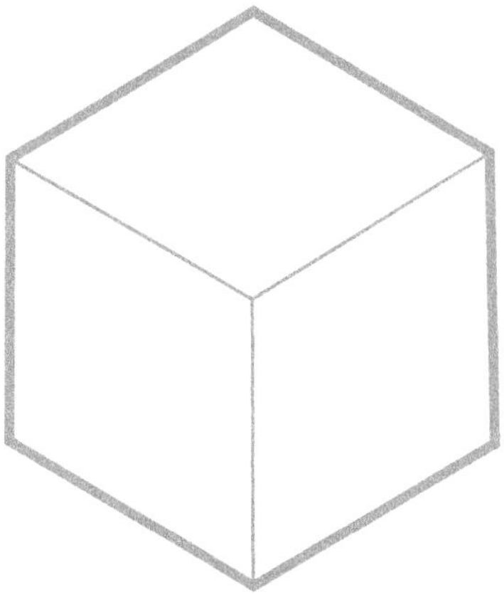

1

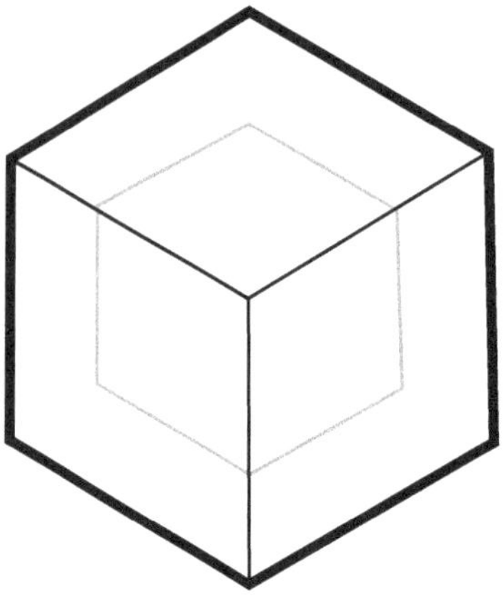

2

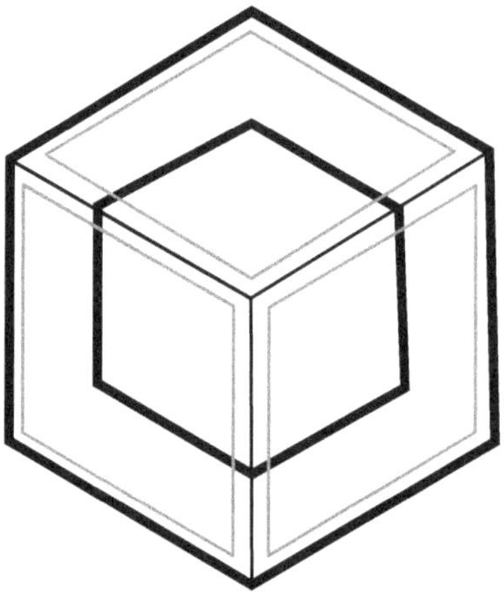

3

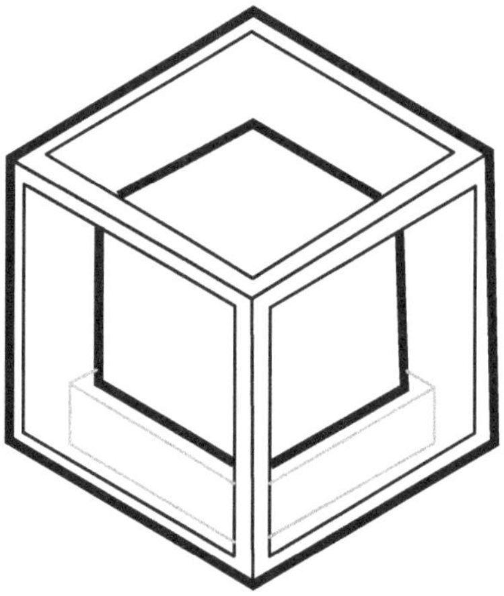

4

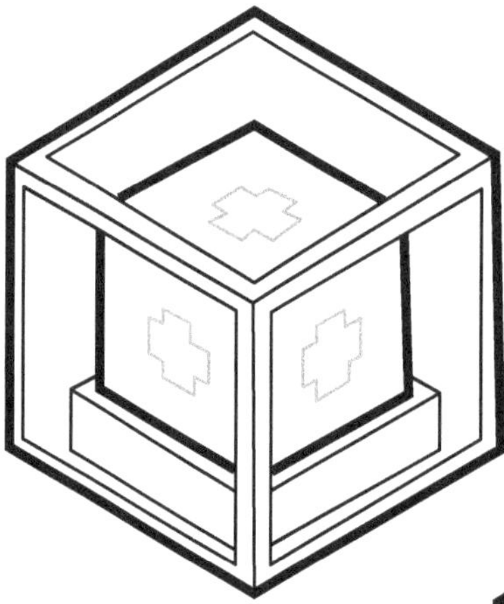

5

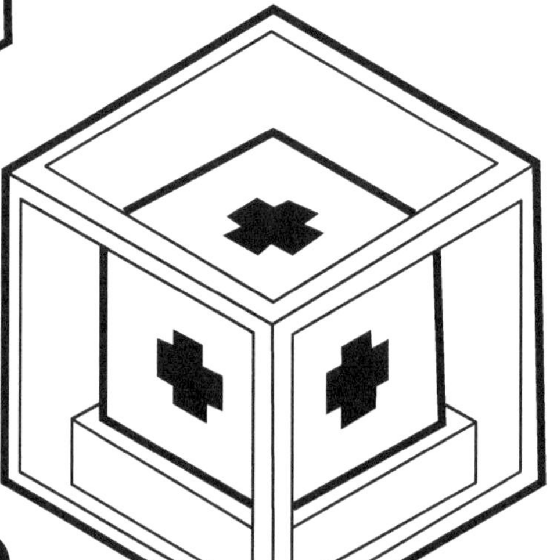

6

NOW, IT'S YOUR TURN

How to draw: Dolphin

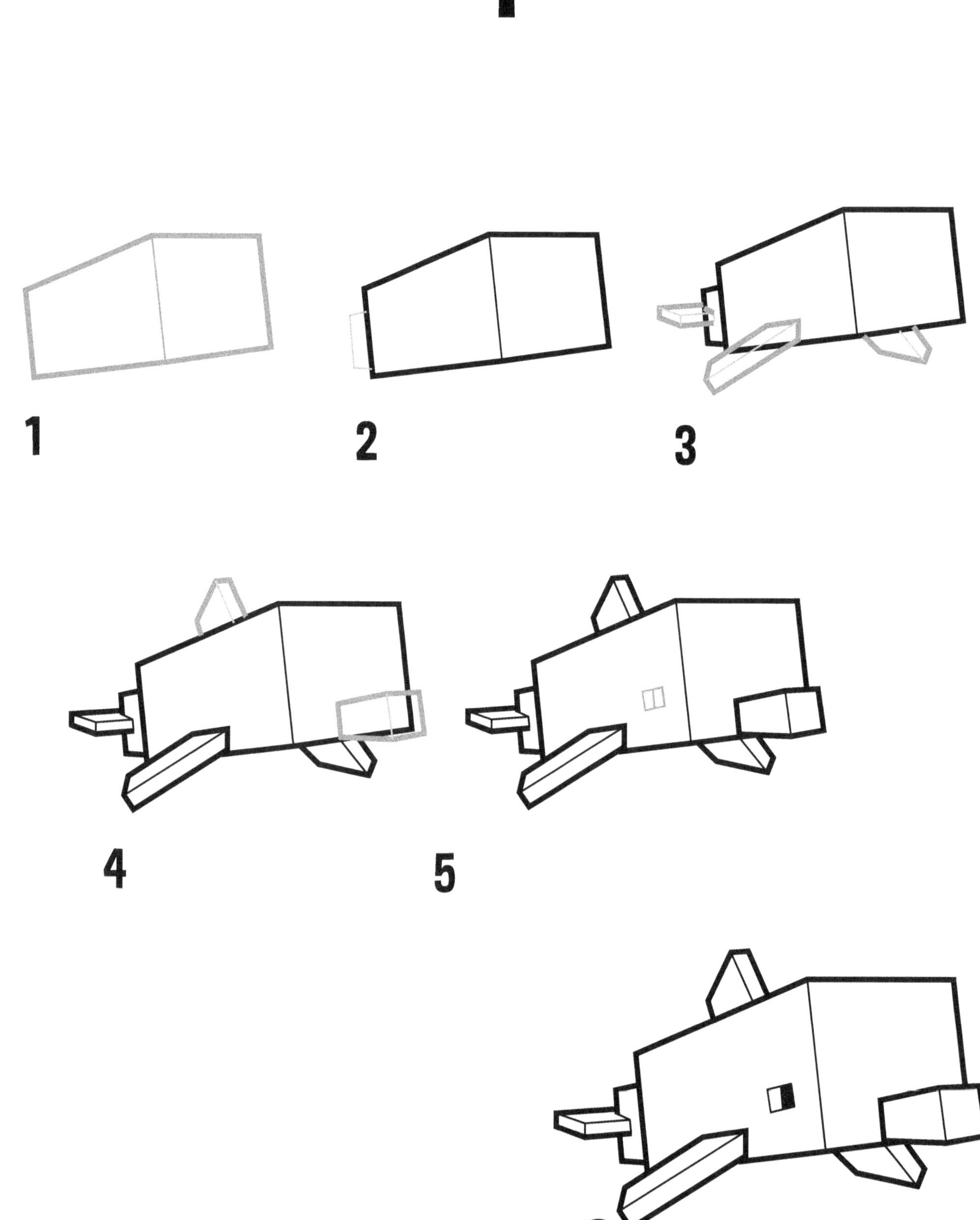

NOW, IT'S YOUR TURN

How to draw: **Ellegaard**

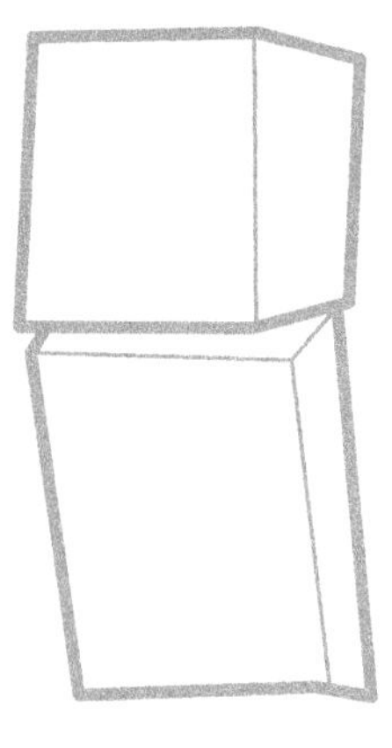

1

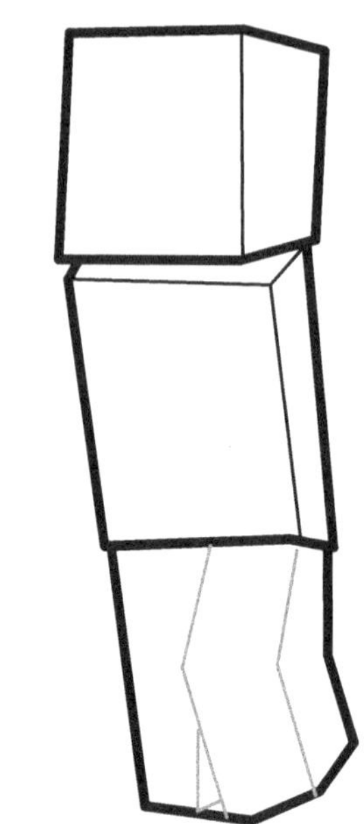

2

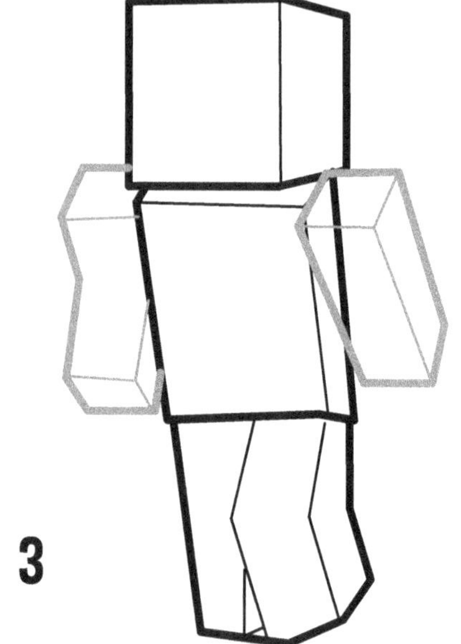

3

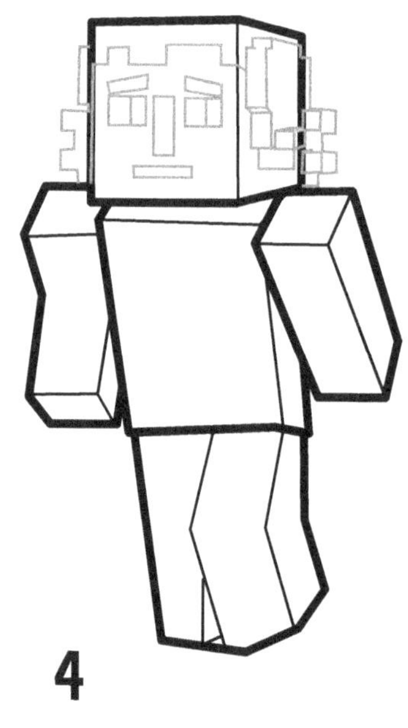

4

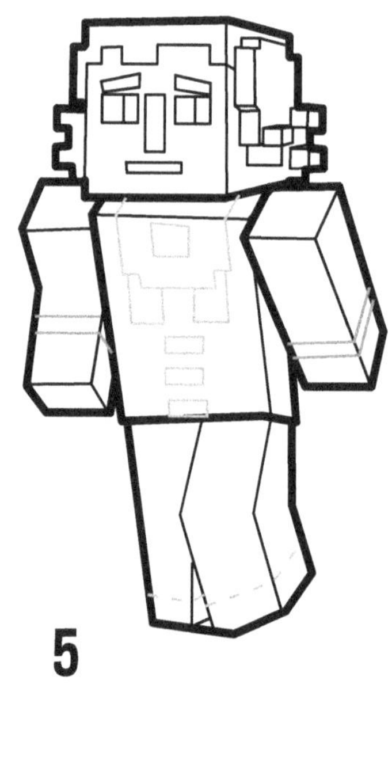

5

6

NOW, IT'S YOUR TURN

How to draw: Enchanter

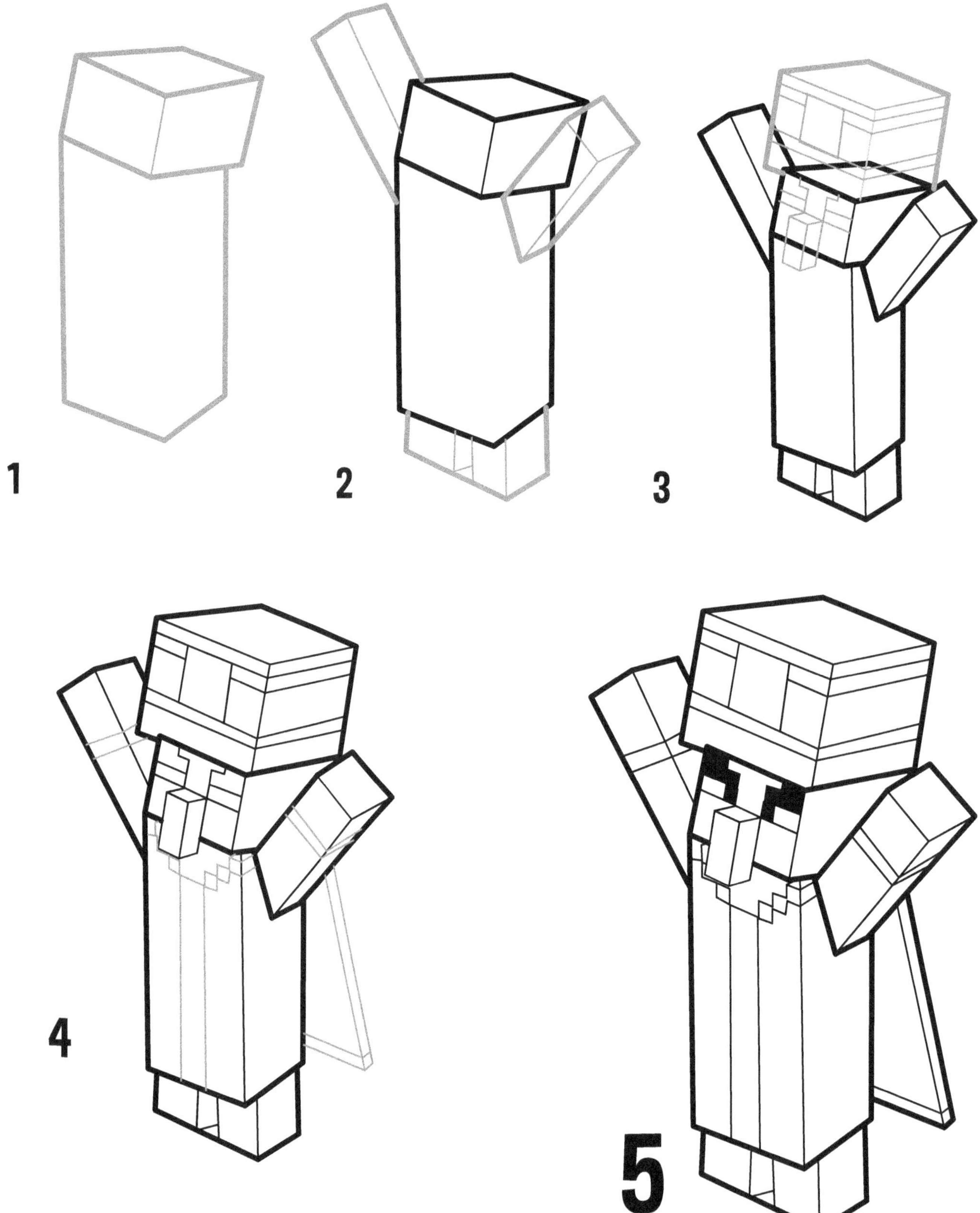

1

2

3

4

5

NOW, IT'S YOUR TURN

How to draw: Fox

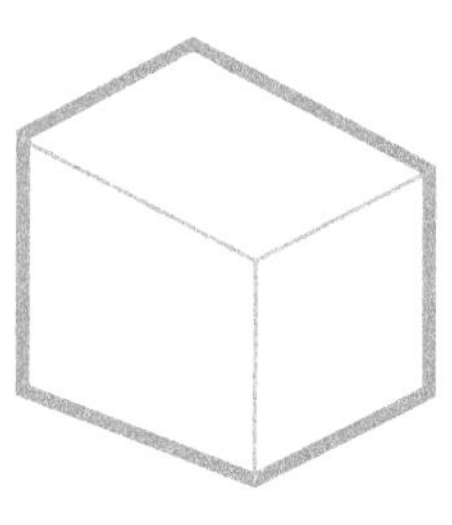

1

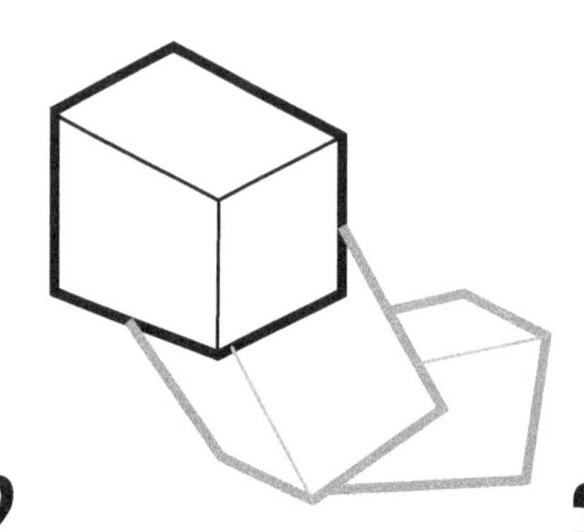

2

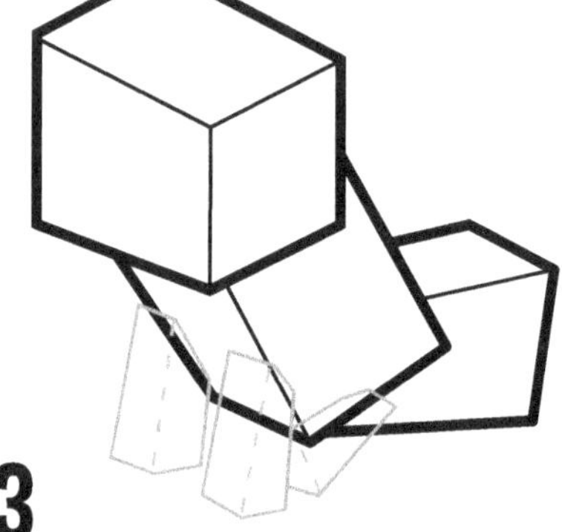

3

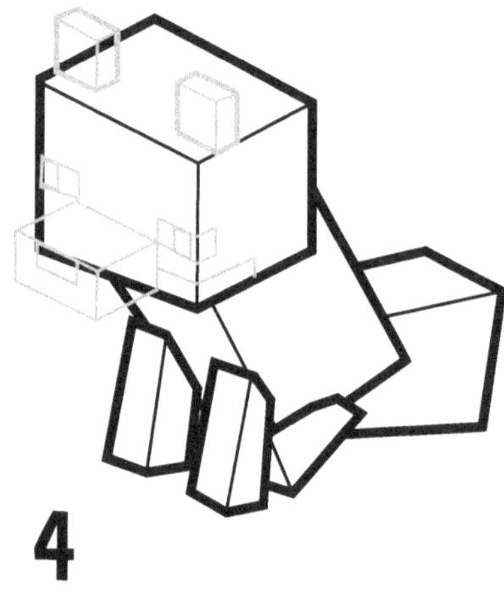

4

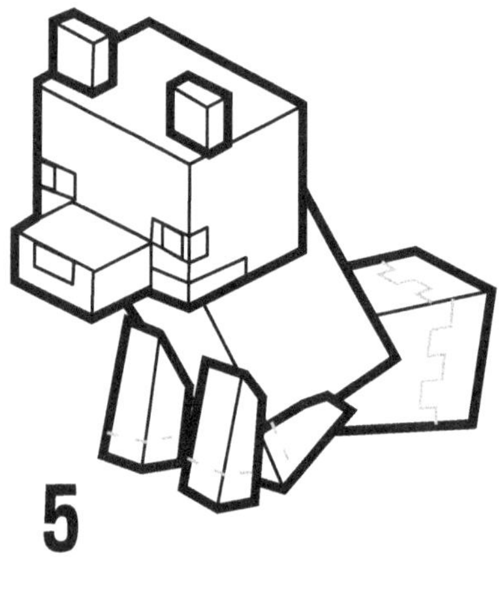

5

6

NOW, iT'S YOUR TURN

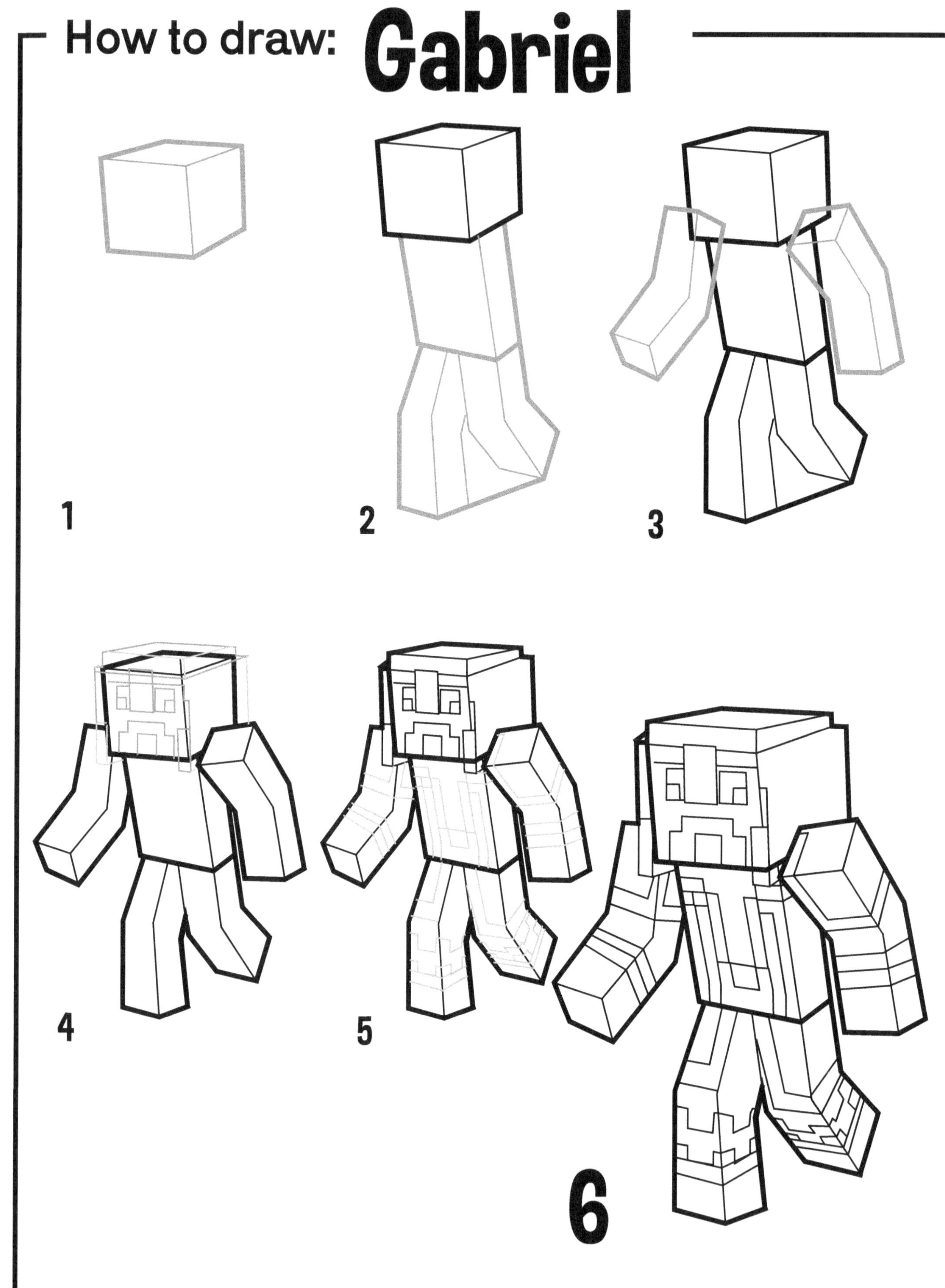

How to draw: Gabriel
1
2
3
4
5
6

NOW, IT'S YOUR TURN

How to draw: Great Hammer

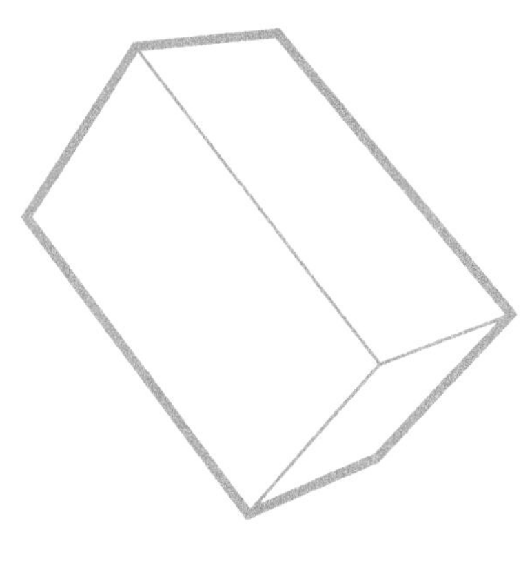

1

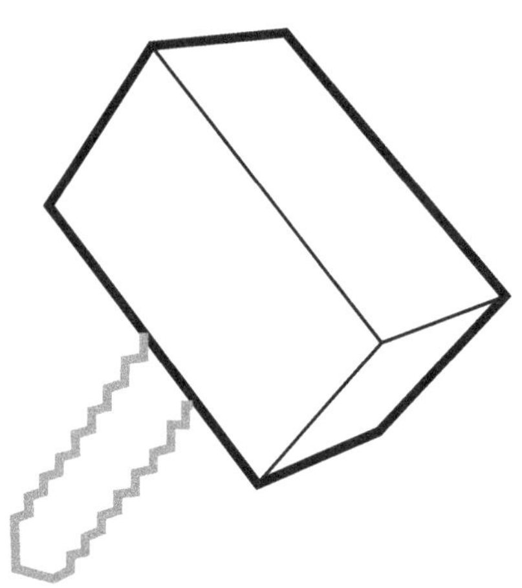

2

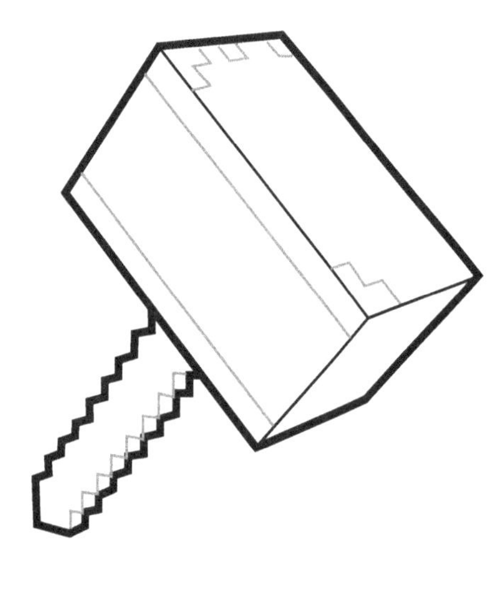

3

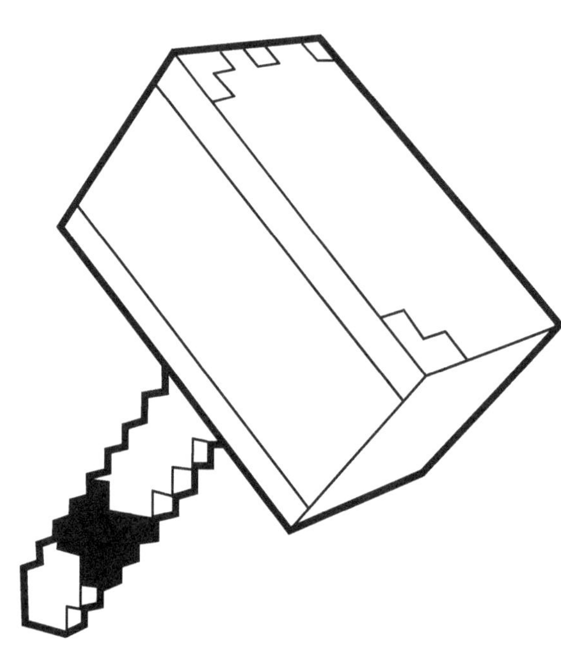

4

NOW, iT'S YOUR TURN

How to draw: **Guardian Bow**

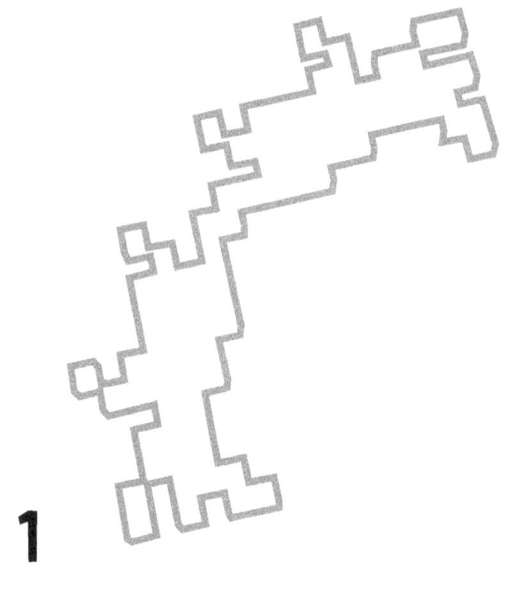

1

2

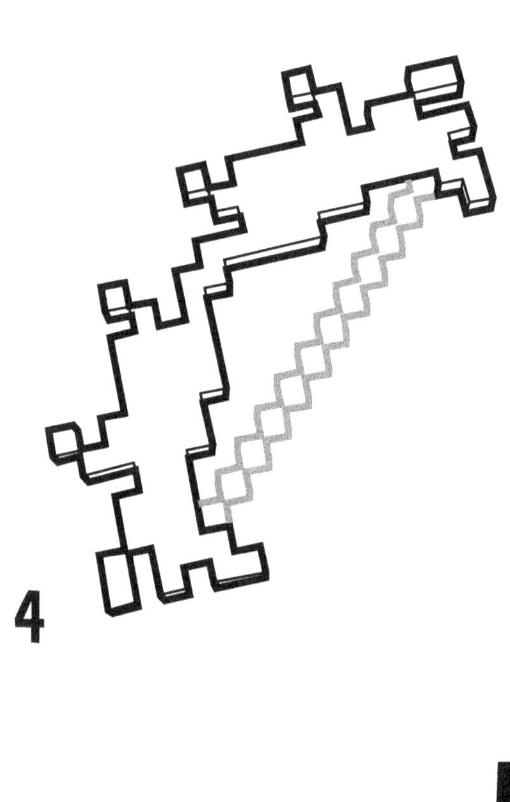

4

5

NOW, iT'S YOUR TURN

How to draw: Ice Wand

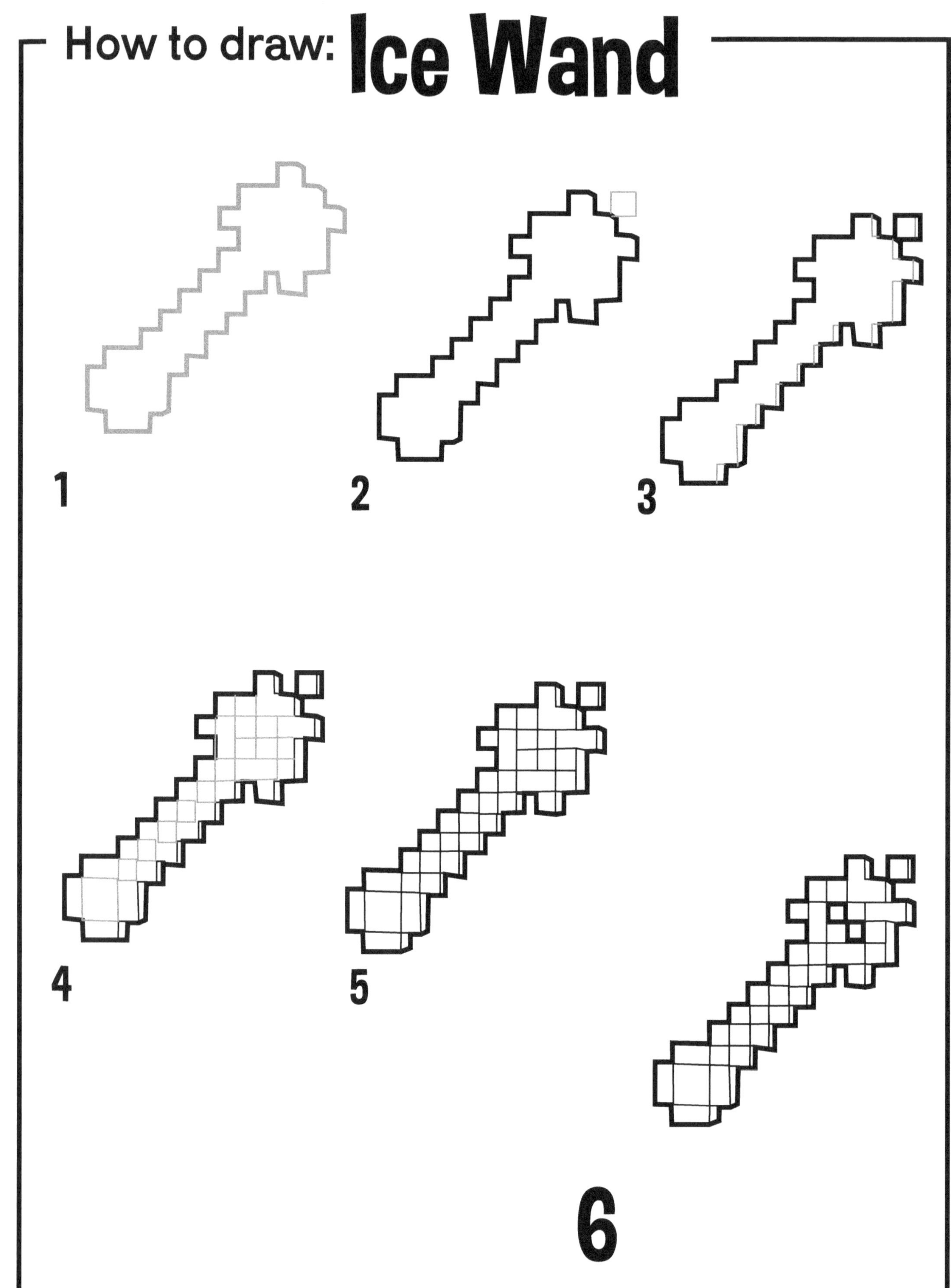

NOW, iT'S YOUR TURN

How to draw: **Ivor**

1

2

3

4

5

6

NOW, IT'S YOUR TURN

How to draw: Jess

1

2

3

4

5

6

NOW, iT'S YOUR TURN

How to draw: Jungle Abomination

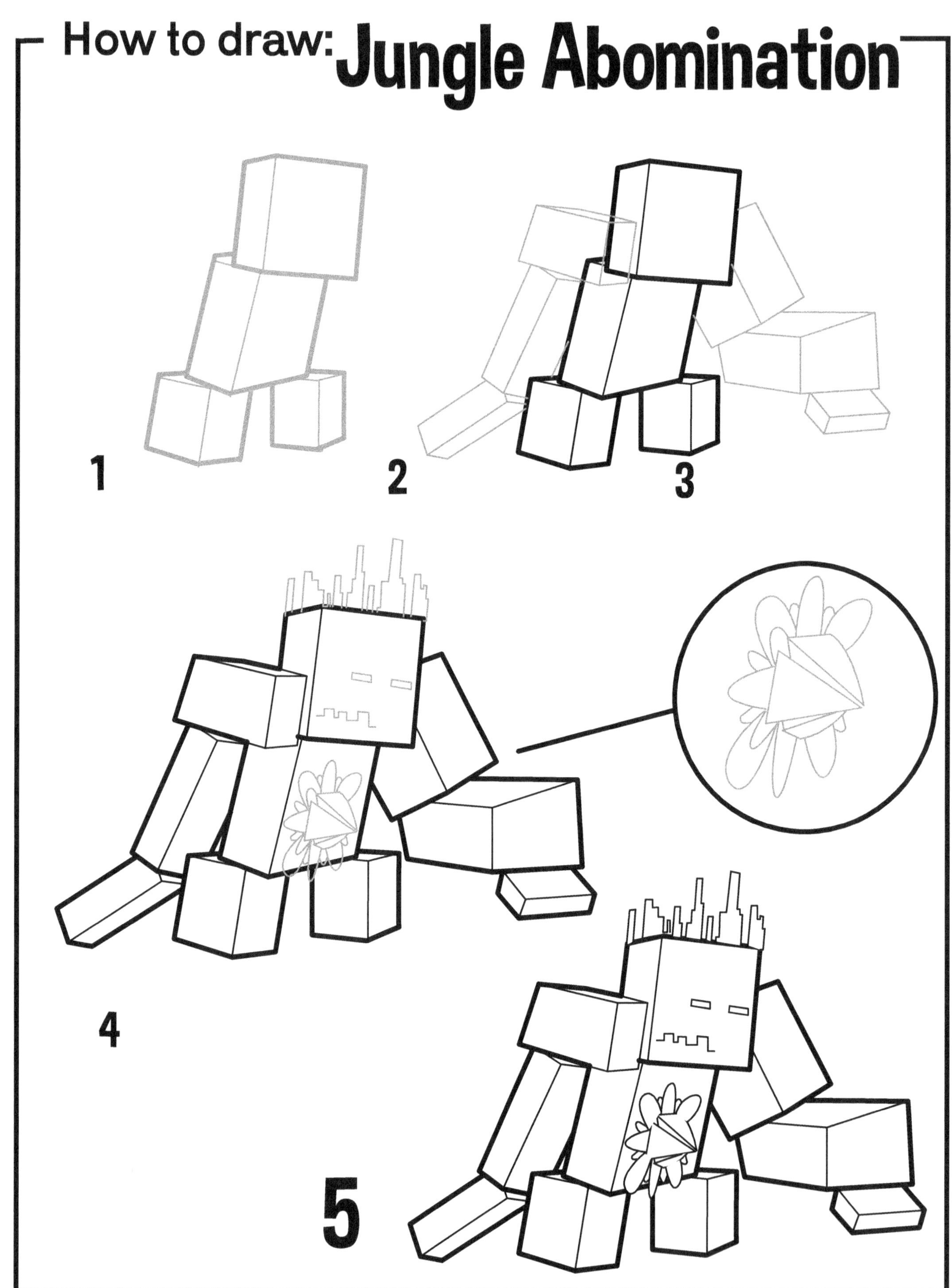

NOW, IT'S YOUR TURN

How to draw: Light Feather

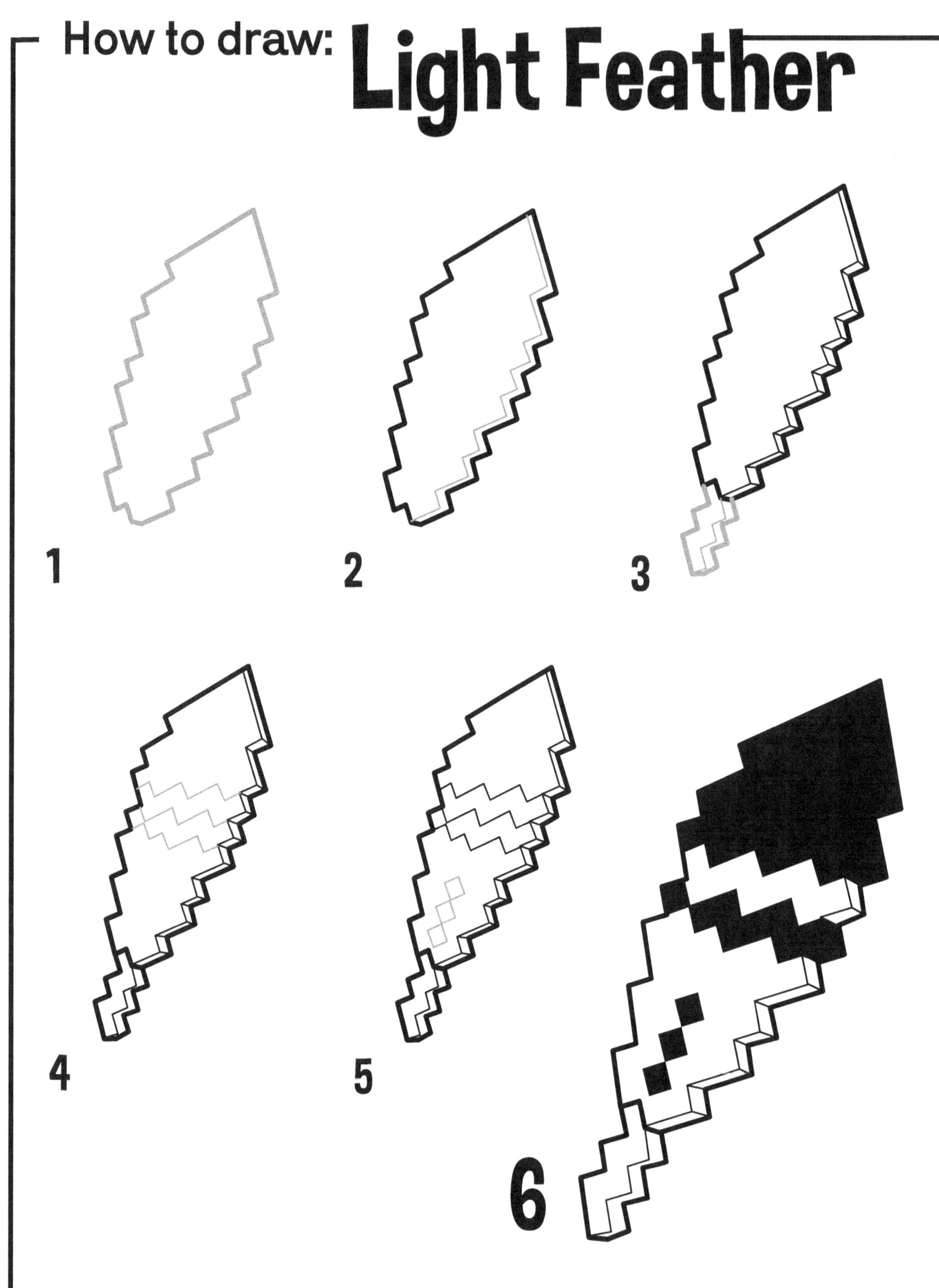

NOW, iT'S YOUR TURN

How to draw: Lighning Rod

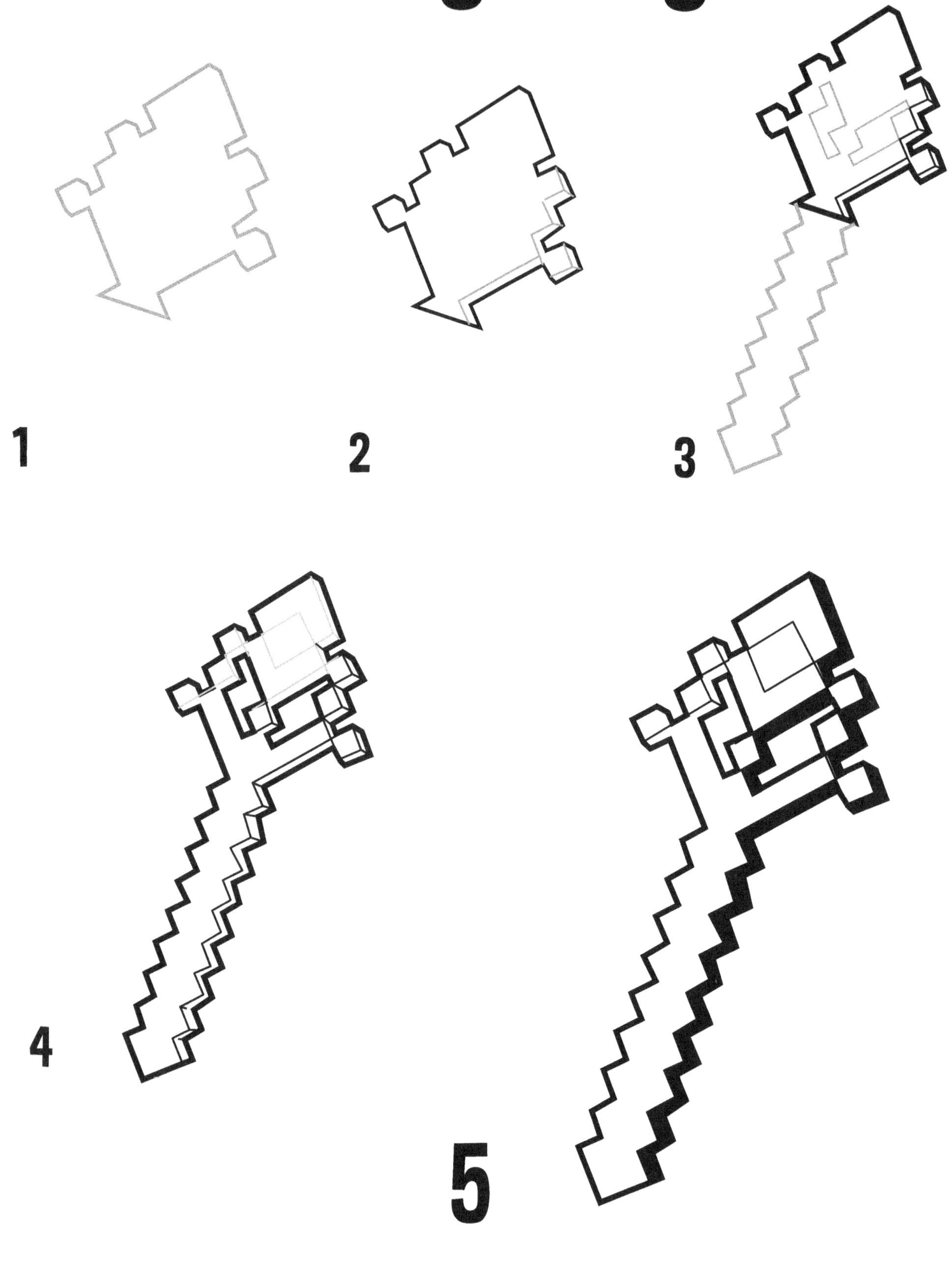

1

2

3

4

5

NOW, IT'S YOUR TURN

How to draw: Lukas

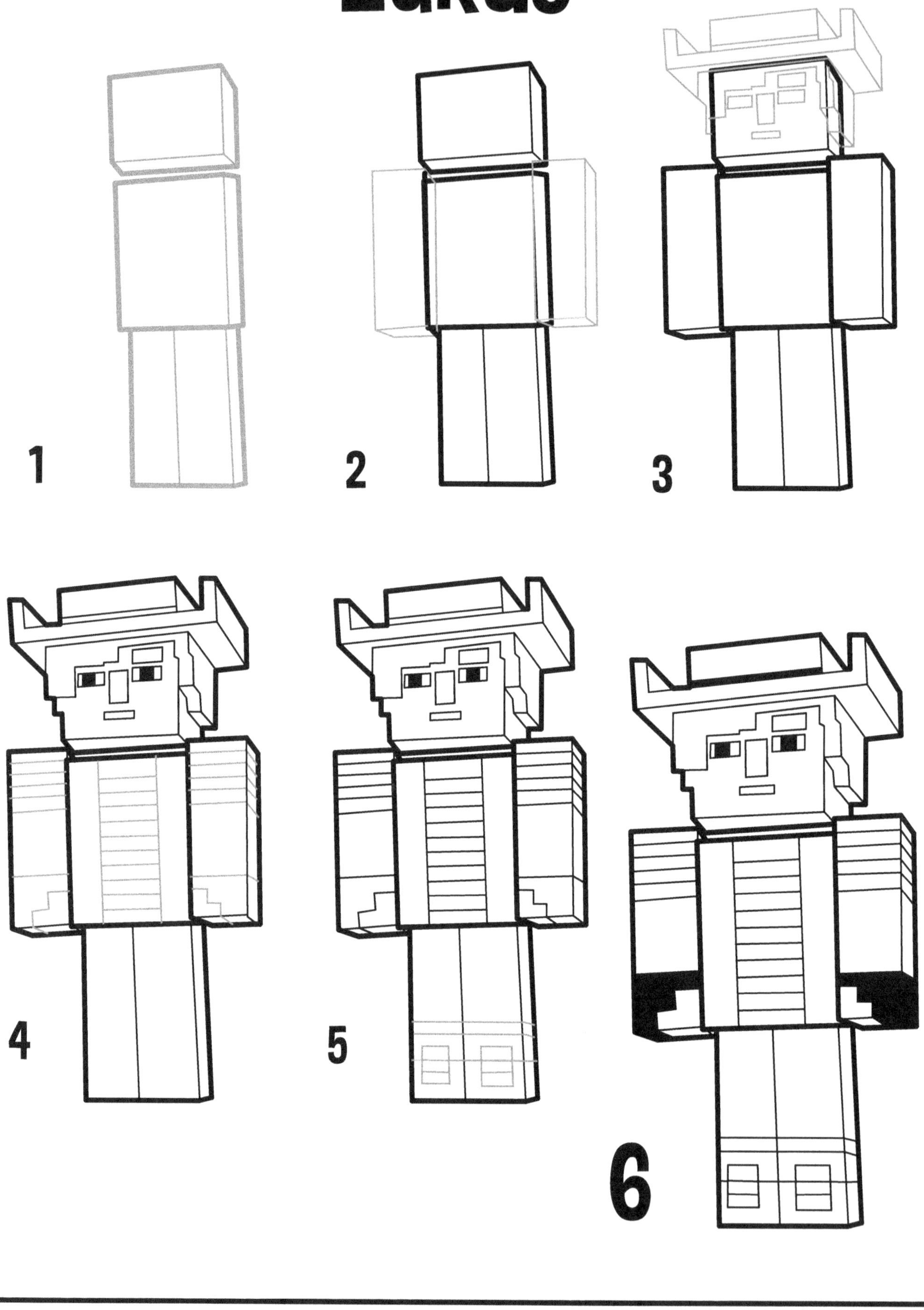

1

2

3

4

5

6

NOW, IT'S YOUR TURN

How to draw: Luxury Merchant

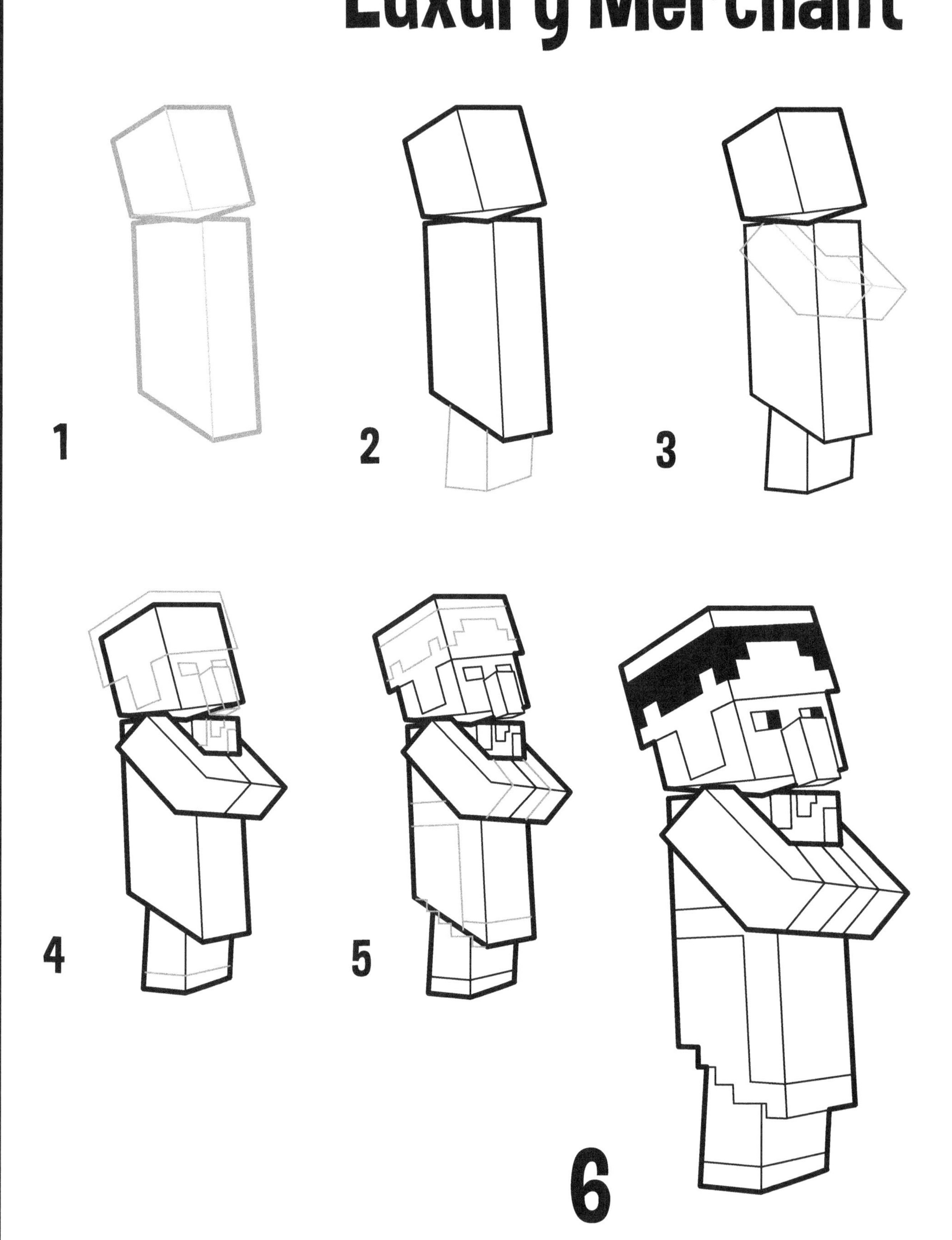

NOW, iT'S YOUR TURN

How to draw: **Mistery Merchant**

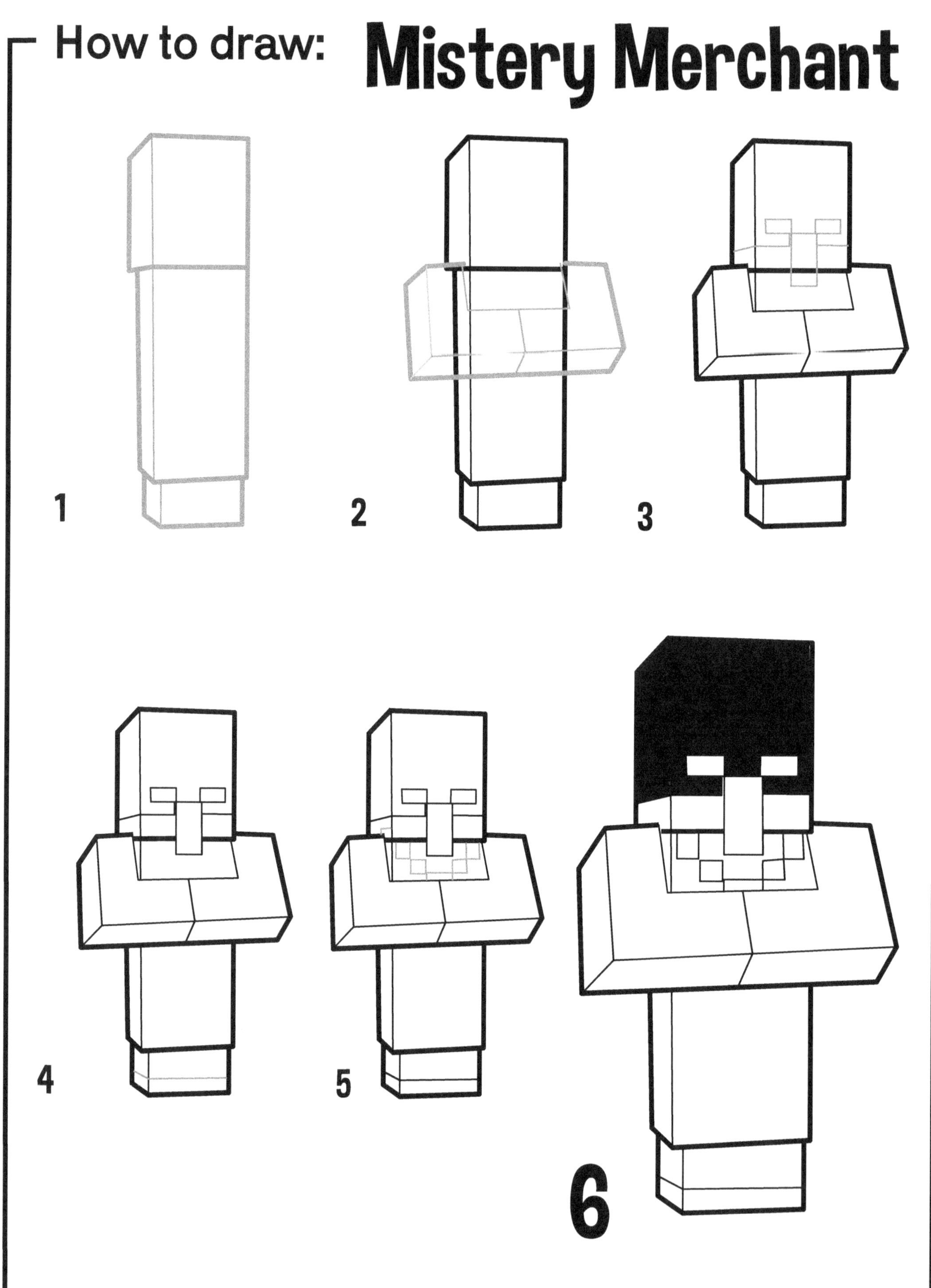

1

2

3

4

5

6

NOW, iT'S YOUR TURN

How to draw: Mushroom Cow
1
2
3
4
5

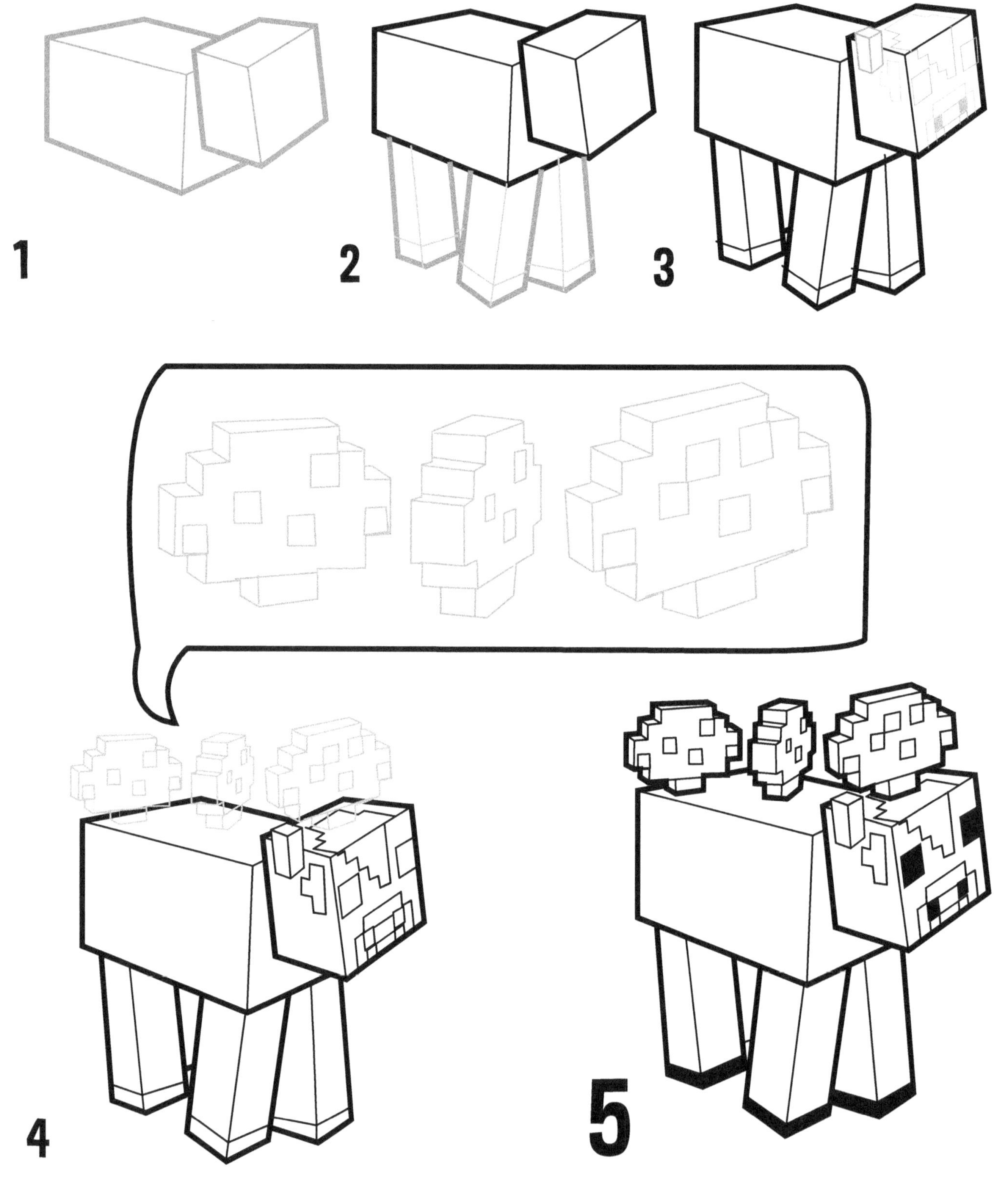

NOW, iT'S YOUR TURN

How to draw: Nameless Blade

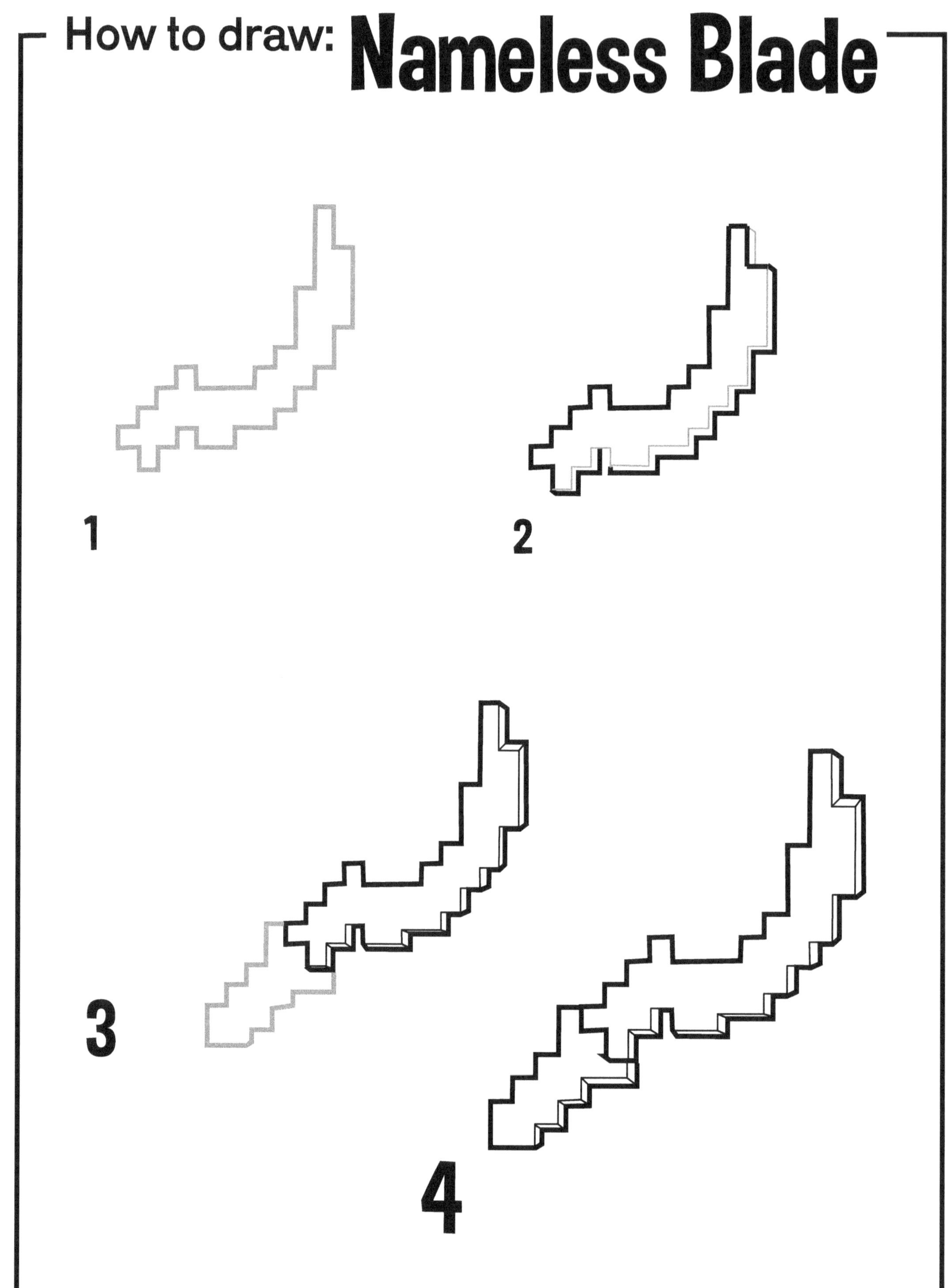

NOW, iT'S YOUR TURN

How to draw: **Nameless One**

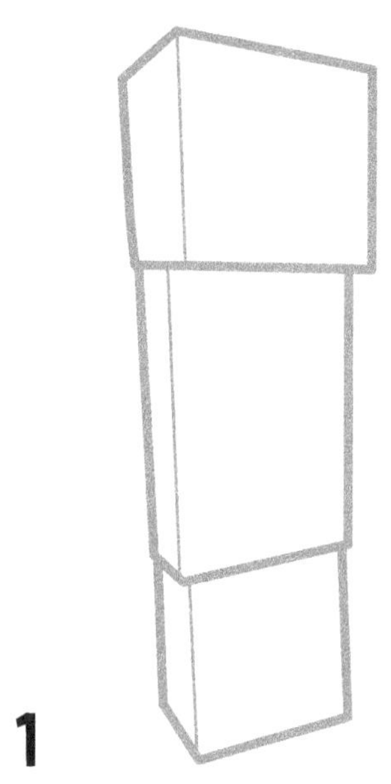

1

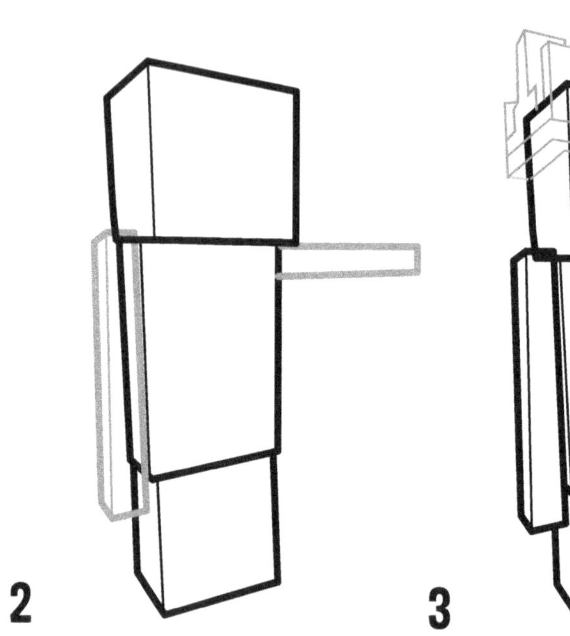

2

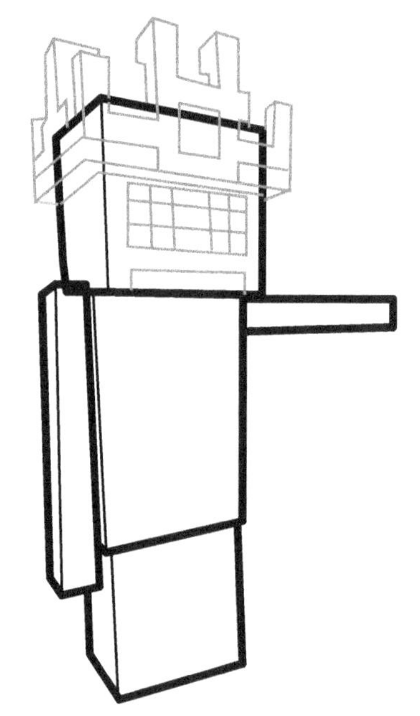

3

4

5

NOW, IT'S YOUR TURN

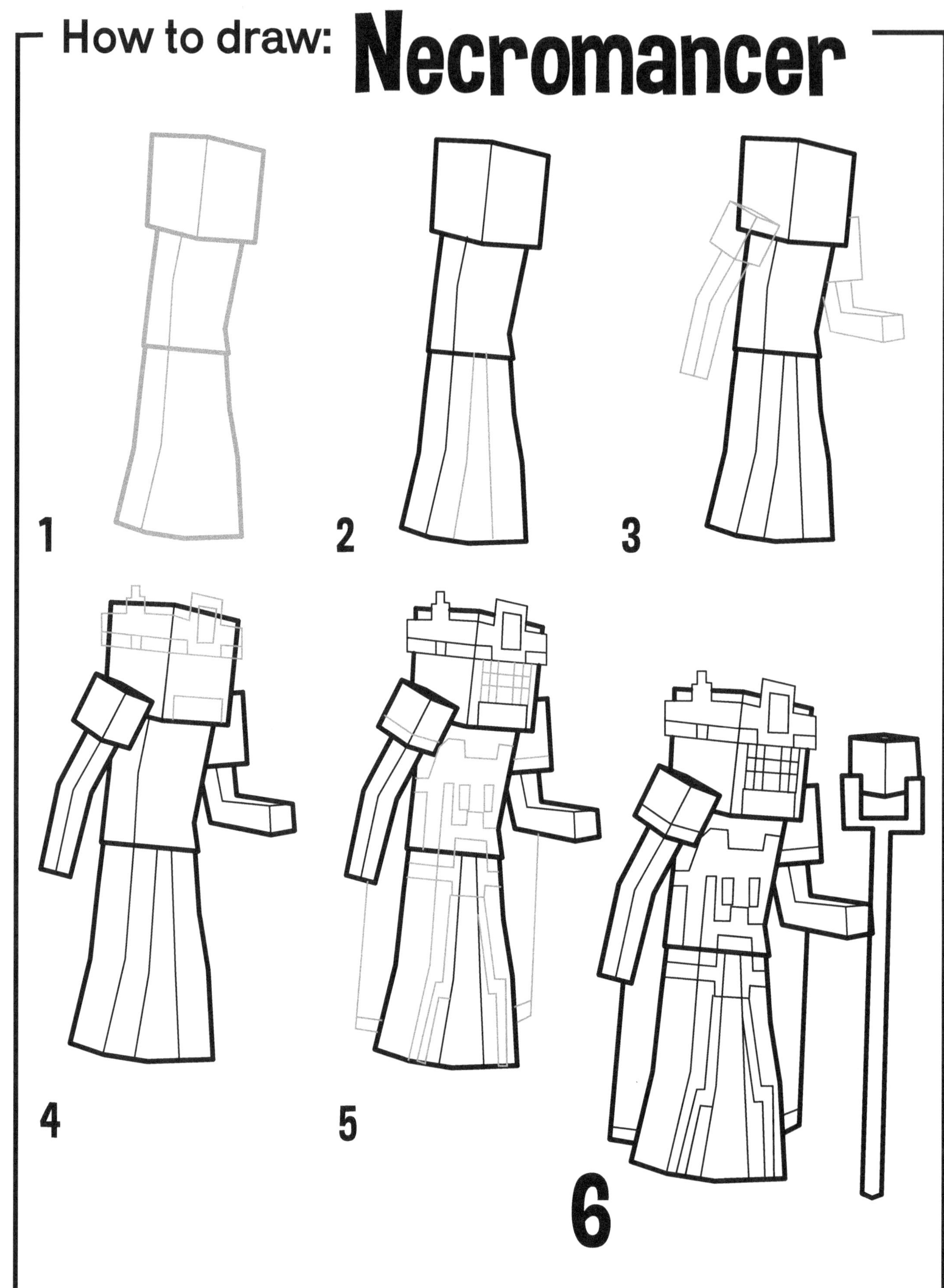

How to draw: Necromancer
1
2
3
4
5
6

NOW, iT'S YOUR TURN

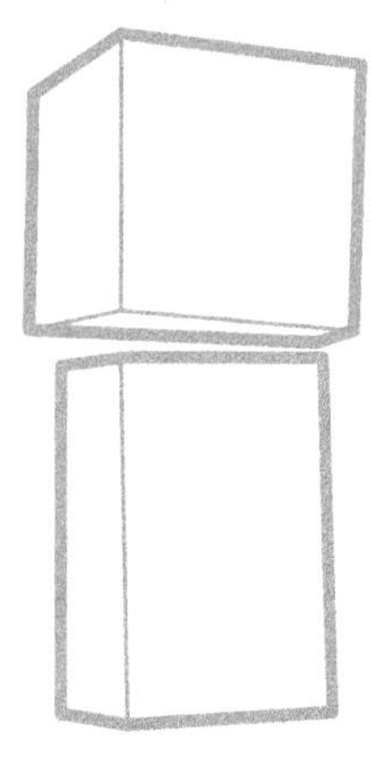

1

2

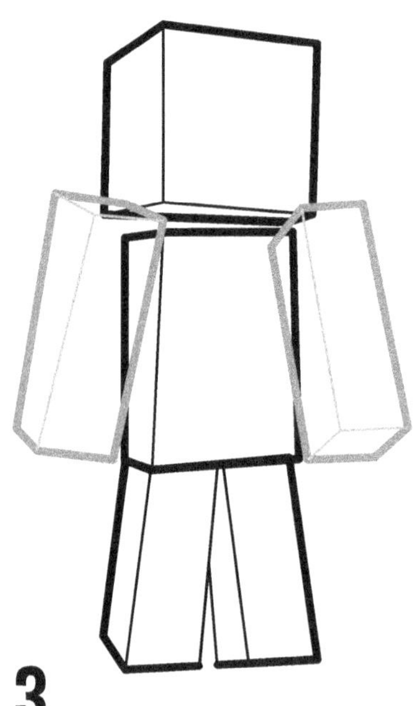

3

4

5

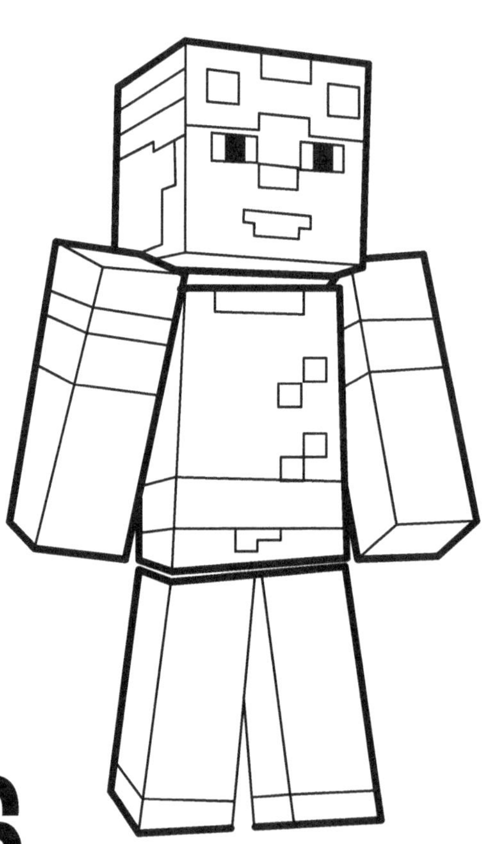

6

NOW, IT'S YOUR TURN

Panda

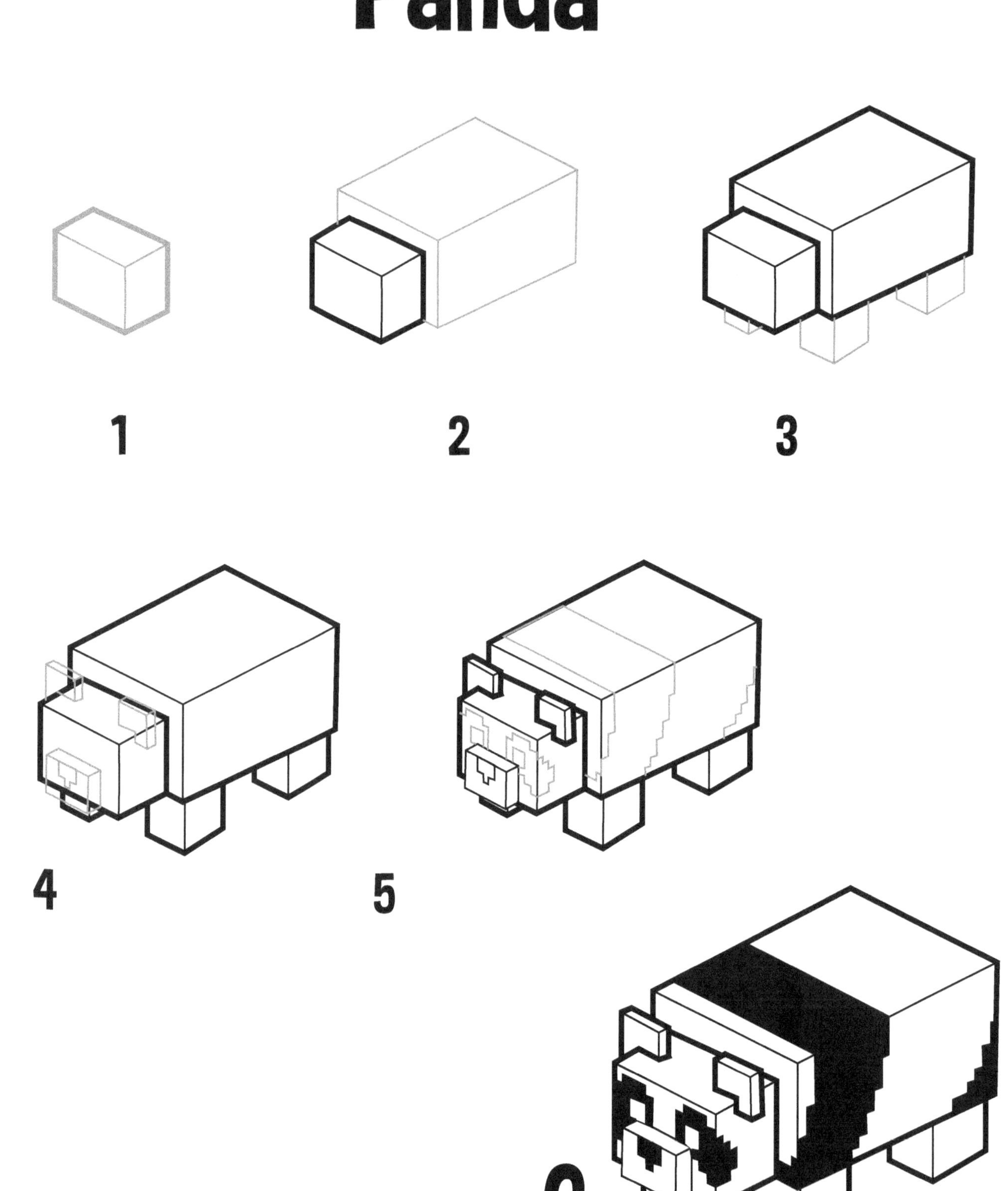

NOW, IT'S YOUR TURN

How to draw: Petra

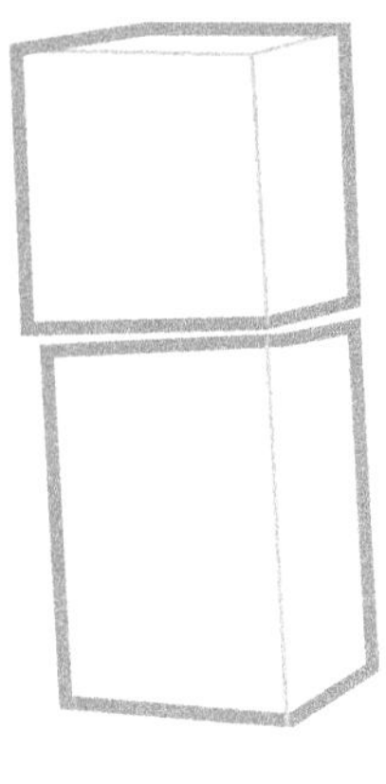

1

2

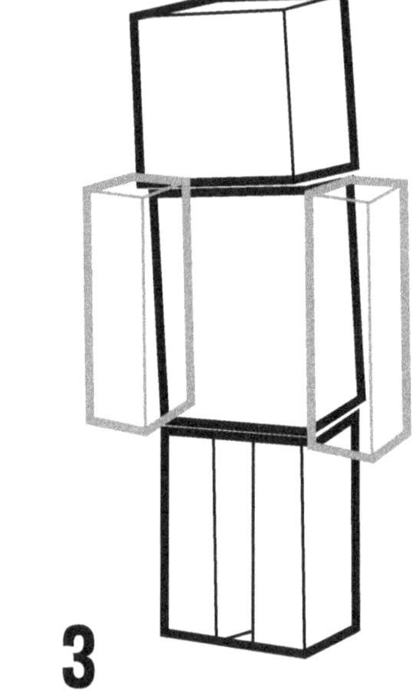

3

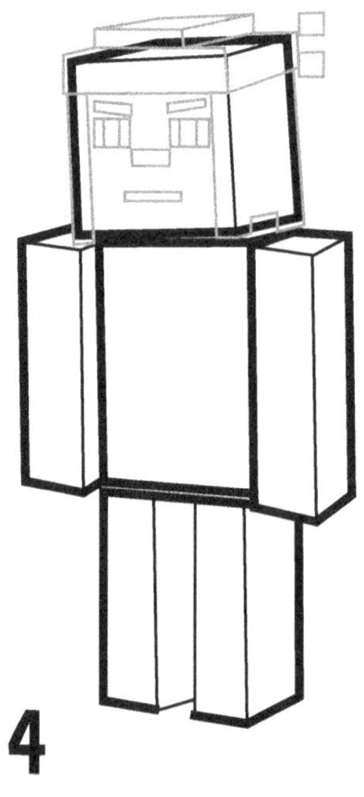

4

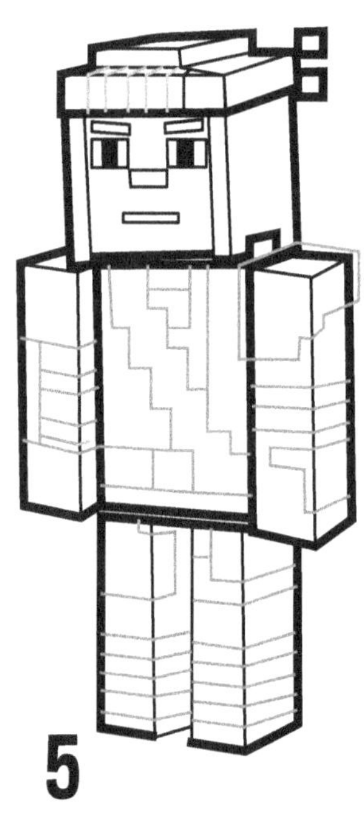

5

6

NOW, IT'S YOUR TURN

How to draw: PIG

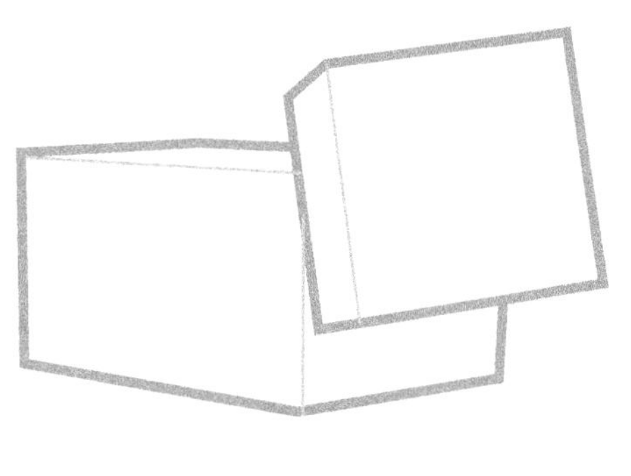

1

2

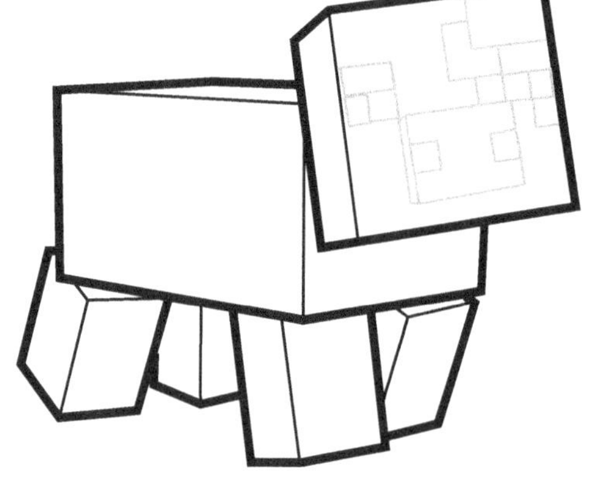

3

4

5

NOW, IT'S YOUR TURN

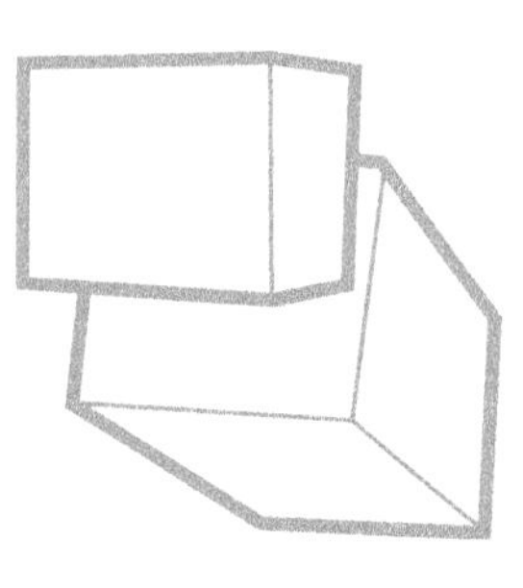

1

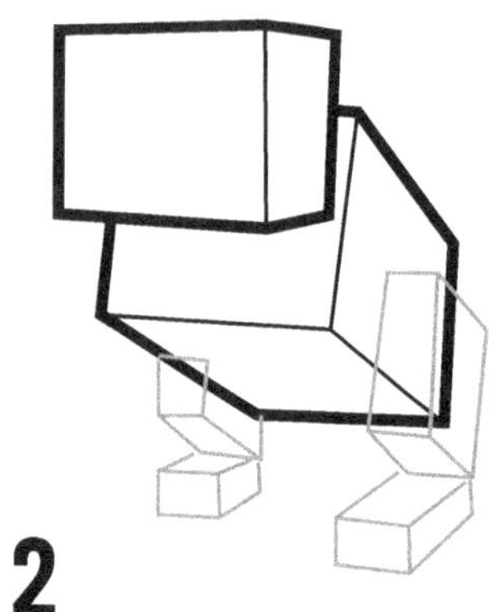

2

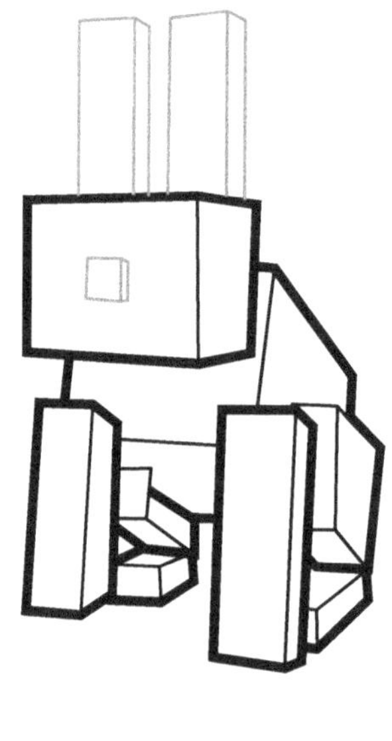

3

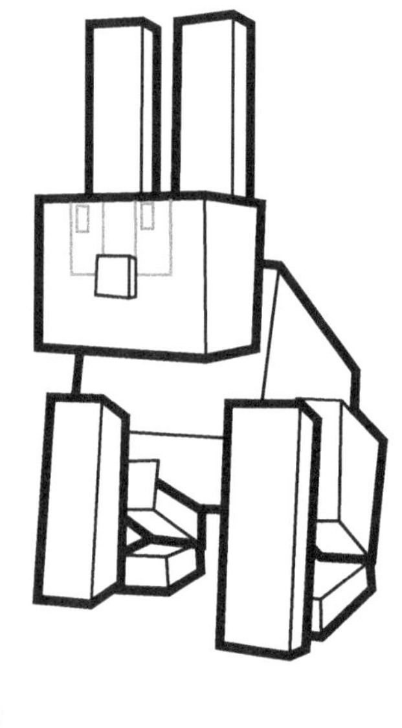

4

5

6

NOW, IT'S YOUR TURN

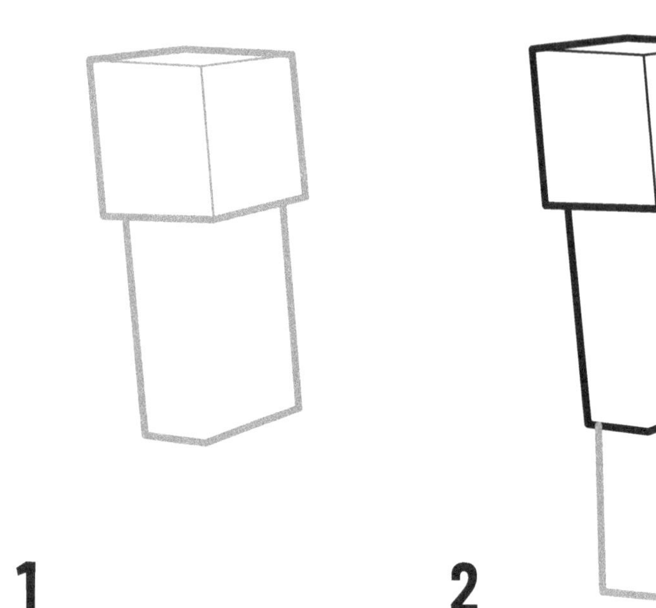

1

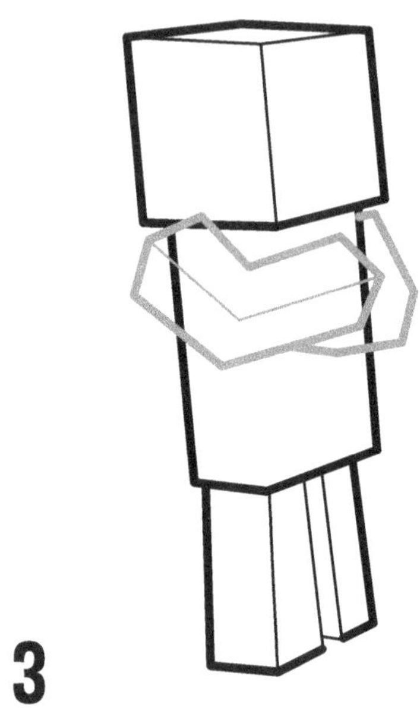

2

3

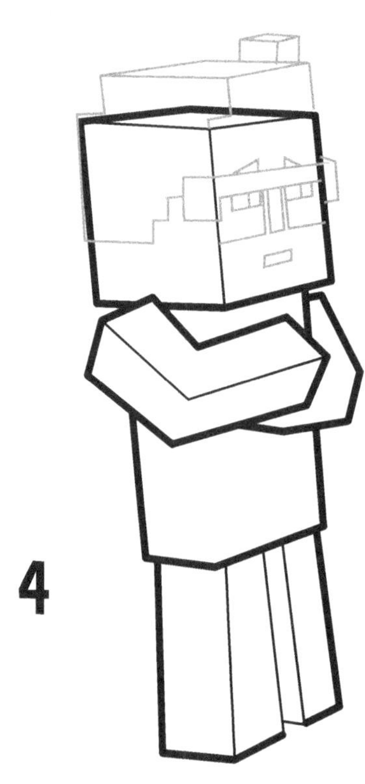

4

5

6

NOW, iT'S YOUR TURN

How to draw: Redstone Monster

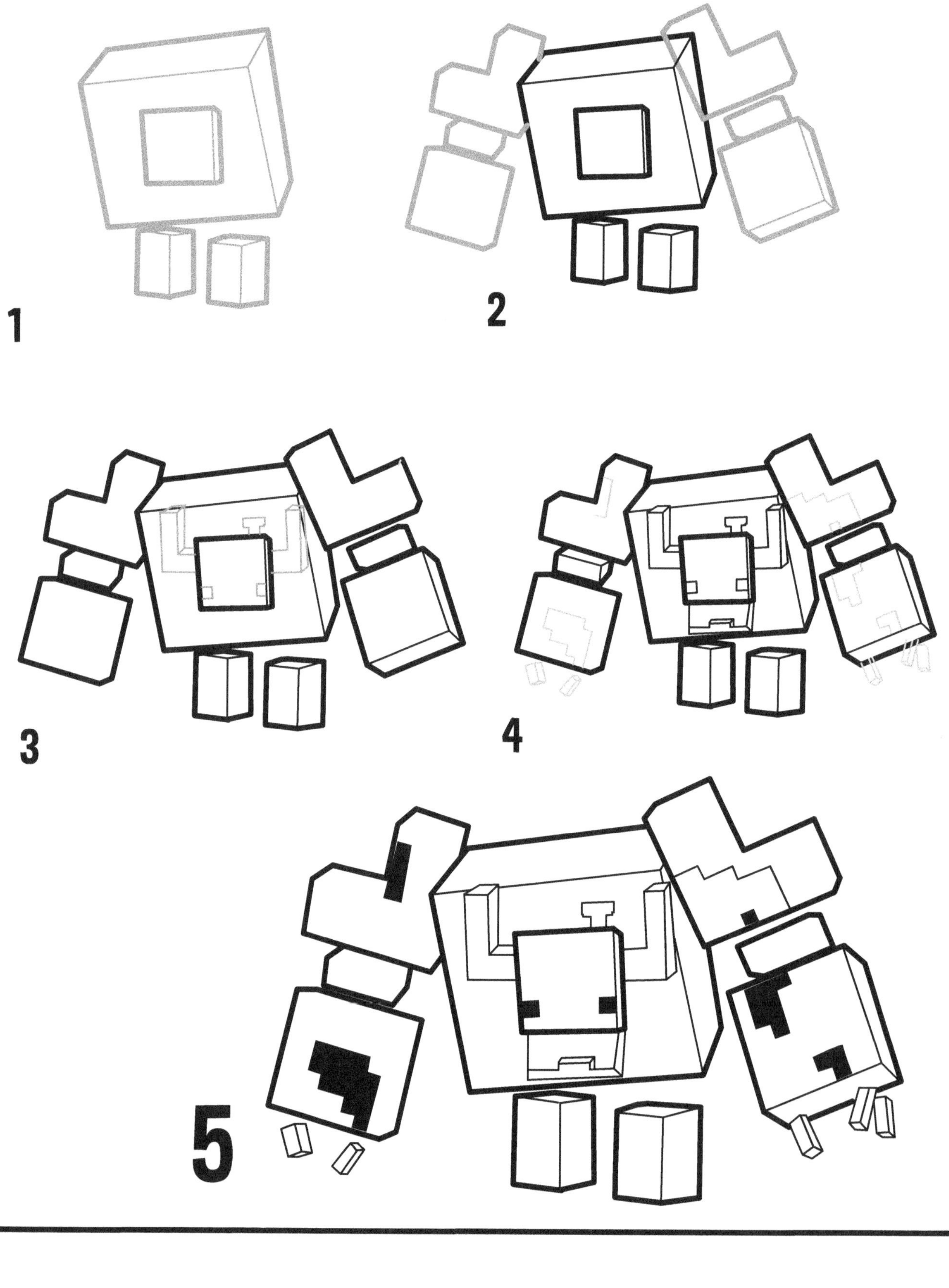

1

2

3

4

5

NOW, IT'S YOUR TURN

NOW, IT'S YOUR TURN

How to draw: Royal Guard

1

2

3

4

5

NOW, IT'S YOUR TURN

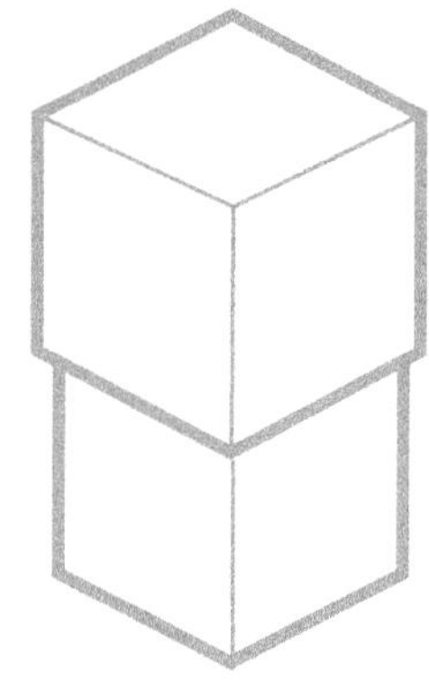

1

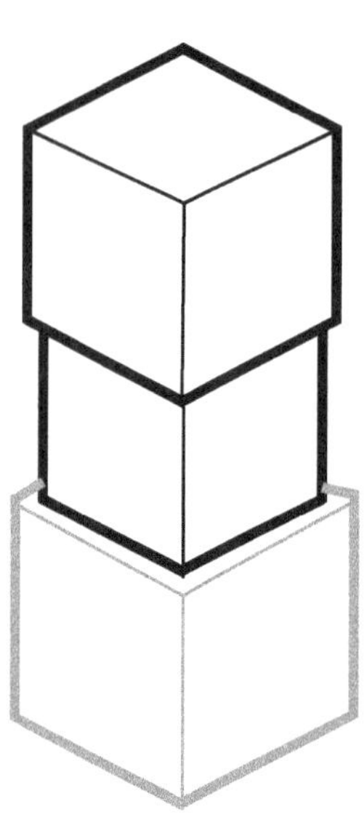

2

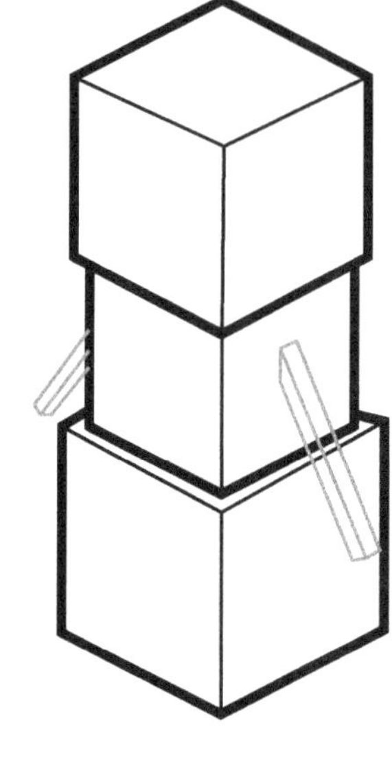

3

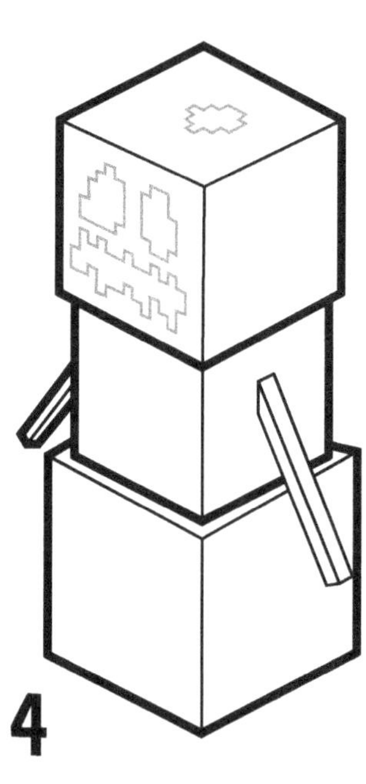

4

5

6

NOW, iT'S YOUR TURN

How to draw: Soren
1
2
3
4
5
6

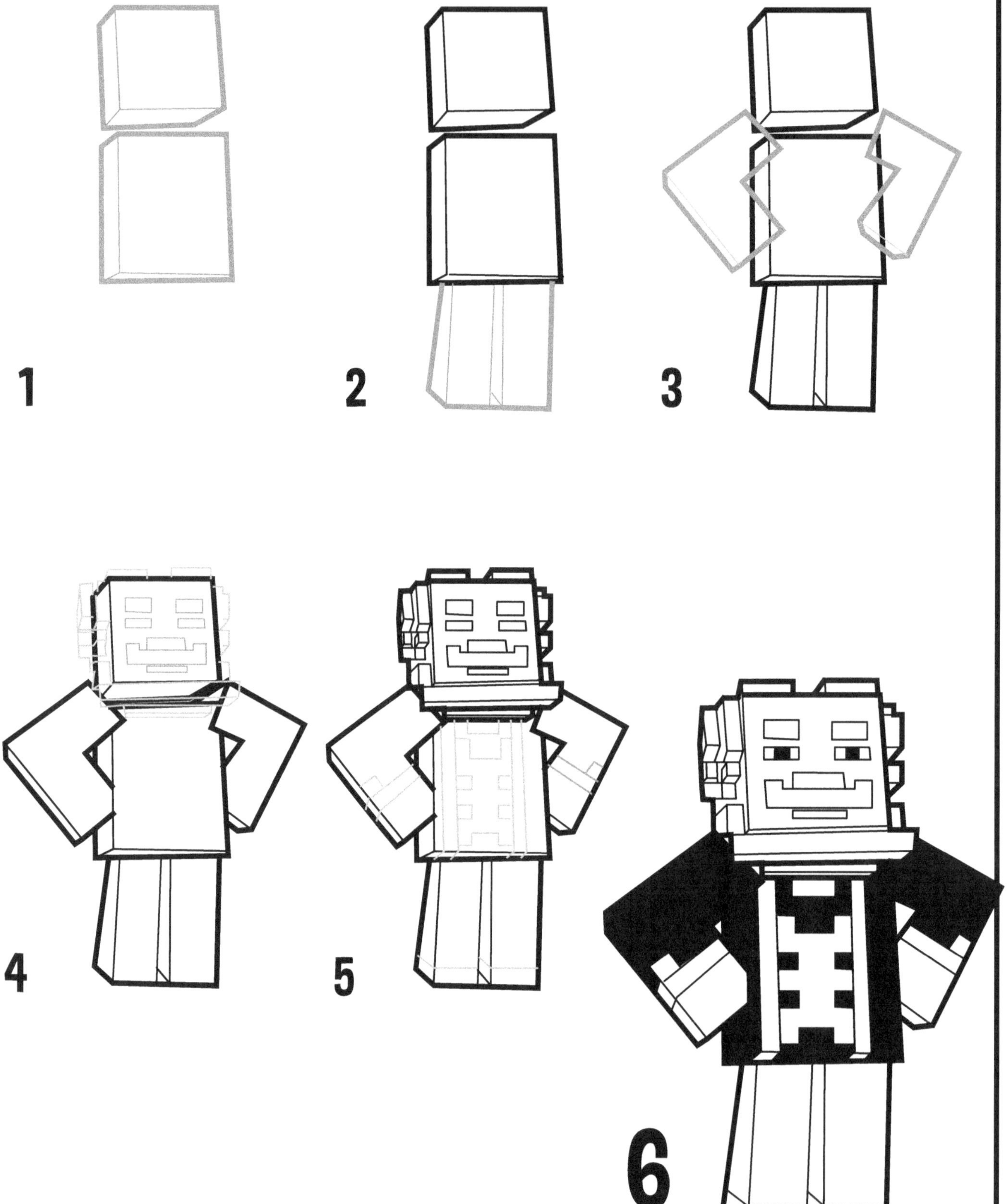

NOW, IT'S YOUR TURN

Soul Healer

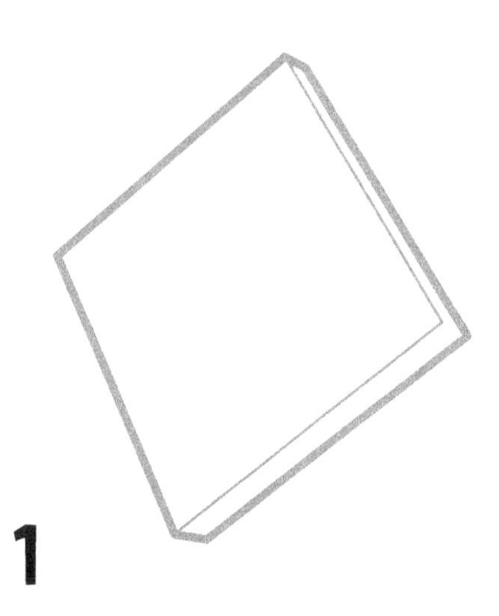

1

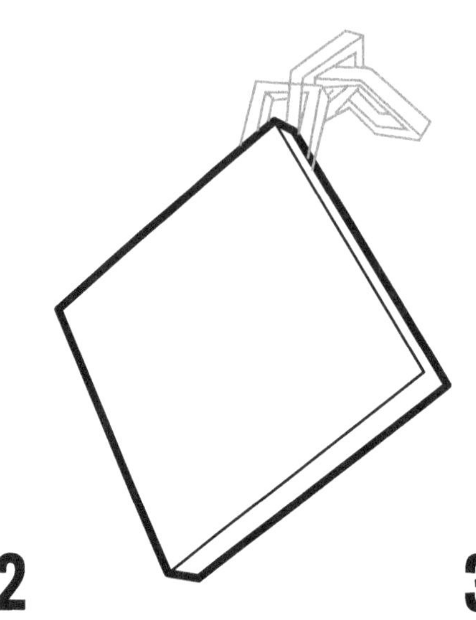

2

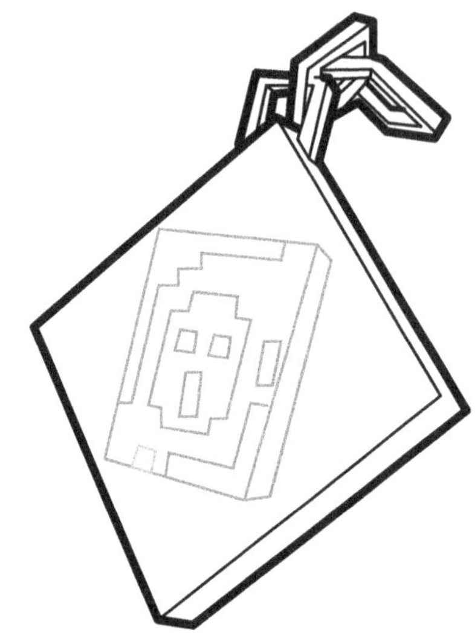

3

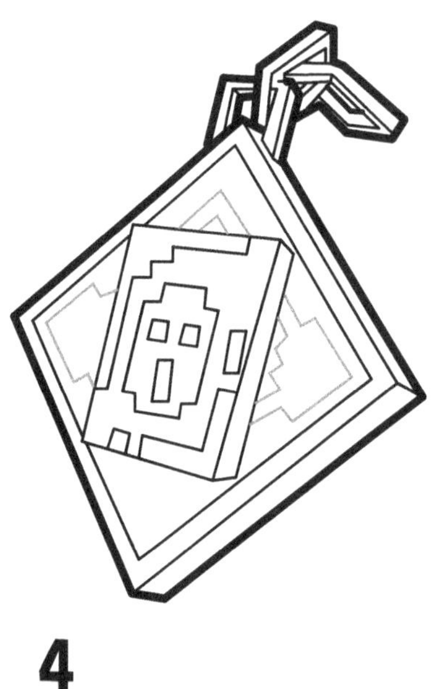

4

5

6

NOW, IT'S YOUR TURN

How to draw: Soul Lantern

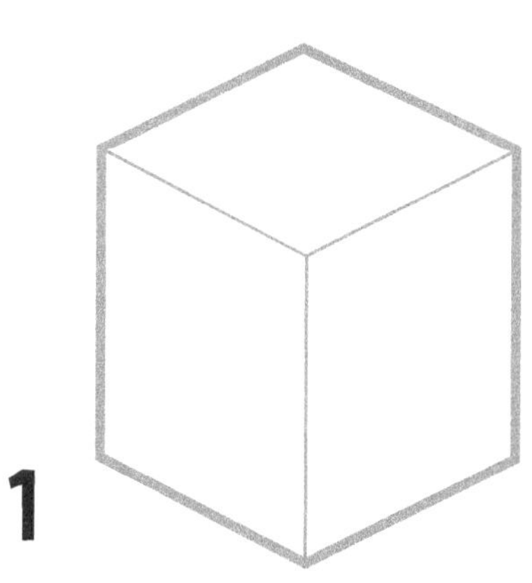

1

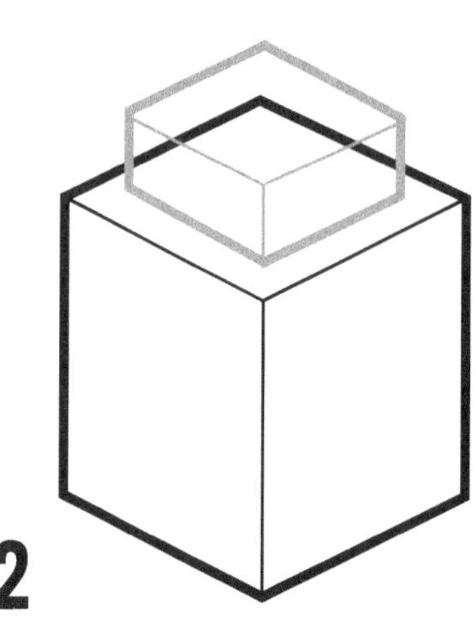

2

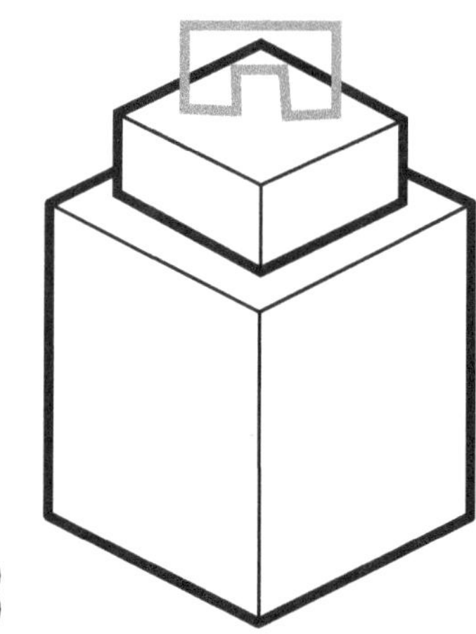

3

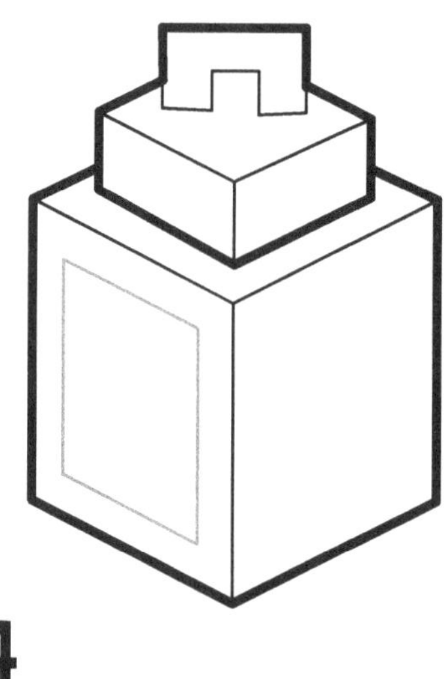

4

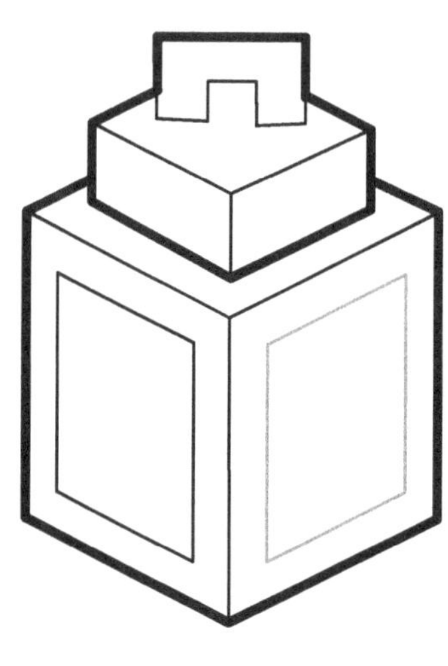

5

6

NOW, IT'S YOUR TURN

Soul Scythe

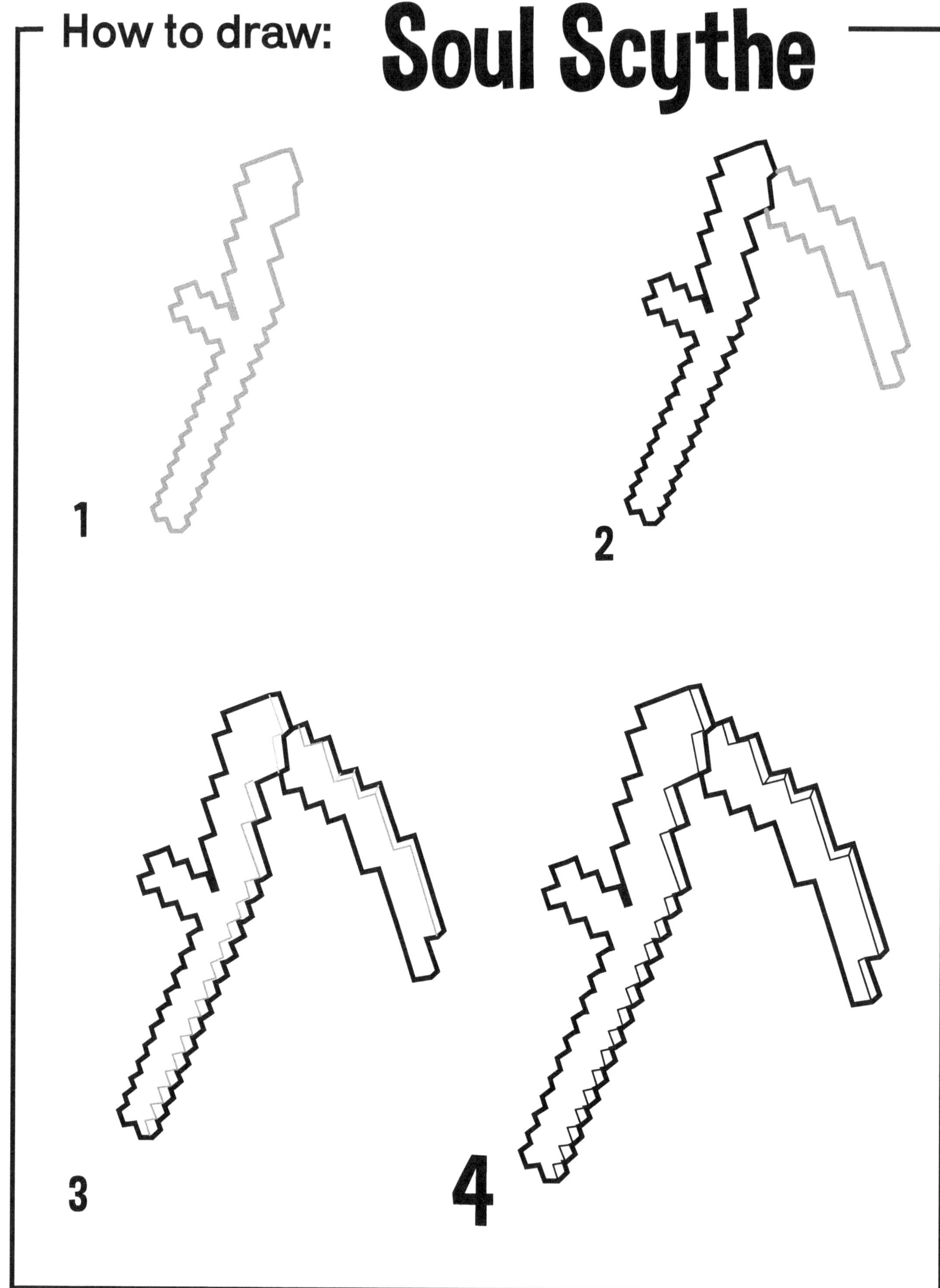

NOW, IT'S YOUR TURN

How to draw: Spider Armor

1

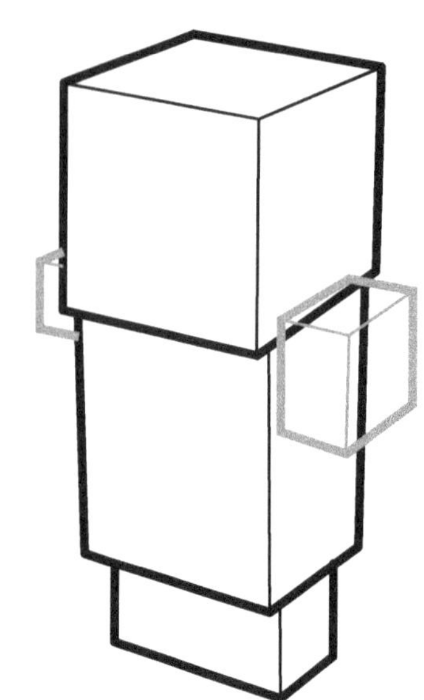

2

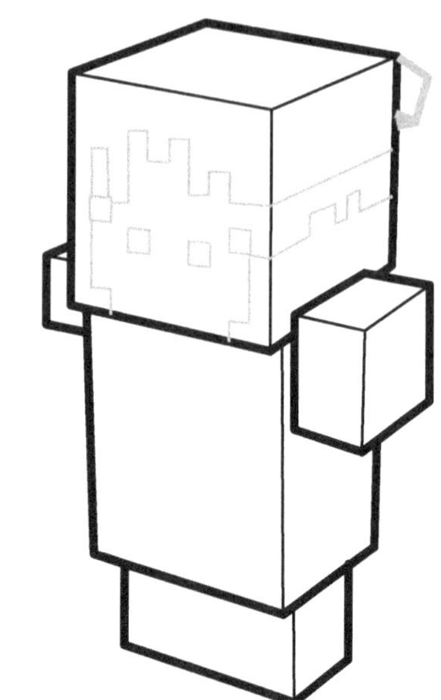

3

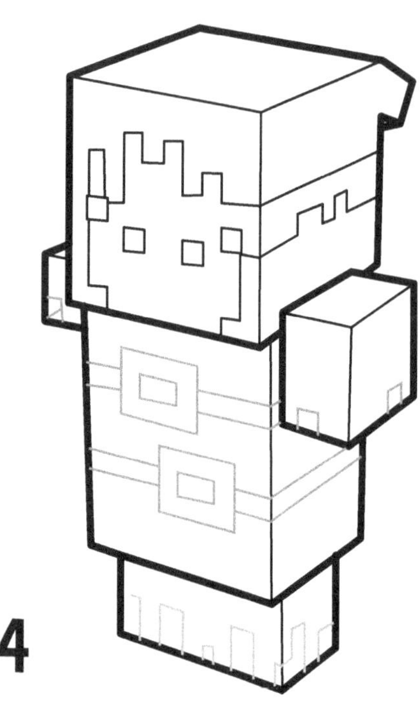

4

5

NOW, IT'S YOUR TURN

How to draw: **Sword**

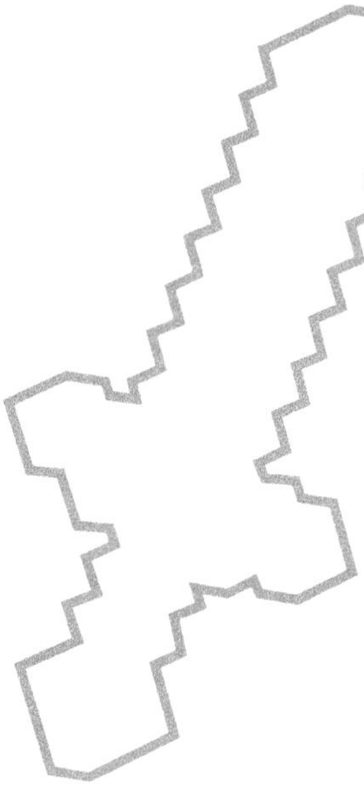

1

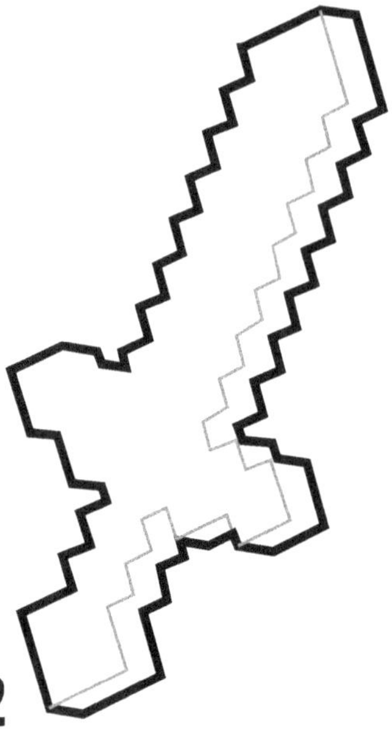

2

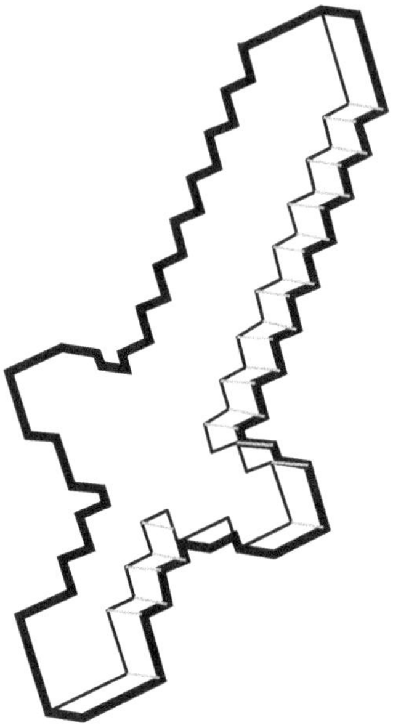

3

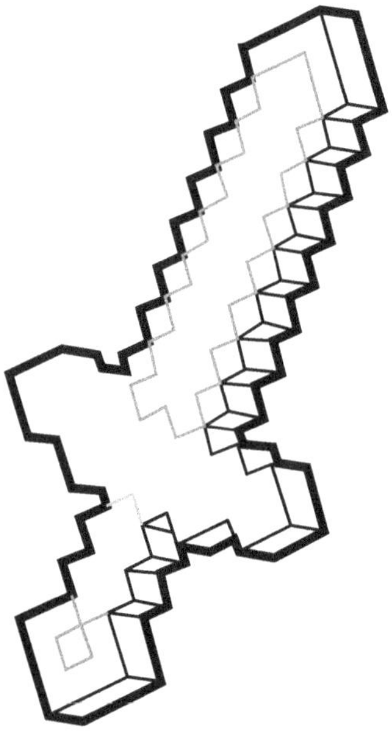

4

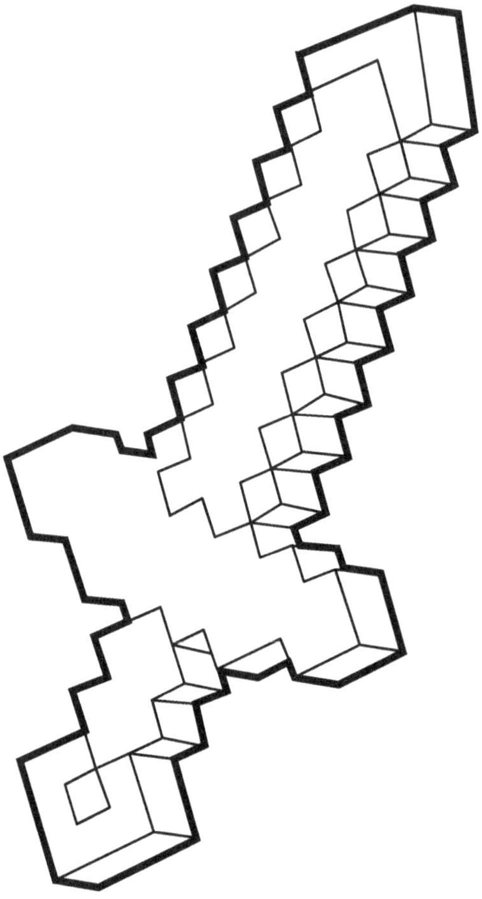

5

NOW, IT'S YOUR TURN

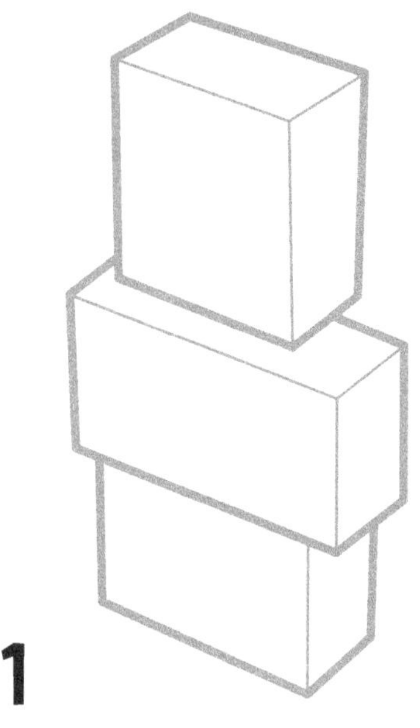

1

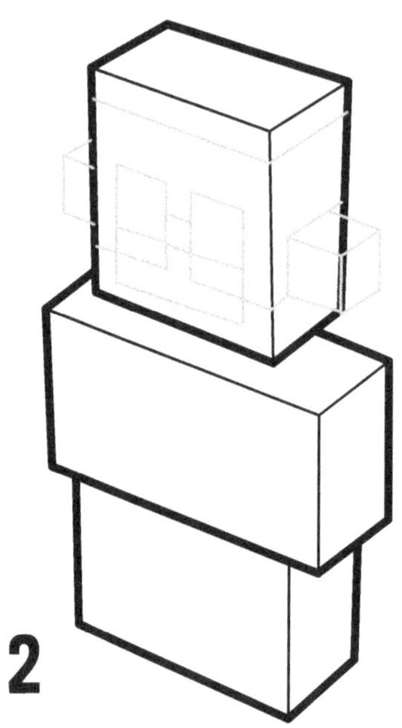

2

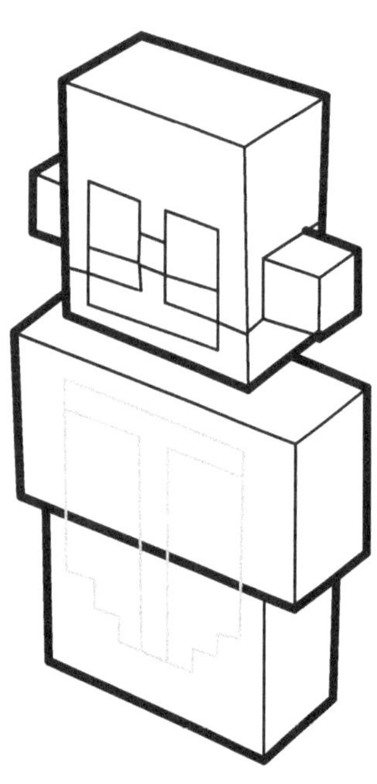

3

4

NOW, IT'S YOUR TURN

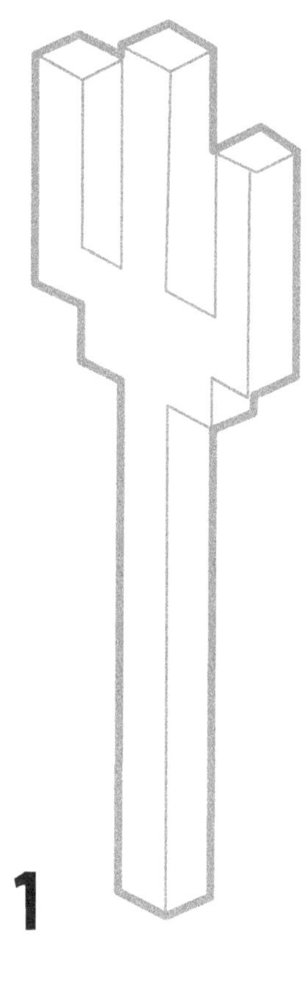

1

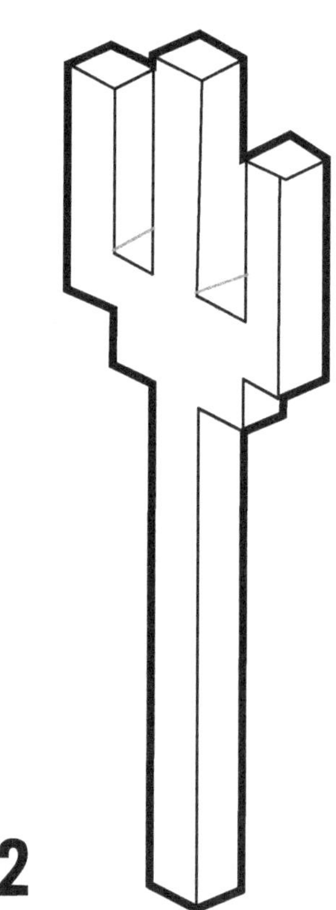

2

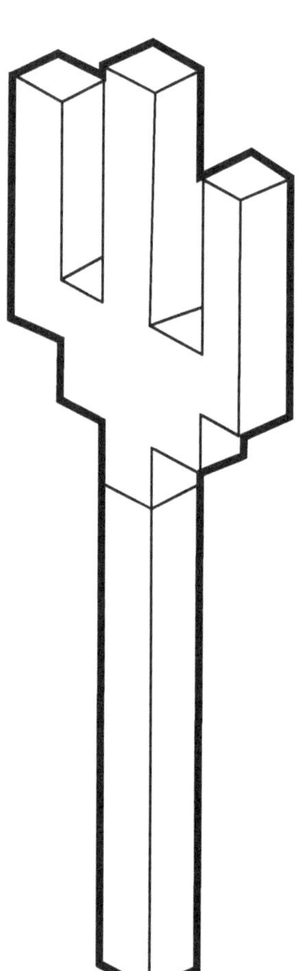

3

NOW, iT'S YOUR TURN

How to draw: Turtle
1 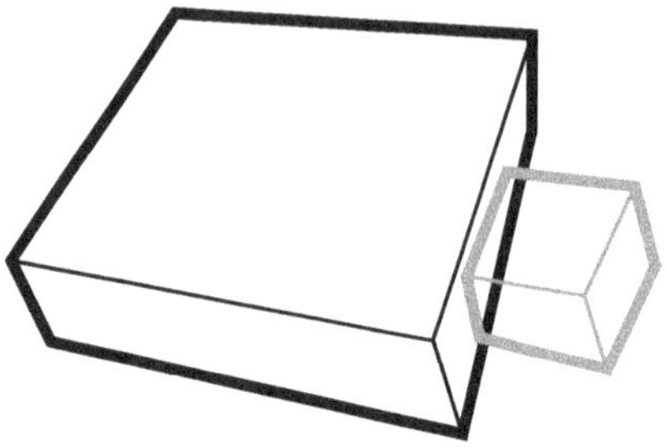
2 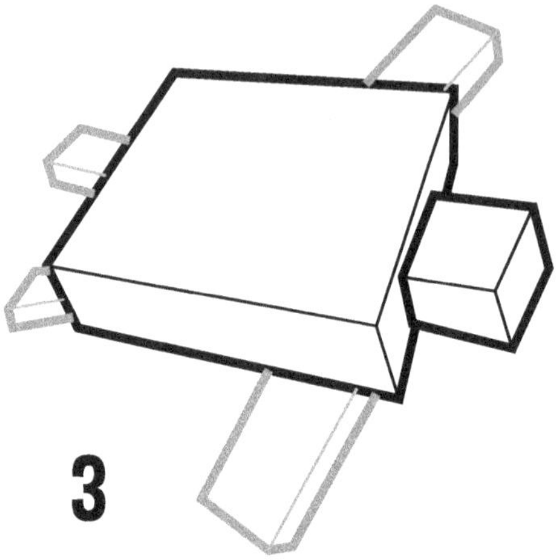
3 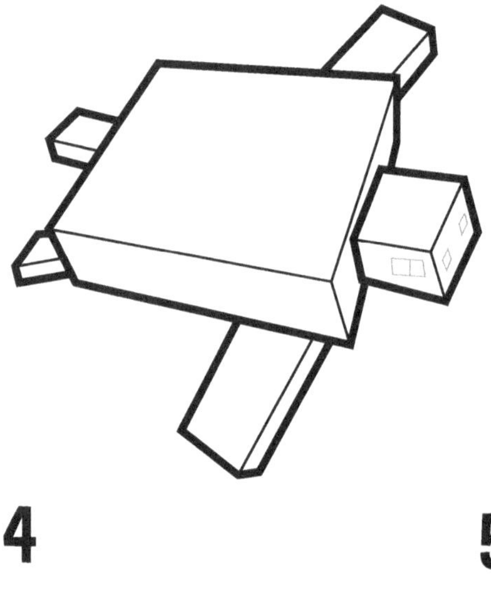
4 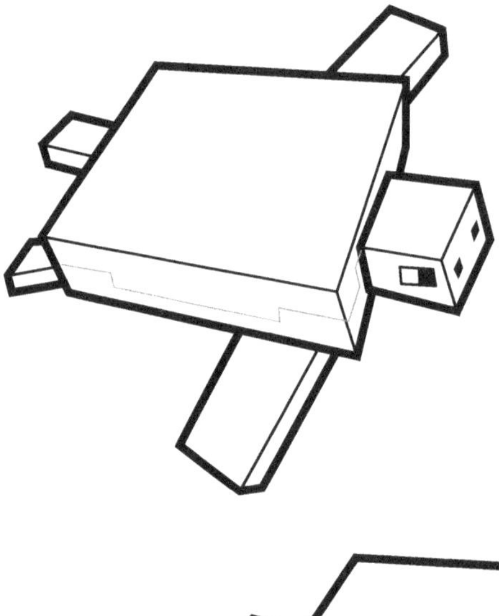
5 
6

NOW, IT'S YOUR TURN

How to draw: Vindicator

1

2

3

4

5

6

NOW, IT'S YOUR TURN

How to draw: **Wolf**

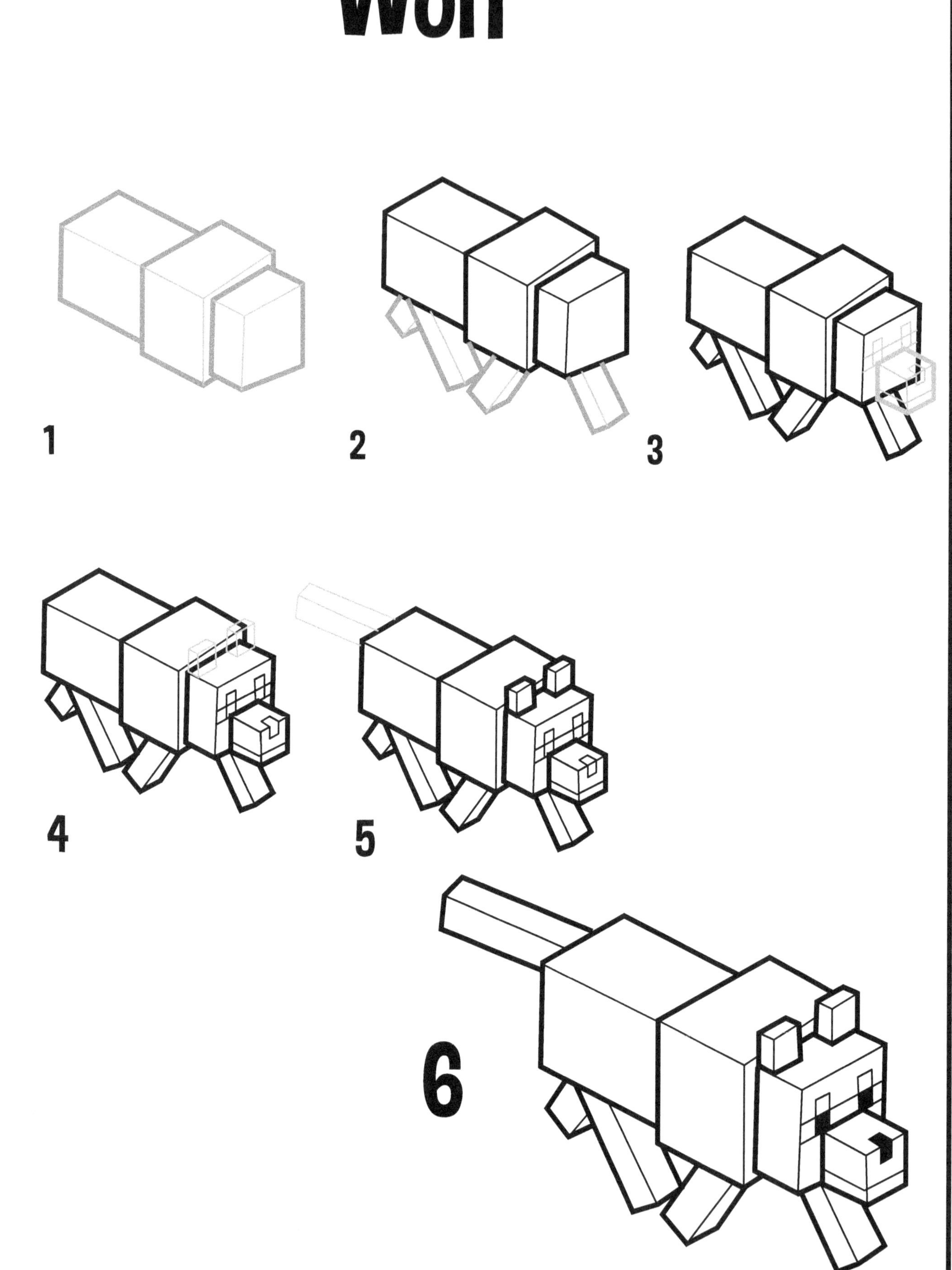

NOW, IT'S YOUR TURN

How to draw: **Wraith**

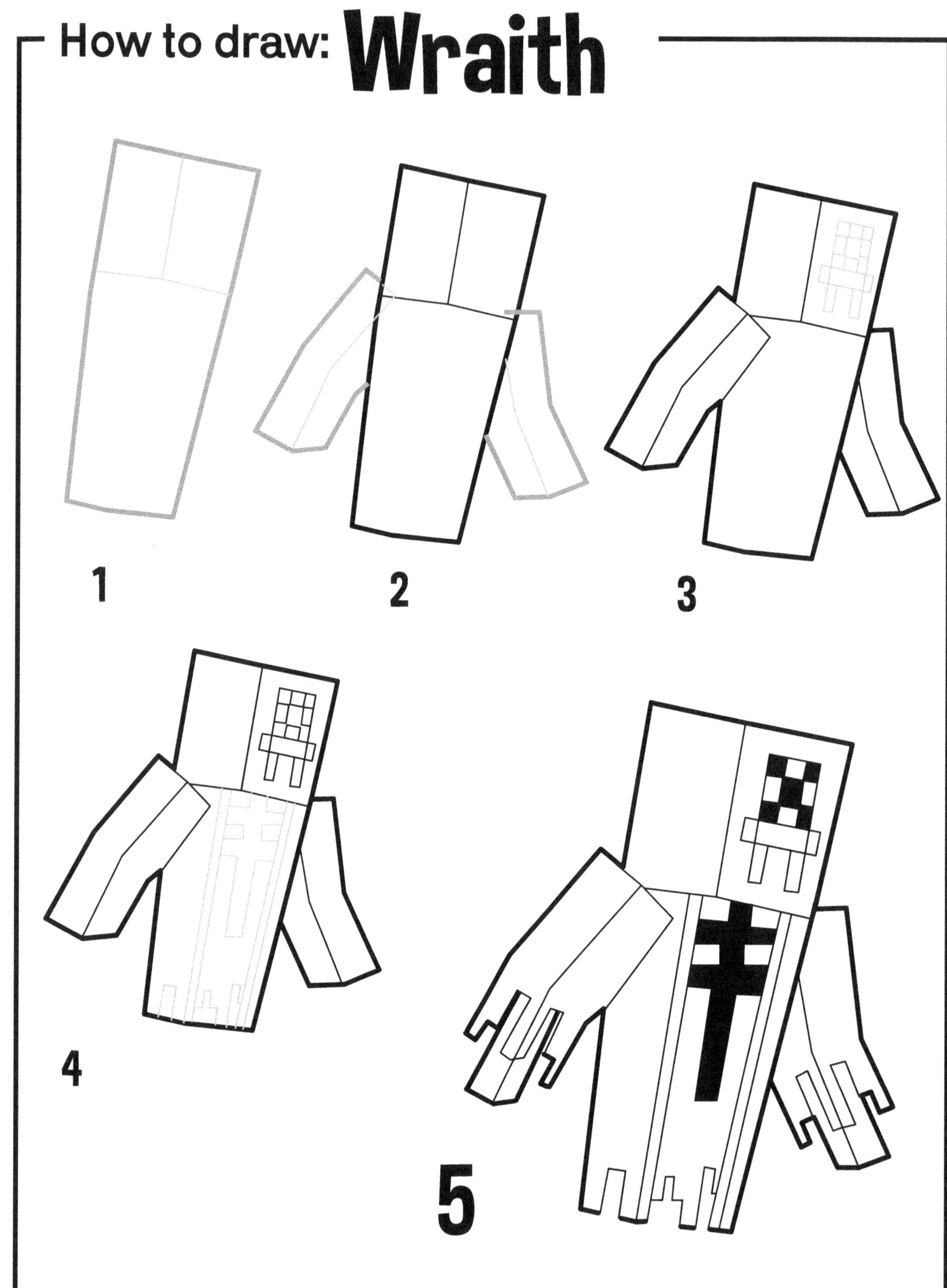

NOW, iT'S YOUR TURN

How to draw: **Wretched Wraith**

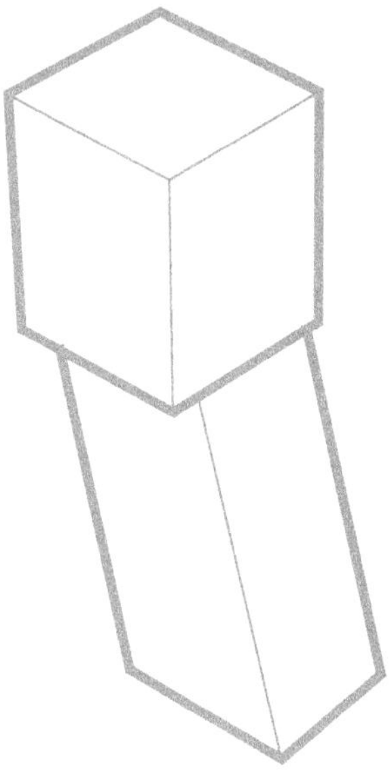

1

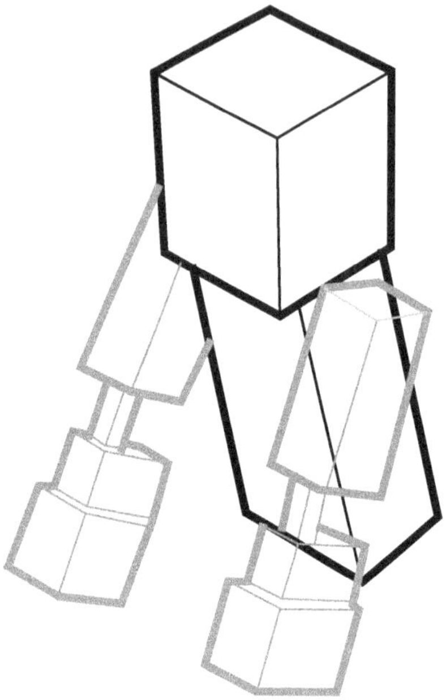

2

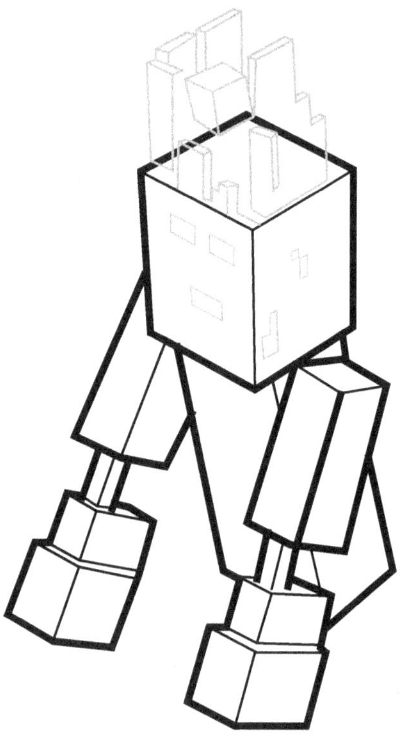

3

4

5

NOW, IT'S YOUR TURN

DOWNLOAD 50
FREE COLORING PAGES

Click the link below
to
DOWNLOAD NOW!